Wedding Etiquette FOR DUMMIES®

by Sue Fox

Wiley Publishing, Inc.

Wedding Etiquette For Dummies®
Published by
Wiley Publishing, Inc.
111 River St.
Hoboken, NJ 07030-5774
www.wiley.com

WILEY

About the Author

Since 1994, **Sue Fox** has provided etiquette products, educational material, group training, and private consultations to business professionals, celebrities, corporations, K–12 schools, and higher education, through her company, The Etiquette Survival Group, which has offices in Central and Southern California. Previously, she was employed in the high-tech industry, with 10 years of experience in event planning and sales and marketing at Apple, Inc.

The Etiquette Survival Group offers etiquette products and mentoring programs for individuals interested in starting their own etiquette consulting businesses. Sue has set up many Etiquette Survival consultants throughout the United States and internationally. She has traveled extensively and is well acquainted with various international cultures. Her travels have taken her to East Africa, Mexico, Central America, and Europe. Sue and her company have provided western etiquette programs throughout the United States, Singapore, Malaysia, Hong Kong, and India. She also is executive producer of *The Etiquette Survival Kit,* a series of educational DVDs featuring dining and social etiquette and proper table settings for adults and teens.

Sue is a professional member of the International Association of Protocol Consultants (IAPC) and has an additional background in image consulting, makeup artistry, and wedding planning. She is the author of *Etiquette For Dummies,* 2nd Edition, and *Business Etiquette For Dummies,* 2nd Edition (Wiley).

The Etiquette Survival Group and MCE International have partnered to jointly develop etiquette and diversity products and programs. Sue and her business partner, Linda Cain, are working together to create a better understanding of people in diverse business and social environments by emphasizing the importance of respect, diplomacy, and civility in every aspect of life.

Sue and The Etiquette Survival Group have been featured in many national and international publications, including *Woman's Day, Vogue, Ladies' Home Journal, Real Simple, American Baby, Newsweek, Fortune, New York Magazine, US Weekly, People, Los Angeles Times, The New York Times, The Wall Street Journal, New York Post, Chicago Tribune, Washington Times, San Francisco Examiner, The Boston Globe, USA Today, Sunday London Times, Australian Financial News, Folha de S. Paulo, Brazilian Daily News, Nikkei Business Journal, Times of India,* and *The Hindu Businessline.*

Sue's media credits include radio interviews and feature stories on CNBC, KRON-TV (San Francisco), Knowledge TV, San Francisco Mornings on 2, KOVR-TV (Sacramento), ABC World News, ABC News with Sam Donaldson, KQED-TV (San Francisco), CNET.com, and KABC-TV (Los Angeles).

Sue is the mother of two grown sons, Stephen and Nathan, and she has two grandsons, Joseph and Michael Fox.

Dedication

This book is dedicated to my two charming grandsons, Joseph and Michael Fox, who continually make me smile!

Author's Acknowledgments

I'd like to express my sincerest thanks to the dedicated team at John Wiley & Sons who generously contributed to the preparation of *Wedding Etiquette For Dummies*.

My deepest gratitude goes to my acquisitions editor, Tracy Boggier. Thank you for your continual faith in me. My sincere appreciation goes to my tireless project editor, Georgette Beatty. Thank you so much for your ongoing assistance, guidance, and professionalism.

A special thank you to assistant editor Erin Calligan Mooney, to copy editor Amanda Langferman for her meticulous editing, and to the additional talent at Wiley, illustrator Liz Kurtzman and cartoonist Rich Tennant, who all contributed to the development of this book. I gratefully acknowledge and thank my technical reviewer, Nancy Mitchell, for her editing expertise and knowledge, and a special thank-you to my agent, Reid Boates. I am most grateful for the assistance of Sandra M. Monahan, MBC, for her expertise, insights, and graciousness. It's been a pleasure working with all of you!

Among those who deserve an enormous thank-you are my talented etiquette colleagues, friends, and family who pitched in to help shape this book — Colette Swan, Kimberly Seth Smith, Roberta Kay, Julia Todd, and Anne Fox. You are all an inspiration, and there are no words that can describe my gratitude for your generous assistance, your encouragement, and especially your enthusiasm and humor! Thank you from the bottom of my heart for giving your time.

To my dear friend and business partner, Linda Cain, thank you for your friendship and support. My ongoing appreciation and gratitude goes to the Etiquette Survival consultants who continue to motivate me to stay focused on our quest to raise awareness of the importance of treating others (and ourselves) respectfully. And a big thanks to all my colleagues and friends at The Monarch Club. I want to thank all of you for your patience and understanding while I was working on this project.

I gratefully acknowledge the love of all my family — my sons Stephen and Nathan, my sisters Shirlee and Sandy, my brother Rick, and your families — thank you for always being there for me. And to my two extremely precious grandsons, Joseph and Michael, how you tug on my heartstrings!

Finally, I would like to thank all the faithful readers of the *For Dummies* series, and to every couple planning to marry — may your wedding planning be absolutely seamless and your wedding day faux pas free!

Publisher's Acknowledgments

We're proud of this book; please send us your comments at http://dummies.custhelp.com. For other comments, please contact our Customer Care Department within the U.S. at 877-762-2974, outside the U.S. at 317-572-3993, or fax 317-572-4002.

Some of the people who helped bring this book to market include the following:

Acquisitions, Editorial, and Media Development

Senior Project Editor: Georgette Beatty

Acquisitions Editor: Tracy Boggier

Copy Editor: Amanda M. Langferman

Assistant Editor: Erin Calligan Mooney

Editorial Program Coordinator: Joe Niesen

Technical Editor: Nancy Mitchell

Editorial Manager: Michelle Hacker

Editorial Assistant: Jennette ElNaggar

Art Coordinator: Alicia B. South

Cover Photo: © Marnie Burkhart/Corbis

Cartoons: Rich Tennant
   (www.the5thwave.com)

Production

Project Coordinator: Sheree Montgomery

Layout and Graphics: Karl Brandt, Ana Carrillo, Joyce Haughey, Christine Williams

Special Art: Elizabeth Kurtzman

Proofreaders: Rebecca Denoncour, Toni Settle

Indexer: Sherry Massey

Publishing and Editorial for Consumer Dummies

Diane Graves Steele, Vice President and Publisher, Consumer Dummies

Kristin Ferguson-Wagstaffe, Product Development Director, Consumer Dummies

Ensley Eikenburg, Associate Publisher, Travel

Kelly Regan, Editorial Director, Travel

Publishing for Technology Dummies

Andy Cummings, Vice President and Publisher, Dummies Technology/General User

Composition Services

Debbie Stailey, Director of Composition Services

Contents at a Glance

Table of Contents

Introduction

People constantly ask me whether *wedding etiquette* still exists today or is merely something from the past. Well, the answer to this question is really two sided. Yes, today's engaged couples toss out traditional etiquette faster than they throw the wedding bouquet. And, yes, the rules have relaxed a bit since the Victorian era; however, a certain level of common sense and basic etiquette is still necessary in every facet and phase of wedding planning, not to mention the protocol needed for the big day itself. Familiarizing yourself with what to do before, during, and after the wedding will help you ensure that everyone, from the ring bearer to the caterer, enjoys the ceremony and all the wedding festivities. *Wedding Etiquette For Dummies* is here to help you do just that.

About This Book

You've announced your engagement, your phone is ringing off the hook, and your mother, future mother-in-law, sister, aunt, and cousin are all calling to ask questions and give opinions. Plus, you're looking into possible ceremony and reception locations and talking to caterers, florists, photographers, and wedding planners — just to name a few folks. Are you feeling overwhelmed, yet? Well, buckle your seat belt because the ride is about to begin! *Wedding Etiquette For Dummies* guides brides, grooms, and friends and family of happily engaged couples through the basics of appropriate wedding behavior, from the engagement announcement throughout the planning process to the big day itself and beyond.

Use this book as a reference guide, reading any section that interests you. You can start at the back, in the middle, or at the beginning — it's your choice.

Conventions Used in This Book

To help you make your way through this book, I use the following conventions:

- *Italics* highlight definitions and emphasize certain words.
- **Boldface** text indicates key words in bulleted lists and actions to take in numbered lists.
- `Monofont` highlights Web addresses.

When this book was printed, some Web addresses may have needed to break across two lines of text. If that happened, rest assured that I didn't put in any extra characters (such as hyphens) to indicate the break. When you're entering one of these Web addresses, just type exactly what you see in this book, pretending the line break doesn't exist.

What You're Not to Read

Throughout this book, I share information that may be interesting to you but isn't essential to your understanding of a given wedding etiquette topic. So feel free to skip the sidebars (shaded gray boxes) within the chapters. They don't provide vital information you need to know to incorporate etiquette into your wedding.

Foolish Assumptions

In short, I assume that those of you who pick up this book are planning to marry or perhaps that you're a family member or friend of someone who's engaged. You may want to clear up some confusion about the complexity of planning a wedding, or maybe you're seeking some guidance on the finer points of wedding etiquette. Whatever your reason is for reading this book, I hope you find it helpful and have fun as you incorporate some wedding etiquette that often gets overlooked!

How This Book Is Organized

I organized this book into 5 parts and 18 chapters, separated according to specific topics and situations. You don't need to read any previous chapters to understand a later one that's of interest to you. Just jump around to find what you need or check out the table of contents to locate the specific subject matter you're curious about. I provide cross-referencing between the chapters to help you find more information on certain topics.

Part 1: Engaging in Proper Wedding Etiquette from the Start

In this part, I walk you through all the etiquette involved at the beginning of the wedding planning process. Many questions come up when it comes to how to properly share the news of your engagement, whether to throw an engagement party, and how to gracefully handle friends and family who may not be excited about the announcement. I address all these issues in Chapter 2. If you're interested in technology, turn to Chapter 3, where I talk about the etiquette behind creating a wedding Web site and using e-mail during wedding planning. If you need to figure out who pays for what, check out Chapter 4, where I explain everything from the traditional expenses for the couple and their families to how to stay on a budget while keeping your cool.

Part II: The Main Event: Planning Your Ceremony and Reception

In this part, you find details for creating a memorable and taste-ful wedding celebration. In Chapter 5, I describe different types of ceremony styles (such as religious, civil, military, and others). In Chapter 6, I offer advice on choosing an appropriate ceremony site and officiant and personalizing your wedding with readings, music, and more. I explain all the details for selecting a proper reception venue along with tips for planning different aspects of your reception in Chapter 7.

Part III: Working on Wedding Details with Your Manners Intact

This part addresses all the etiquette you need to know as you plan your big day. Chapter 8 helps you through the highly personal and subjective task of choosing a wedding party. I offer etiquette advice specifically to help you through the selection process, along with tips on determining the number of attendants and advice for breaking away from the norm. You find advice on choosing your wedding attire in relation to the various levels of formality in Chapter 9. And, if you're struggling with the guest list, check out Chapter 10, which lays out the etiquette ground rules.

That's not all! In Chapter 11, you find the details for composing your wedding invitations and the all-important etiquette involved with assembling, addressing, and mailing them. Chapter 12 offers you advice on registering for gifts and the proper way to present gifts to family members and the bridal party. Finally, Chapter 13 addresses the major etiquette involved in the prewedding festivi-ties, from the bridal shower to the rehearsal dinner.

Part IV: Behaving on the Big Day and Beyond

This part covers everything that occurs on your wedding day. Chapter 14 helps you specifically with the ceremony, from how to properly greet and seat guests to what steps to follow for a proper processional, recessional, and other ceremony rituals. Chapter 15 includes etiquette advice on events at the reception: giving toasts, cutting the cake, and more. Chapter 16 finishes up the wedding festivities with tips on celebrating after the big day, including the protocol involved with sending thank-you notes.

Part V: The Part of Tens

This part is chock-full of good advice, given concisely for your convenience. In Chapter 17, I offer you ten tried-and-true tips for getting along with vendors and the wedding planner. And in Chapter 18, I provide some important etiquette guidance for marriages the second time around.

Icons Used in This Book

I use little pictures, called *icons,* to flag important bits of information throughout the book. Here's what these icons mean:

This icon points out take-home messages you can use before, during, and after your wedding.

Wherever you see this icon, you find small hints that help make the bumps you may encounter as you plan your wedding a little easier.

When you see this sign, pay attention — or watch out!

Where to Go from Here

If you're new to the whole wedding etiquette thing, I suggest you start off with the basics in Part I; otherwise, feel free to skip to the section you're interested in. I hope that, as you read, you pick up ideas and information that make your wedding day the day you've always dreamed of!

Part I

Engaging in Proper Wedding Etiquette from the Start

The 5th Wave   By Rich Tennant

"Along with the invitations, announcements, and save-the-date cards, I'd like some 'I told you so' cards for people who thought I'd never get married."

In this part...

1n this part, I provide suggestions and advice on incorporating etiquette and grace into the beginning of your wedding planning — starting with the proper way of announcing your engagement. I talk about the basics of save-the-date cards and engagement parties, and I give you helpful information for creating a wedding Web site. I also offer some gentle guidance on how to politely handle sticky situations, such as dealing with family or friends who may object to your marriage. Finally, I offer advice on the all-important task of managing your wedding finances — and keeping the peace at the same time!

Chapter 1

Incorporating Etiquette into Your Wedding

. . . .

In This Chapter
▶ Announcing your happy news
▶ Properly using technology during wedding planning
▶ Determining the budget and planning duties
▶ Coordinating all the details
▶ Acting appropriately on — and after —your big day

. . . .

*N*ow that you're newly engaged, it's time to start the planning! As exhilarating and fun as wedding planning can be, you need to keep in mind that weddings scream etiquette more than just about any other event in life, so, before you get started, take some time to understand the guidelines — which is where this book comes in.

From the moment you become engaged to the moment you and your beloved wave farewell to your guests after the reception (and beyond!), this book provides all you need to know to plan your wedding, walk down the aisle, and receive your guests with grace, dignity, and good manners. This chapter introduces you to the essentials. Gracious planning, and best wishes!

Etiquette (in other words, good manners) is a way of honoring and showing respect to other people in any circumstance, no matter what.

Sharing the News of Your Engagement

Announcing your engagement can be thrilling, intimidating, stressful, or all of the above, depending on whom you're telling. But properly announcing your engagement is more than just informing your family and phoning your friends: It's alerting the media. (Just kidding — sort of.)

Really, though, you need to give careful thought to how and when you tell your parents, children (if you have any), siblings, grand-parents, other relatives, friends, and co-workers. What should you do if someone objects to your engagement? How do you word the newspaper announcement? And what about save-the-date cards — are those really necessary?

Chapter 2 covers all these concerns in detail. It also explains every-thing you need to know about the etiquette of having engagement parties and handling the unfortunate situation of calling off the engagement.

Putting Technology to Proper Use during Wedding Planning

A wedding Web site is an excellent tool for publishing details about your engagement and wedding. For example, you can pro-vide a place for guests to select their meal preferences, as well as share information about accommodations for out-of-town guests. You can even tell your personal engagement story or the tale of how you met. And don't forget to share photos — just make sure they're appropriate for all your guests.

Chapter 3 gives you all the Web site etiquette and pointers you need to know. It also discusses the use of e-mail during wedding planning. In some instances, e-mail is completely inappropri-ate (such as in place of formal wedding invitations or thank-you notes), but there are a few times when using e-mail is okay.

As wonderful as a wedding Web site can be, know that such sites (along with e-mail) don't take the place of formal announcements and invitations. After all, Grandma probably doesn't have access to the Internet, and even if she does, she still wants a printed invita-tion for a keepsake.

Establishing the Budget and Planning Responsibilities

Over the years, the people responsible for funding the wedding have changed. Traditionally, the bride's family paid for a good portion of the costs, but today about 30 percent of couples pay for their own weddings, sometimes with a little help from both their families.

Knowing who pays for what can be tricky. Trickier still is graciously managing overly ambitious (yes, pushy) people who want to have a major say in how you plan your wedding. Fear not! You don't have to go at it alone. Chapter 4 focuses on handling budget and planning responsibilities with grace.

Making Plans for Your Ceremony and Reception

Although etiquette certainly plays a major role on your wedding day, good manners are also crucial when you're planning the basics of your ceremony and reception, as you find out in this section.

Understanding different ceremony styles

In addition to choosing whether to have a formal or informal wedding, you have to choose to have either a religious or secular service — both of these decisions somewhat determine your ceremony's overall style. Various faiths/denominations have unique customs. A Christian wedding is vastly different from a Hindu wedding, for example. Military weddings have a certain protocol. Destination weddings and commitment ceremonies involve their own etiquette guidelines. Each of these choices helps define your particular wedding style.

Chapter 5 gives etiquette considerations for a variety of wedding ceremony styles.

Deciding your ceremony's details

After you settle on a ceremony style, it's time for the fun stuff: figuring out the ceremony details. You have to choose everything from the date and time to the content of your programs — all while keeping your manners intact and ensuring that the ceremony itself is appropriate. Here are a few of the topics I cover in Chapter 6:

✔ Making sure your ceremony style matches your location

✔ Agreeing on a date and selecting a time that works for your ceremony's level of formality

✔ Graciously communicating to the officiant your desires for the ceremony and working well with the officiant throughout the entire planning process

✔ Selecting your music, special readings, and vows

✔ Appropriately honoring deceased loved ones

✔ Assembling wedding programs

✔ Planning your transportation to and from the ceremony

Preparing for your reception

After you become engaged, the ceremony and reception sites are among the first things you need to select and book (after the officiant, if possible). In fact, many couples pick their wedding dates from the list of available dates they get from their chosen venues. (Gee, how romantic!)

After you've booked a site, what do you have to consider as you plan the rest of your reception? Chapter 7 is your go-to chapter for helpful etiquette guidelines about this step of the planning process.

Working Out the Details of Your Wedding

Working out the details of your wedding means selecting your attendants, choosing appropriate attire, assembling your guest list, putting together invitations and wedding announcements, giving and receiving gifts graciously, and attending a variety of festivities before the wedding. This section introduces guidelines on how to effortlessly navigate through these details.

Choosing your wedding party

After you know the style of your wedding, you can figure out the appropriate number of attendants to have. You probably have two special people in mind to be your maid or matron of honor and your best man, but you need to come up with a few more attendants, too. I discuss the main wedding-party considerations in Chapter 8.

Carefully considering the bridal party you want to surround yourself with on this special occasion is an important part of ensuring that your wedding day becomes a wonderful memory for years to come.

Shopping for wedding attire

Wedding attire doesn't have to translate to fashion disaster for your attendants. A little planning, a little compromising, and *voilà* — everyone wins.

You can have the wedding of your dreams without sentencing your attendants to the wedding of their nightmares. Chapter 9 covers the important points you need to know to help you choose wedding attire that's both appropriate and stylish. It also discusses how to outfit the happy couple.

Putting together the guest list

A cold, hard fact of life is that unless you're a gazillionaire, you have to make your guest list match your budget, which often means you can't invite everyone you've ever known. Some guests will be on your *must*-invite list; some will be on your *should*-invite list; others will be on your *could*-invite list. Chapter 10 explains all the etiquette details for assembling your guest list.

Assembling invitations and announcements

Invitations and announcements should, of course, match the style (formal or informal) of your wedding. But you're no longer forced to choose either white or ivory. Not at all. Today you can choose from a beautiful array of wedding stationery — something to fit every wedding style and budget.

But you can't stop after you pick out your invitation style. You have to word your invitation properly and then figure out how to stuff all the enclosures into one nice, neat packet to mail to your guests. And, of course, you have to address those packets correctly, too. Find out all these details in Chapter 11, which also explains when to mail your invitations, what to do if your wedding is canceled or postponed after the invitations are out, and when (and why) to send wedding announcements.

Giving and receiving gifts

Current research indicates that more than 91 percent of couples register for — and receive — gifts from an average of 200 guests. Most of these gifts are between $85 and $100. Not to mention you and your spouse-to-be have to give your own gifts to all your wedding party members and a few other special helpers. With so many people involved, you better believe you have a few etiquette guidelines to follow as you register for, receive, and give gifts. Chapter 12 includes details to help you get through the gift process gracefully.

Acting appropriately at prewedding parties

Wedding festivities aren't limited to just the big day. Prewedding celebrations include bridal showers and the all-important rehearsal dinner. Like at the wedding, guidelines for etiquette prevail at these parties, too. Have fun at your parties, but keep your manners intact! Chapter 13 discusses these events and the appropriate etiquette guidelines that go with each one.

Behaving on and after Your Wedding Day

You've finally arrived at your big day, and everyone's etiquette antennae are up and running. You just have to get through the ceremony and reception, and then you can focus on happily ever after. Here's what you need to know and where you can find it:

- ✔ **The ceremony:** Chapter 14 guides you and your star players through the nerve-wracking event known as the ceremony.

  Knowledge is power. Knowing what you're supposed to do will help you remain confident and radiant as you marry the love of your life.

- ✔ **The reception:** Finally; it's time for the party you've waited for all your life . . . your reception! Take note: The reception is no time to throw etiquette to the wind. After all, you've had a wonderful wedding up until now; why give your guests a lasting memory that, at best, embarrasses you or, at worst, seriously offends someone else? For all the details on reception etiquette, check out Chapter 15.

- ✔ **After the big day:** After the wedding day is over, you need to tie up a few loose ends to make your wedding experience a complete etiquette success and to give yourselves a positive place to start your new life together. Chapter 16 is your guide to a happy ending.

Chapter 2

Announcing Your Engagement with Elegance

*B*ecoming engaged may be one of the most significant moments of your life. At the time, it may seem like you and your beloved are the only two people on earth, but, in reality, a wedding typically isn't just the uniting of two people — it's the joining together of two families (sometimes more!). Therefore, you need to know a few things about engagements to ensure that everyone involved feels nothing but joy for you and your spouse-to-be when you make your announcement. This chapter tells you what you need to know.

Traditional etiquette dictates that a man should ask for permission from the bride's father before proposing. Modern convention, on the other hand, suggests that most men propose first and then seek parental permission (but you still may want to talk to your girlfriend's parents before you pop the question if they're traditional in their ways). If your future in-laws live too far away to meet them face to face, writing a letter or making a phone call shows respect for your spouse-to-be and her family.

And for those of you brides-to-be who took it upon yourselves to pop the question, more power to you — it's totally acceptable for the woman to do the proposing. However, this practice may be difficult for some parents to appreciate, so keep that in mind before you tell your parents. At the end of the day, regardless of who asked whom, you're still getting married, so hopefully everyone involved will support you.

Informing Your Immediate Family

When you first become engaged, you want to shout the happy news from the rooftops, and who can blame you? But traditional etiquette maintains that your immediate family — meaning your parents and your children, if you have any — should find out first. In the following sections, I explain how to share the news with these important folks; I also show you how to gracefully handle first-time meetings among all the parents involved.

Sharing the news with your parents

As excited as you may be — and as tempted as you are — to tell that one really close friend right away, think again. Protecting the feelings of your parents is most important at this time. If word of your engagement gets back to any of your parents before you personally inform them, you may find yourself having to deal with hurt feelings from the get-go. You and your spouse-to-be must make sure your parents are the first to know of your plans.

And, *how* you tell your parents is just as important as when. Sending a group e-mail or announcing your engagement on Twitter may seem like the simplest way to spread the word to everyone quickly — but hang on just a minute. Before you head to cyber-space, you need to inform your parents — in person if possible. In the following sections, I explain a few important considerations for telling your parents about your engagement.

If parents live in distant states or other countries, letting them know by telephone is fine (not e-mail or text, please!). Being with your spouse-to-be when you make the call is thoughtful because doing so gives everyone a chance to share the happy news together.

Which set of parents should find out first?

Back in the dim reaches of history, the custom was for the groom's parents to find out the big news first and then contact the bride's family. Today, however, etiquette states that you should inform the bride's parents about the engagement first (if her parents are divorced, tell the mother of the bride first) and then the groom's parents immediately afterward. However, you don't have to stick to this tradition — it's a matter of personal choice.

Planning a lunch or dinner at a special restaurant and announcing the news to all the parents at the same time is a nice idea! If you can have all your parents in the same place, short and sweet is the best way to go. The groom should stand up, get everyone's attention, and say, "We are so happy to share with you that Sarah has agreed to be my wife." If you've chosen a date (or at least a month), you may choose to share these details at this time, too.

What about telling divorced parents?

If your parents are divorced, they still deserve to hear the news from you personally and as soon as possible, even if bad feelings about the divorce still exist between you. Choosing one parent over the other to tell first may be difficult, but the goal is for you to avoid hurting either parent.

You may want to tell the parent you feel the closest to or the one who raised you and then let the other parent in on the news shortly thereafter. Even if you're estranged from one parent, consider announcing the engagement to that parent, as well. After all, you're starting a new life — what a great time and way to begin to put the past behind you. You may choose to tell an estranged parent by writing a brief note or making a phone call. Whatever you choose, just say something like: "I just wanted to let you know Tom and I will be getting married this March." You may also want to fill your parent in on the details of your relationship with your intended, and you may consider making arrangements to meet in person.

Smoothing over the big surprises

If you think your parents may at all be caught off guard by your news, take time to discuss matters with them before you make any public statements. Giving your parents time to digest the news is extremely important — you can always have a follow-up discussion to reassure them of your decision. Make it clear that you respect your family's feelings; however, make sure you're firm about the fact that you and your spouse-to-be are moving forward with your plans. Say something like: "I know you and Dad may need a few days to get used to the idea of our engagement, but I hope you'll give us a chance to address any specific concerns you have. Why don't we talk about it more in a day or two?"

If your parents have never met your spouse-to-be, don't drop the bomb on your first visit. If possible, arrange a few family gatherings before you announce your engagement.

If any issues, such as concerns about age differences, backgrounds, or religions, may cause tension with your parents, you may wish to tell your parents the news alone, without your spouse-to-be — or you may want to take your spouse-to-be along for moral support. Whatever the situation may be, make certain that your parents know that neither of you has any reservations about your differences. Say something like: "Todd and I are more than aware of the age difference between us. We've discussed what this means for our future and are prepared to handle the challenges we may face together. We hope you'll support our marriage and be confident in our partnership." However you choose to tell your parents, be sure to resolve matters amicably early on because doing so will pave the way for smooth wedding planning later.

Telling your children tactfully

Consider speaking with your children about your marriage plans as soon as possible, even before you talk to your parents, and do so alone, without your spouse-to-be. Children may need time to fully understand what your marriage will mean for them. If you have an ex in the picture, you need to tell him or her, too.

Reassure your children that how you feel about them hasn't changed at all, and make a point to listen carefully to all their concerns. If they're old enough, ask them whether they'd like to help with the wedding planning and then give them specific tasks. Be sure to let them know what their role will be in the wedding. For example, you may say: "We're really looking forward to getting our new family off to a joyful start at this wedding. We'd love for you both to be in the wedding as junior bridesmaids."

Even if your children have spent a lot of time with your spouse-to-be and they seem to get along great, tread lightly. Children may not be prepared to hear news that will have such a major effect on their lives. You can try dropping a few subtle hints to see how they feel. But depending on their age and maturity, expect some unpredictable reactions, confusion, reluctance, and possibly even initial anger. The most important thing to do is validate your children's feelings; never dismiss a feeling or concern. Set clear boundaries and make commitments you know you can keep (that you will spend one night a week with just your kids, for example) to help your children feel secure during the transition period.

Introducing the parents to one another

In the past, the groom's parents traditionally contacted the bride's family soon after the engagement was announced, but, today, either set of parents can make the first move. In either case, getting your parents together for an in-person get-together soon after the engagement is always a good idea. If a personal meeting isn't possible because of distance, a phone call is fine. If one set of parents lives close to the couple, a conference call is a nice idea to get everyone involved from the beginning. A written note or card is also acceptable, but, if the parents go this route, they should follow up with a call at a later date.

If divorce is part of either family, you need to give the utmost care to planning a get-together; you don't want to force anyone into a potentially uncomfortable situation. For example, if the groom's parents are divorced, ask both of them how they feel about being in the same room together. If one is adamantly opposed to the idea, you may choose to have separate gatherings or to skip this particular step entirely.

To introduce future in-laws successfully, make a point of giving both sets of parents some information about the other one before the first meeting. For example, you can tell your parents where your in-laws went to college. Or maybe the groom's parents just returned from a trip to Africa or the bride's parents are avid skydivers — either topic makes for a great conversation starter! The point of all this planning is to help all the parents learn about one another before the meeting so they have some common ground on which to start a conversation.

Plenty of minefields already exist when two families unite. Prepare your parents for any unexpected lifestyles or idiosyncrasies that the other set of parents may have. These differences may range from food preferences (strict vegan, for example) to devout religious beliefs. Alternative-living nudists may not have much in common with a military general and his wife, for instance. It's up to you as a couple to inform each family of the appropriate considerations and potentially offensive issues. Be accepting, understanding, and nonjudgmental when you inform your parents of anything you think may surprise or shock them. Say something like: "I know you and Dad may find it a little hard to swallow, but Joan and Allan are big tarot card readers. Don't be surprised if they try to do a reading on you. For tonight, please just humor them."

Sharing the News with Relatives, Friends, and Colleagues

After you tell your parents (and children, if you have any), you need to tell your closest family members, friends, and co-workers. I give pointers for telling these groups in the following sections.

Sending formal engagement announcements isn't appropriate. You may choose to have an engagement party, for which you may send out invitations. You may also send out save-the-date cards, but only to the people you plan to invite to the actual wedding.

Telling your relatives

Family pecking order is sometimes appropriate when you share news of your engagement. For example, out of respect, you want to tell your grandparents the news before you tell your siblings, aunts, uncles, cousins, and other relatives (but after you tell your parents and children). However, if you're not close to your grandparents or you never see them, you can skip this step. Whether you tell your grandparents first or not, next you should make a list and decide who's most special to you and your spouse-to-be — in both families. Ensure that you tell these people before you release your news to the rest of the world. You can do so with a phone call or, if possible, in person, either on your own or with your spouse-to-be.

Be sensitive to what's going on in your family members' lives, and make the announcement to them accordingly. For example, if your cousin is going through an ugly divorce, be extra sensitive when sharing your happy news with her. Say something like: "I realize you're going through a really tough time right now, but I wanted to share this with you myself before you heard it from your parents: I'm getting married next year."

Tradition doesn't offer an exact timeline for announcing your engagement to other family members (the ones you aren't close to), but taking a little time before spreading the word is perfectly fine. In most families, word spreads quickly on its own, and for the relatives you don't plan to invite to the wedding, that's the only notice they need. For the relatives you're not particularly close to but still intend to invite to the wedding, calling them is better than e-mailing them, but some form of direct contact is a must.

Letting your friends in on the happy news

Close friends merit special priority. Let them know about the engagement immediately after family, but if your friends were there during the proposal or see you immediately afterward with your new engagement ring, you likely can't keep the news from them. Just remember to stress how important their discretion is until you've contacted your families. It's up to you to choose whether you want to tell your friends individually (in person or with a phone call) or get them all together for lunch or an evening out to surprise them. When you have friends living out of the country and a phone call is out of the question, sending an e-mail is perfectly acceptable.

Like with your relatives, you need to take into consideration the events going on in the lives of your friends. If your good friend recently went through a bad breakup, for example, let her know of your happy occasion in a low-key manner during some one-on-one time; say something like: "I know you're still having a hard time dealing with your break-up, but I hope you can still be happy about the fact that Joe and I are getting married."

In all the excitement, be careful if you're making the announcement with a group of friends and end up discussing the bridal party at the same time. You may have a close friend who expects to be a bridesmaid or a groomsman, but you may not be thinking the same thing — try not to hurt anyone's feelings. (Flip to Chapter 8 for full details on selecting your wedding party.)

Informing your co-workers

In terms of co-workers and colleagues, you have free reign to decide whom you tell, when you tell them, and where you tell them. Clearly, some co-workers are closer to you than others, so you can let them know the exciting news either at work, at an after-work get-together, or via a phone call or *personal* e-mail. Going out to lunch with your close office buddies and announcing the news all at once is a nice idea. As a courtesy, you may want to inform your boss or direct reports before you tell other co-workers and colleagues, particularly if you have the dates picked, so they can begin to arrange schedules accordingly.

What you don't want to do is send a group e-mail — doing so is frowned upon in etiquette circles because sharing news of your wedding is very different from sharing information regarding the new location for the paper shredder. An individual message lends a feeling of importance to the announcement.

To share or not to share? Telling folks you know won't be invited

Is it appropriate to announce your engagement to people you know you won't invite to the wedding? The answer is yes. Most people today are aware of the financial cost of having a wedding and normally understand that you can't invite a cast of thousands.

If you anticipate that your wedding will be small, you may want to mention this fact when you announce your engagement to people. That way, you can avoid disappointment when you can't invite everyone. (Of course, I don't advise this tactic if you plan to have a wedding with 300 guests!)

When you discuss your wedding with a potential uninvited guest, be as gracious as possible. You don't need to say anything about an invitation, but if the other person happens to ask, you can simply say something like: "As much as I'd like to have you join in the festivities, I'm really limited in the size of the guest list. I hope you understand." You don't have to apologize or feel bad.

Dealing with Folks Who Object to the Engagement

Although you may be jumping over the moon about your engagement, be warned that a family member or friend may voice strong disapproval of the match. The following are some typical reasons why a loved one may object to an engagement:

- ✔ Uniting two people of different cultures, religions, or races can be a potentially difficult situation. Ignorance and misunderstanding of other cultures, races, and/or religions can lead to lack of support from loved ones.

- ✔ Fears of losing you as a best friend after you marry can lead some friends or siblings to be less than supportive of your engagement. Or some friends may harbor deeper feelings of envy or jealousy.

- ✔ Some people may decide that they just don't like your choice of a mate. Their reasons for this dislike may be logical and reasonable (he's been married twice before, for example), or they may be purely emotional and unreasonable (he went to your rival university, for example).

If you have a loved one who disapproves of your engagement for any reason but refuses to talk to you about it, set up a time for a private discussion as soon as possible. This kind of situation isn't something you can sweep under the rug. Before you talk to your loved one, though, take some time to consider the following guidelines (they can help you and your loved one move forward):

- ✔ Be sensitive to fears about your marrying someone of a different culture, race, or religion, but seek to educate and diffuse potential issues, such as arguments about which religion you'll choose for your children's upbringing. For example, try to have an open conversation with your family about the concerns you and your future spouse have already discussed. If the issues are religious, consider inviting a member of the clergy to be part of the conversation to clarify or explain any misunderstood elements of the religion.

- ✔ Listen to your loved ones without judging them. Hear them out and let them know you'll try to look at the issues from their perspective. Try not to make matters worse by arguing.

- ✔ Realize that if you're young and very close to your parents, they may have a hard time letting you go. Make sure that any negative feelings they have about your engagement aren't simply masking their pain from losing their baby. Take the same approach with your best friends. They may feel left behind, particularly when you're getting married first or are planning to move to another town to be with your spouse. Let them know your friendship won't change.

✔ Keep in mind that getting married in a way that doesn't involve a lot of ceremony may not be a bad idea if you and your spouse-to-be sense discord that you can't set aside temporarily. Hopefully, with open and honest dialogue, you can eventually bring your loved ones around.

Whether it's a parent, another relative, or a friend who disapproves of your engagement even after your best efforts, ask the person to hold his or her peace, trust your decision, and go along with the wedding. You certainly don't want to damage your relationship or alienate a family member or close friend; however, in the end, you have to be true to yourself — after all, it's your happiness.

Announcing Your Engagement in the Newspaper

The most traditional way to announce an engagement is to put a notice in the newspaper. It's a simple way to get the word out to a wider audience. I explain where, when, and how to make a newspaper announcement in the following sections.

You can also set up a personal Web site to announce your wedding plans; see Chapter 3 for details.

Figuring out where and when to submit announcements

Publishing the engagement announcement in the newspaper is normally the responsibility of the bride's family, but they should also ask the groom and his family whether they want the announcement published in their local newspaper if they live in a different area — it's the polite thing to do. You may want to place the article in two or three newspapers — for example, one in the bride's hometown paper, one in the groom's hometown paper, and one in the paper of the city where the couple currently lives. Just beware newspapers charge high fees for placing announcements.

Call the newspaper or check the paper's Web site to find out how to submit an announcement. Most papers allow you to submit your article and photo online, or they have a hard-copy form you can submit with details about your engagement. If you need help with the writing or correct wording, someone on the newspaper staff should be there to help — check out the paper's Web site for contact information. (I provide pointers on appropriate wording for announcements in the next section.)

Most people put their announcements in the paper about two to three months before the wedding, although you won't find a strict rule on this time frame and some people choose to print their announcements a whole year in advance of the wedding.

If either member of the engaged couple has a divorce pending, it's inappropriate to place an engagement announcement in the newspaper until after the divorce is final.

Publishing your engagement without mentioning the actual wedding date is perfectly acceptable. In fact, you may wish to omit the actual wedding date to prevent potential thieves from turning up at your empty home on the day of the wedding. Instead, you can say something like: "The bride and groom plan a spring wedding."

Wording announcements for different situations

Traditionally, the engagement announcement contains information about the couple, including full names, parent's names, hometowns, and the wedding month (if scheduled). However, the exact wording depends on certain circumstances, as you find out in the following sections.

Basic wording (when the bride's parents make the announcement)

A basic engagement notice, in which the bride's parents make the official announcement, reads something like the following:

> Dr. and Mrs. George Roberts of Carmel announce the engagement of their daughter, Miss Melissa Roberts, to Mr. Charles Green, son of Mr. and Mrs. Frank Green of San Francisco.

> Miss Roberts is a graduate of the University of San Francisco and is currently an art teacher at Los Gatos High School in Los Gatos. Mr. Green is a graduate of Stanford University and a lawyer with the firm of Sweeton, Martin, and Watt in Palo Alto. The couple plans an autumn wedding.

Wording when parents are divorced

When you're dealing with divorced parents, you name them both as individuals, by their current legal names and places of residence. You never refer to them as a couple. If the bride's parents are divorced, the bride's mother usually makes the announcement (and her name appears first). However, if the bride's father is the custodial parent, he may make the announcement (in which case his name appears first). For example, an announcement involving divorced parents reads like the following:

> Ms. Adele Smith of Sherman Oaks, California, and Mr. Bill Smith of New York, New York, announce the engagement of their daughter, Miss Lauren Smith, to Mr. John Clark, son of Mr. and Mrs. William Clark of Los Angeles.

If the groom's parents are divorced, the announcement reads something like the following:

> Mr. and Mrs. Budd Emerson of Indianapolis announce the engagement of their daughter, Miss Sally Emerson, to Jeremy Harold Owens, son of Mrs. Jenny Martin of Chicago, Illinois, and Mr. Clint Owens of Centerville, Ohio.

Wording when one or more parents are deceased

When one of the bride's parents is deceased, the surviving parent makes the announcement, and it reads like the following:

> Ms. Jane Lowell of Harrisburg announces the engagement of her daughter, Miss Leslie Lowell, to Mr. Carl Johnson, son of Steven and Karen Johnson of Chicago. Ms. Lowell is also the daughter of the late James Lowell.

When one of the groom's parents is deceased, the announcement reads like the following:

> Mr. and Mrs. Eugene Black of Blacksburg announce the engagement of their daughter, Miss Rebecca Black, to Thomas Payne, son of Mrs. Roberta Payne and the late Norman Payne of Harrisburg, Pennsylvania.

When both the bride's parents are deceased, the bride usually asks a close family member to make the announcement, and it reads something like the following:

> Mr. and Mrs. Randy Harris of Pasadena announce the engagement of their granddaughter, Miss Heather Harris, to Mr. Nathanial Jones, son of Mr. and Mrs. Richard Jones of San Jose. Miss Harris is the daughter of the late Mr. and Mrs. Jim Harris.

If both the groom's parents are deceased, the announcement reads like the following:

> Mr. and Mrs. Steven Hughes of Annapolis announce the engagement of their daughter, Miss Amelia Hughes, to Mr. Lewis Watson, son of the late Mr. Thomas Watson and the late Mrs. Edna Watson.

Wording when only the groom's parents make the announcement

Traditionally, the groom's parents don't make the announcement. However, they may choose to do so in certain circumstances, such as when the bride's parents are deceased or when the bride has been married before and her parents choose not to make an announcement themselves. The wording reads as follows:

> Mr. and Mrs. Eric Thompson of Albany are honored to announce the engagement of Miss Joanne Green of Albany to their son, Mr. Allan Thompson. Miss Green is the daughter of the late Mr. and Mrs. Arthur Green of Boston.

Wording when the couple makes the announcement

In the case of a couple with no close relatives, a couple who has lived independently of their parents for some time, a couple in which one or both people have been married for many years before, or a couple who's already living together, the couple may make the announcement. The wording reads something like the following:

> Miss Barbara Watson and Mr. James Martin of Lexington are pleased to announce their engagement. They are both professors at the University of Kentucky. They plan an autumn wedding.

Wording for a same-sex couple

If you're a same-sex couple and you want to announce your engagement in your local paper, call the editor of the Lifestyle, Social, or Weddings section of the paper to find out the paper's policy regarding announcements for same-sex unions. If the paper hasn't yet considered this kind of announcement, your call may encourage the paper to embark on a more inclusive attitude regarding such announcements.

The wording in this situation doesn't change from the wording of engagement announcements for heterosexual couples. Just be sure that you inform the readers whether you plan to have a wedding or a commitment ceremony. An announcement for a commitment ceremony with the parents involved reads like the following:

> Mr. and Mrs. Ethan Grey of San Diego have the pleasure of announcing the engagement of their daughter, Miss Alison Grey, to Miss Belinda Jackson, daughter of Mr. and Mrs. Stephen Jackson of Thousand Oaks. Miss Grey is a graduate of UCLA and is a lawyer with the firm of Brendon and Steele in Los Angeles. Miss Jackson is a hairstylist in Los Angeles. The couple plans a July commitment ceremony.

A notice in which a same-sex couple announces their own engagement reads like the following:

> Miss Alison Grey and Miss Belinda Jackson of Los Angeles have the pleasure to announce their intent to be joined in commitment. Miss Grey, a graduate of UCLA, is a lawyer with the firm of Brendon and Steele in Los Angeles. Miss Jackson is a hairstylist in Los Angeles. The couple plans a July ceremony.

Composing and Mailing Save-the-Date Cards

Sending your intended guests save-the-date cards is a nice gesture. These cards are especially helpful when some people have to travel to your wedding from long distances or when the date of your wedding falls on a major holiday. When you're planning a destination wedding, save-the-date cards are a must for all your invitees because they need time to make the proper arrangements for time off and travel expenses. In this section, I describe the style and wording you can use in save-the-date cards; I also explain who receives them and when.

Using the right format and wording

Normally, save-the-date cards aren't as formal as wedding invitations, although many couples choose a design that mirrors their wedding invitations to brand their printed pieces. Either way, feel free to let your imagination run wild. These cards can be mini versions of the wedding invitations, magnets, postcards, or photo cards — the design choices are endless. You should be able to find or create a card that blends nicely with the style of your wedding.

If you're an especially informal person with a wedding style to match, you can use an e-mail or an e-vite (e-mail invitation) for a save-the-date announcement. However, keep in mind that not all your guests are comfortable using a computer, so you have to inform some guests with a phone call or a note.

Make sure that you include the names of you and your spouse-to-be, the date and location of the wedding, and an explanation that a formal invitation will follow (because the save-the-date card may be a new concept to some of your guests). You can word your card quite informally, as in the following examples:

> Save the weekend of June 19, 2010! Jane Jones and John Baker are getting married in Boston! Formal invitation to follow.

> Jane Jones and John Baker are getting married! You'll be invited to the wedding that is to take place on June 19, 2010, in Boston. Please save the date!

> Please save the date! Jane Jones and John Baker will be getting married on June 19, 2010 in Boston, Massachusetts. Invitation and details to follow.

A more formal approach for a formal wedding may read like the card in Figure 2-1. The more formal version should be presented in a letter-style format and include the names of the wedding hosts.

Dear Mr. and Mrs. Myers,

Please save the date of Saturday, June 19, 2010, for the wedding of our daughter, Miss Jane Jones, and Mr. John Baker in Boston, Massachusetts. Invitations are to follow.

Sincerely,

Mr. and Mrs. William Jones

Figure 2-1: A formal save-the-date card.

Understanding who should receive cards and when

Make *certain* that all the people to whom you send save-the-date cards are invited to the wedding! Keep a corresponding list of people to whom you're sending save-the-date cards and cross-reference that list with your wedding guest list. (I discuss etiquette guidelines for assembling a guest list in Chapter 10.)

Generally, you send out save-the-date cards about three to four months before the event. In the case of a destination wedding, you may want to send them sooner — six months or more to give attendees a chance to prepare their finances, passports, visas, legal and medical documents, and vaccination shots if needed.

Throwing an Engagement Party

The *formal betrothal party* dates back to the time when families formed alliances through marriages; in general, the party was an opportunity for the bride and groom to meet each other's families. This custom evolved into what you call an *engagement party* today. Although some customs have changed, this event is still the perfect venue for families to meet and celebrate. I explain a few basic etiquette rules for engagement parties in the following sections.

You must be officially engaged to hold an engagement party. Also, neither one of you may be in the midst of divorce proceedings.

Do you need to have a party?

No etiquette rule requires you to have an engagement party. In fact, the trend for having formal engagement parties may be slowly fading out, and nontraditional ways of announcing wedding details, such as wedding Web sites (see Chapter 3), are becoming the norm.

If you happen to live a long distance from your parents, a party may be difficult to arrange. In that case, you can announce your engagement simply by telling friends and family individually (I explain how to do so properly earlier in this chapter).

Who hosts the party, where, and when?

Most of the time, the bride's parents host the engagement party as a way of announcing the engagement of their daughter, which may be left as a surprise for the rest of the guests. As far as etiquette is concerned, letting the bride's parents have the honor of hosting the party is a good idea because doing so gives the bride's parents the first opportunity to celebrate the engagement. Today, however, letting other family members or friends host the engagement party is perfectly acceptable. The groom's parents may even offer to put on their own party or co-host with the bride's family.

If you plan a surprise announcement, the host makes an excuse to host a party for relatives and friends. Then, during the party, the host may drop subtle hints of an upcoming announcement.

If guests are meeting for the first time at the party, the host should assign someone to welcome the guests and make proper introductions. Or they may consider having people wear name tags with their relationship to the couple included on their tags.

The party can be held in the home of the bride, a friend, or another family member or at a restaurant. The formality is up to the host and the bride and groom; it can be a casual barbeque, a clambake on the beach, or an exotic meal at a Japanese steakhouse.

If the purpose of the party is to announce the engagement, it should take place within a few weeks of the proposal. If the goal is simply to celebrate the upcoming nuptials and give family members a chance to mingle, the party can take place up to two months after the engagement.

Who should be invited and how?

Normally, the host sends the invitations for the engagement party, with the assistance of the bride and groom. Typically, invitations go to close family and friends, as well as any other people the couple wants to include in the celebration. Depending on the formality of the party, the host may choose to send invitations via the mail, with a phone call, or through e-mail or e-vites.

The basic invitation for an engagement party includes the following:

- ✔ Announcement of the event (unless it's a surprise)

    If the announcement is a surprise, list a pretend reason for the get-together, such as "Bring on the Spring BBQ."

- ✔ Date, time, and duration
- ✔ Location (including address, driving directions, and map)
- ✔ Theme if there is one
- ✔ Contact information for RSVP

Be certain that you don't invite anyone to the engagement party whom you don't plan to invite to the wedding!

Should you expect gifts?

You shouldn't register for gifts before the engagement party, and you shouldn't expect gifts from the guests who attend. If a few guests choose to bring gifts to the party, store them discretely during the event and open them afterward (sending immediate thank-you notes to the gift-givers, of course). (See Chapter 16 for more on sending thank-you notes.)

What about the announcement and toasts?

When the time feels right, the bride-to-be's parents stand up, call for order, and express their great pleasure at their daughter's intentions to marry. The host of the party, often the father of the bride, makes the announcement at the party if it's a surprise. The host says something like, "I'm so glad to be able to have you all here today to celebrate the engagement of Rebecca and Thomas."

Someone, normally the father of the bride, then proposes a toast to the couple's future happiness. If the bride's father can't or doesn't want to give the toast, the bride's brother or the party host can do the honors. The person making the toast raises his glass and says something like, "To Thomas and Rebecca, may your future be as bright as the smiles we've seen today," at which time all the other guests pick up their glasses and take a sip.

Never drink to a toast made in your honor. The bride and groom just smile and thank the person making the toast.

The groom responds with a toast of his own, praising his future in-laws for the reception they've given him and saying how much he looks forward to becoming part of the family. (He may then take a drink.) A nice touch is for the bride to toast her parents and thank them for their love, support, and help with the wedding planning.

Don't forget to send thanks!

Don't forget thank-you notes! Write these notes promptly (within a week of the party, 48 hours is best) to any guests who brought gifts. For guests who didn't bring gifts, you may verbally thank them for attending the party and taking part in the special event. If any guests traveled a particularly long distance to attend, a note of gratitude is a lovely gesture, even if they didn't bring a gift.

Your thanks can be informal (but don't send it via an e-mail); use a simple card — you can either buy one or have one custom made for you. A handwritten note is especially nice, and it should be from both the bride and the groom.

Canceling the Engagement

The purpose of an engagement is not only to test your commitment, but also to build a stronger bond and learn more about your spouse-to-be's values and his or her approach to dealing with a variety of situations and circumstances. If you discover issues about your beloved that you don't like, or that may cause you serious concern, don't feel obliged to go ahead with your plans.

If you begin to question the relationship, do some serious soul searching and be honest with what you're feeling. If you're confused about what to do, speak to your parents or a close friend. You may just have a case of the jitters, which can make you extra sensitive to everything, so listening to another person can help. However, in the end, the decision is yours, so follow your instincts.

If you do decide to break off your engagement, call your family first and let them know. Then tell your friends. Keep your explanation brief, and be fair to your ex. You wouldn't want your ex to say awful things about you, so don't say awful things about him or her, either. Simply say that the decision to break off the engagement was mutual, even though that's rarely the case.

Your family and close friends can spread the word by making phone calls. You should speak with the officiant, the people you've contracted for services, and the people who've agreed to be part of the ceremony as soon as possible. You also should send a note or card to all the people who received an invitation or save-the-date card. This note requires only the following level of detail:

> Dr. and Mrs. George Roberts announce that the marriage of their daughter, Melissa, to Mr. Charles Green, which was arranged for July 24, 2010, will not take place.

If the woman breaks the engagement, she should return the ring to the man. If the man breaks the engagement, she may keep the ring, although she often returns it because she doesn't want a reminder of the relationship. However, she may be able to exchange the ring for another piece of jewelry.

You may have already received wedding gifts, so keep notes about who gave you which gift and return them as soon as possible. You should return any and all gifts you received, whether at showers or as wedding gifts. *Never* keep wedding gifts when you cancel your engagement, and make sure you return them to the people who gave them to you, not the stores.

Chapter 3

Tastefully Using Technology during Wedding Planning

. . . .

In This Chapter

▶ Checking out reasons for creating a wedding Web site

▶ Putting together your own wedding Web site

▶ Understanding wedding e-mail etiquette

. . . .

*E*tiquette changes with the times, as I often like to say. And you won't find better proof of that than with technology, specifically the Internet. What does changing technology have to do with planning a wedding? In a nutshell, the ever-improving technology means that you can share the details of your big day with all your loved ones, no matter where they are. Your 80-year-old grandmother who can't travel to your destination wedding can still find out how you met your spouse-to-be and get the scoop on the planning — all thanks to technology!

In this chapter, you find out how to launch a tasteful wedding Web site that's informative and appealing to your family and friends. You also discover when using e-mail is appropriate (and inappropriate) during your wedding planning.

Why Have a Wedding Web Site?

For most couples today, a wedding Web site has become a necessity. Having a Web site is one of the easiest and most affordable ways to communicate to all the people you know (all over the world) about all the details of your engagement and upcoming wedding. In this section, I discuss popular reasons why you may want to consider setting up a wedding Web site.

Telling your story

A wedding Web site gives you and your spouse-to-be the opportunity to share your personal stories and reflections about your relationship with just about everyone you know. By opening up to family and friends, you deepen your understanding of what you and your spouse-to-be mean to each other, and you allow your families to share in your happiness.

You can get creative by adding separate accounts of your time together. For example, each of you can add your viewpoint of the day you met or other meaningful events you've shared (such as graduating from college or moving to a new city together). See the later section "Including appropriate content" for more information on choosing suitable material for your site.

Providing wedding details

A wedding Web site is really a kind of one-stop shop — so to speak. You have the ability to provide visitors to your site all the details of both prewedding activities and the actual wedding — all in one place! This system saves time not only for you but also for your family and friends. Here are some examples of wedding details you can post to your site:

- ✓ **The location and time of both the ceremony and the reception:** These details are the most important of all the information you include on your site. Post the times and locations as soon as you confirm them so that your guests can mark their calendars. Being mindful of other people's schedules is always good etiquette! (Flip to Part II to get the scoop on ceremony and reception planning etiquette.)

- ✓ **The formality of the ceremony and the reception:** Mentioning the formality of your wedding and appropriate guest attire (including any restrictions for a religious ceremony) is important — otherwise, you'll be swamped with calls and e-mails asking for this information. Be as specific as possible, noting that "casual" has various meanings to most people. (You can use the terms of formality I provide in Chapter 9 if you're stuck on what to include.)

- ✓ **The travel information for a destination wedding:** Getting hitched in an exotic locale? Post travel information (such as hotel check-in times, means of transportation to the hotel, and weather updates) in one spot that everyone has access to. Guests appreciate not having to do all the hard work themselves. You can also post tourism information and attractions, which is a great idea for guests who have never been to your wedding's destination before.

✔ **A description of your wedding's theme:** Having a theme wedding? Theme weddings can be quite exciting, and you don't want your guests to miss out on all the fun! After you've picked a theme, share the details on your site. The more details your guests have beforehand, the more comfortable they'll be at your wedding.

✔ **A place where guests can select their meal choices and other preferences (such as vegetarian meals and meals meeting certain dietary restrictions):** Adding a meal-preference section to your Web site is useful for whoever is coordinating the meal. Providing this option to guests gives them peace of mind and shows that you're thinking of them.

✔ **Information on local accommodations for out-of-town guests:** You can include a link to the hotel you've chosen for out-of-town guests so that your guests can take a peek at the accommodations and easily make reservations.

If you've negotiated a group rate (and you should), be sure to mention the details on your site so that guests know to ask for your rate when they make their reservations.

✔ **A schedule of events:** If you plan any additional events around the time of your wedding, you can list a schedule with times, locations, and directions.

✔ **Details about your gift registry and instructions on how to access it online:** Placing details of where you're registered for gifts is extremely helpful to guests. You can list all the stores on your site, along with Web site information for people interested in shopping online. Providing this information online reduces the number of calls and e-mails you'll receive in the weeks leading up to the big day. Chapter 12 has details on setting up a gift registry.

Managing RSVPs

Providing an online RSVP feature is becoming more acceptable, and it can save time and money. Send wedding guests to your Web site so they can RSVP for the wedding online; you can note this option on your response card (see Chapter 11 for details on this invitation enclosure), along with an e-mail address for those guests who would like to respond via e-mail.

You can set up a database system that organizes your RSVPs for you. After a guest completes the RSVP form, the system automatically sends an e-mail to your inbox. To keep track of the guests who haven't responded, all you have to do is log in to your site and take a look at the saved RSVPs. Simple as that!

If you're more traditional and are planning a very formal wedding, an online RSVP feature may not be for you.

Maintaining a guest book

Traditionally, the bride and groom provide a guest book at the wedding service so that their guests can share a thoughtful sentiment. The book becomes a special wedding keepsake and history of all the people who attended the wedding. Similarly, you can provide an interactive guest book on your Web site for all the people who want to leave a note of well wishes, a personal sentiment, or a fun comment.

Your guest book should allow you to remove or edit comments. Make sure you leave a thoughtful message to remind visitors that only appropriate comments will be published.

Your online guest book is in no way a substitute for your wedding day guest book.

Setting Up a Wedding Web Site

With advances in software and Internet technology, designing and developing your own wedding Web site is easier than ever. In this section, I describe the basic process of setting up a site.

Getting started

The easiest route for setting up a wedding Web site is going through a general wedding planning site. The following popular Web sites offer a variety of services, including help with writing, editing, hosting, designing, and developing your wedding Web site:

- www.engagepage.com
- www.ourweddingday.com
- www.theknot.com
- www.weddingwindow.com
- www.wedshare.com

For more options, check out www.weddingwebsites.com. This site has a long list of wedding Web site developers and makes it easy and convenient to sort through all the choices so that you can decide on a provider that fits your needs.

Including appropriate content

Your written content — more than fancy design — is the most important aspect of your Web site. One example of proper content is the story of how you became engaged; other appropriate content includes the date and time of your ceremony and reception (among other details), an option for sending online RSVPs, and a guest book for visitors — all of which I cover in the "Why Have a Wedding Web Site?" section.

Include a few fun interactive features like a wedding etiquette quiz (guests will love that!) or a poll in which visitors can vote on everything from where you should go on your honeymoon to what you should name your first baby.

Telling every detail about your relationship isn't necessary. As humorous as you may think an experience is, keep your site's content tasteful. The purpose is to allow visitors to get to know a little more about you and your spouse-to-be.

Writing and editing Web site content are unique specialties. If you don't feel experienced enough, consider hiring a professional, or seek out a friend or relative who has this talent. For most people, writing in general — let alone writing personal stories and informational content — doesn't come easily.

Two more important features of your Web site are photos and videos. Displaying pictures and videos, especially videos with audio, of you and your spouse-to-be can tell a visual story from your early relationship, through your engagement, and up to your wedding. Your media gallery also can include tasteful photos of the people in the bridal party or photos and video from the bridal shower or other prewedding events. And don't forget to include wedding and honeymoon photos! Having a photo gallery is a thoughtful way to make people who can't attend the wedding feel like a part of your big day.

Grammatical errors, typos, broken links, and pages that state "under construction" are embarrassing, so you need to avoid them at all costs. Here are a few other important guidelines to keep in mind as you develop your own wedding Web site:

- ✔ Make sure your home page loads in fewer than 30 seconds.

- ✔ Don't go overboard with too many links, images, or pages; doing so can overwhelm visitors. Your site should be user friendly and easy to navigate.

- ✔ Some Web design templates allow you to display the same photo or image on each page of your site, so selecting that photo carefully is important. Any images you select should be tasteful; this isn't the time or place to display photos that are too intimate. Childhood photos through college and more recent pictures of you together are appropriate.

✔ Photos may be worth a thousand words, but they're worthless when they don't open quickly. So make sure all your photos and videos open fairly quickly.

Politely spreading the word

After you set up your site, you need to launch it. What's next? Well, after your site goes live and you've tested all the features, consider the best way or ways to spread the word to your family and friends. What better way to announce the launch of your new Web site than through technology? Yes, sending an e-mail with one tasteful announcement to a group is acceptable today. Here are a few rules to keep in mind when you're sending a group e-mail to announce your wedding Web site:

✔ Be concise and to the point; avoid using long sentences.

✔ Be sure to use proper spelling, grammar, and punctuation.

✔ Be judicious in your use of slang, dialects, and other unusual forms of expression unless you know the people you're e-mailing appreciate such things. Sticking to normal conversational language is best.

✔ Make it personal, and try to show both of your personalities in the e-mail.

✔ Use humor carefully. A face-to-face conversation lets you see the emotions, body language, and nuances of another person. Because e-mail doesn't let you see these nuances, the people receiving your e-mails often don't notice your sarcasm and humor, or, when they do, they may take it the wrong way.

✔ Always proofread your e-mail before you send it.

Here is an example of a properly worded Web site announcement from an engaged couple:

Greetings, friends and family! We're so excited to announce our upcoming marriage!

Many of you know that we've been sweethearts since high school. For those of you who may not know us as well, we've put together a record of our journey to share with all of you. Please visit our wedding Web site (VeronicaAndJason.com) to view all the events we've planned, tidbits of our wedding theme and venue, travel tips, recommended accommodations, and much more.

We look forward to sharing our wedding day with you!

Love,

Veronica and Jason

You may want the style and design of your e-mail announcement to match your Web site design. Or, you may want someone else to do most of the work for you. In that case, you can find some online sites that sell electronic announcements that are ready to go. All you have to do is drop the wording and photo into the template and hit send! Some of the sites listed in the earlier section "Getting started" offer this feature.

Other options for spreading the word about your Web site include save-the-date cards (see Chapter 2) along with response cards and other invitation enclosures (see Chapter 11). You can always ask a friend, a relative, or someone in your wedding party to make a few phone calls or send a group text message with the Web site address. And if you use Twitter or have a profile on a social networking site like Facebook, the news of your Web site will spread like wildfire.

Including your wedding Web site address on your wedding invitation is *always* inappropriate.

What about the friends and family who may not have access to a computer or an e-mail address? How can they see your Web site? Go the extra mile to make sure that all your close friends and family who want to see your Web site have an opportunity to do so. You can call and suggest they try accessing the site from an Internet café, the library, or a neighbor's house. If you're extra thoughtful, you can print out each page of the Web site (in color!) and mail them to the people who don't have computers or e-mail addresses.

When Is E-mail Appropriate during Wedding Planning?

When, if at all, is communicating via e-mail acceptable during the planning stages of a wedding? The decision is really based on whether you're very traditional or very modern — or maybe a little of both. Here are a few acceptable guidelines for when to use e-mail:

✔ To announce your engagement in an individual e-mail

✔ To send save-the-date notices

✔ To communicate with your wedding party and vendors (for example, to tell your groomsmen where and when they need to get measured for their tuxes or to set up meetings with your photographer or caterer before the wedding)

✔ To invite people to bridal showers and other prewedding events or activities

✔ To respond to questions from your guests (especially about travel to the wedding's location, local accommodations, and the like)

✔ To allow your guests an e-mail option for their RSVPs (mention the e-mail address to respond to on your printed response card)

✔ To send online wedding invitations

As shocking as it may be, more couples today are sending wedding invitations via e-mail, not only for the convenience factor but also to save money. An e-mail wedding invitation is recommended *only* for an informal or very small wedding; you can find templates that are designed tastefully for this purpose. Couples may not want to go for this option if traditional etiquette is very important to them or their families.

✔ To announce your marriage to invited guests who couldn't attend your wedding

Be sure you don't go overboard in sending too many e-mails. To get around this issue, many couples create their own personal e-newsletters. This clever idea solves the problem of overwhelming people with too many individual e-mails.

Beware that e-mail isn't acceptable in the following instances:

✔ **For formal weddings:** The more formal the wedding, the more formal your communications should be.

✔ **For working out a conflict with a vendor or wedding planner, or for any personal disagreement:** A phone call or a meeting in person is a must.

✔ **For thank-you notes:** It's still considered good etiquette to send a handwritten note through the mail.

Keep in mind that some people may not be online savvy or have e-mail addresses, so you have to share information with them over the phone or via another method. You also have to account for firewall issues — many e-mails end up in spam catchers, so some of your recipients may never receive your e-mails. You may want to follow up with a call to people who haven't responded by a requested time.

Chapter 4

Deciding on Finances and Planning Responsibilities Upfront

*E*tiquette changes with the times, and the sheer number of unconventional weddings taking place today stands as proof of this simple fact. But one area of wedding etiquette that hasn't changed much over the years is the tradition of who pays for what. Finances can be one of the most contentious and stressful parts of planning *anything* — now throw in the roller coaster of emotions involved in planning a wedding, and you triple the stress!

This chapter takes a close look at the traditional breakdown of expenses for the bride, the groom, and the members of the wedding party; it also covers other money-related issues, such as tipping for wedding services. In addition, I discuss the etiquette you need to follow when dealing with all the people involved in the planning, from future in-laws to wedding planners.

Depending on your situation and circumstances, you can change the budget-related lists in this chapter to suit your own needs. One key point of wedding etiquette — one of a purely practical nature — is that no parent should have to pay more for a wedding than he or she can comfortably afford. The bride and groom need to consider any contribution from their parents as a great gift.

Traditional Expenses for the Bride and Her Family

Tradition calls for the bride's family to pay for the majority of wedding expenses. You can trace the imbalance in responsibility for financing a wedding back to the days when a bride was expected to bring a dowry to a marriage. In some cultures, this rule still applies today. (Poor Mom and Dad!) Although the groom and his family contribute to a few of the expenses (see the next section for details), the following list describes the expenses the bride and her family are traditionally responsible for:

- **Services of a wedding planner or coordinator:** One of the little luxuries of the modern wedding is a wedding planner. The national average cost of using a wedding planner is approximately $3,500 to $4,000. For some couples, hiring a wedding planner is a crucial part of their wedding preparation. Many couples believe that the stress relief that this type of service provides offsets the cost. (I talk about wedding planners in more detail in the "Considering a wedding planner" section later in this chapter.)

- **Ceremony site:** The ceremony site provides the backdrop for the most important part of your wedding — the vows — so make sure you make it a top priority in your budget. The bride's family traditionally pays for all the costs involved in renting the ceremony site.

- **Reception site and related costs:** The celebration following your wedding can range from an afternoon high tea to an all-night dance party. Regardless of the type of reception you have, the bride's parents are expected to host the meal, as well as cover all the other costs related to the reception, including the site rental, any necessary equipment rentals, permits, insurance plans, decorations, and beverages. But because the reception is one of the most expensive costs in any wedding budget, some couples choose to share them today — which is perfectly okay!

  To keep costs down, carefully consider the date and time of your event. A late-night formal wedding is a great option because, if it's late enough, your guests will likely eat dinner before your wedding, which means you can tastefully serve a dessert buffet instead of a three-course meal. (Of course, you need to specify on your invitations that a meal isn't being served.)

A great way to make things more convenient for your guests (and you) is to hold both the ceremony and the reception in the same place. Doing so can help you cut costs, too.

✔ **Floral arrangements for the ceremony and reception and flowers for the bride's attendants:** No one says you have to have a field of flowers on each pew or reception table. Small and simple is often more appealing and less expensive, so choose your flowers wisely.

Buying flowers locally and adding more greenery can add up to big savings. For example, orchids from Thailand are obviously going to cost more than daffodils from down the street. Also remember that the price of flowers varies at different times of the year, depending on holidays and the seasonality of different flowers.

✔ **Music for the ceremony and reception:** A disc jockey (DJ) or recorded music may be more affordable than live music, but you can opt for a hybrid approach, such as a soloist for the ceremony and a DJ for the reception. Whatever you choose, the bride and her family typically pay for the event's music.

✔ **Photographer and videographer:** If photographs and videos of the big day are important to you, paying a professional for these services is worth the extra cost. You can expect to pay anywhere from $700 to $1,200 for a videographer (including 8 hours of filming and an edited, final copy of the video) and as much as $5,000 or more for a photographer (if you want him or her to photograph the entire day). Whatever the cost, make sure you specify whether or not you receive ownership of the original footage and prints.

If the budget is an issue, you may want to try negotiating with the photographer and videographer for a specific amount of time rather than the number of photos — which can get very expensive. You can also ask your photographer to concentrate on formal bride and groom portraits and family photos instead of focusing on candid shots at the ceremony and reception. With technology today, almost everyone has a camera phone or a digital camera, so ask friends and family to take candid shots throughout the day to supplement the professional photos (just know that your friends' pictures may not turn out quite as high quality as a professional's).

✔ **Wedding gown and accessories:** Splurging on a gown is all too easy for a bride to do. The average cost for a wedding dress is approximately $1,500 to $2,500; alterations and accessories also pile on the dollars. Discuss with your partner what percent of your budget you can allocate to the dress and accessories without skimping on other parts of the wedding. Don't let a dream send you deeply into debt.

You can find some great deals by searching Internet auction sites. You can also look for local bridal stores that offer sample sales or seek out vintage gowns from resale boutiques and secondhand stores. Flip to Chapter 9 for full details on choosing wedding attire.

✔ **Groom's wedding ring and gift:** As with all expenses, don't purchase something you can't afford. You can find plain gold or titanium bands between $100 and $200 at most chain jewelry stores. For rings with stones or platinum bands, you can expect to pay upwards of $1,500.

The typical budget for the bride's gift to the groom is around $150. Traditionally, brides gave their grooms such formal gifts as engraved watches and monogrammed cufflinks, but today more modern brides give their grooms personalized grill kits or custom-built toolboxes. (See Chapter 12 for more information on typical wedding gifts.)

✔ **Wedding invitations, announcements, enclosures, and mailing costs:** The average engaged couple spends approximately $1,200 to $1,500 on wedding invitations and reply cards. I'm not talking e-mail invitations here! A standard wedding stationary package includes invitations with professionally printed envelopes, reply cards, and professionally printed reply card envelopes. You may also choose to include reception cards, maps, or direction cards, among other enclosures. And don't forget the cost of mailing everything! For in-depth details on wedding invitation protocol, see Chapter 11.

✔ **Gifts for the bride's attendants:** After you decide on your budget, give your attendants' gifts a lot of thought. The gifts don't have to be extravagant, but they should be memorable, such as a bracelet or an engraved locket. You can give the maid or matron of honor a modestly more expensive gift, or you can give her the same gift you give the other attendants — it's up to you. You may also want to give a small gift to the flower girls. Chapter 12 has more info about giving gifts.

✔ **Luncheon for the bride's attendants:** The bride traditionally has a luncheon as a way to thank her attendants. If you can't splurge, you can show your appreciation in other gracious ways; for example, an afternoon tea or a brunch is also acceptable.

✔ **Transportation for the wedding party and special family members to and from the wedding site:** Although the bride and her family customarily provide transportation for the bridal party, extending the courtesy to special family members (such as grandparents and elderly family members who may not feel comfortable getting themselves around) is gracious, too. For the means of transportation, you can select anything from a horse-drawn carriage to a stretch limo — and everything in between (just keep in mind the logistics of your site's location and the weather before you choose!). (See Chapter 6 for more details.)

✔ **Guest book:** After some of the major expenses in this list, a guest book may seem like nothing! Expect to spend between $30 and $50 for a guest book, although you can find higher priced books ranging from $90 to $100.

Traditional Expenses for the Groom and His Family

Traditionally, the bride was a liability to her father's family and a potential drain on her husband's resources, so the groom wasn't expected to contribute much to the wedding. The groom paid a small price for his bride more to beat out the competition than to woo the girl. Through the ages, this tradition has given way to the groom's family's smaller financial investment in the big day. Although more and more families today split the costs equally, the groom and his family are traditionally responsible for the following expenses:

✔ **Bride's engagement and wedding rings:** Grooms, be sensible and buy the best engagement ring you can afford, but don't worry if you can't afford the biggest diamond in the store — there's no specific standard as far as engagement ring prices go.

Wedding rings vary greatly in price. Some people choose to go with a simple band to match the groom's and spend no more than $150. Others choose a wedding set that includes a bejeweled engagement ring and a matching wedding band. These sets usually start around $1,000.

✔ **Officiant fee or donation:** This fee varies widely, depending on the location of the ceremony and the particular organization represented. Some organizations request a donation to a particular church or other religious institution. Be as generous as possible, and remember to include extra if the officiant had to do extra traveling to get to the wedding location. (Chapter 6 has general guidelines on working with an officiant.)

Professional wedding officiants often request that you sign a contract and pay at least a 50 percent deposit; they collect the balance the day of the ceremony. Normally, the best man, or another member of the groom's attendants, physically gives this fee to the officiant.

✔ **Marriage license:** The cost for a marriage license (and the process for obtaining one) varies from state to state. Check with your city or county clerk's office for details. Just don't turn up at the wedding without this license, or you won't have a wedding.

✔ **Bride's bouquet, bride's going-away corsage, and boutonnieres for the men in the wedding:** In my experience, the groom's family pays for the men's boutonnieres (including fathers and grandfathers) and the bride's bouquet and going-away corsage. Although some brides include these items in the general floral package that I mention in the preceding section, the groom still contributes toward the cost. The bride's family assumes the cost for the flowers for everyone else involved in the wedding.

✔ **Bride's gift:** In terms of the groom's gift to the bride, almost anything goes, from a new sports car to a silver frame with a photo of hers truly. Although you need to consider your budget, you also need to make her gift extra special and meaningful (see Chapter 12 for the scoop on the bride's gift).

✔ **Gifts for the groom's attendants:** Take some time to decide what to give your attendants; your wedding isn't the time for a gag gift — that's just tacky. Perhaps you may consider tickets to a live sporting event or concert. If you're on a tight budget, you may want to go with personalized key chains, a nice set of golf balls, or keepsake cigar cutters instead. You can buy gifts of this sort in quantity to help bring down the cost. And don't forget a small gift for the ring bearer, such as a novelty item from the city where the ceremony is being held.

You also want to give a small gift to the ushers and readers to make them feel like part of the wedding party. If money's an issue, you can give them simple cards letting them know how much you appreciate their involvement in your special day.

✔ **Rehearsal dinner:** A rehearsal is essential, and the dinner is traditional (and typically an expense that the groom's family pays for). Weddings are complicated and extremely stressful occasions; use the rehearsal dinner to have some fun and put your mind at ease. Chapter 13 has the details.

✔ **Transportation and accommodations for the groom's family:** If the location of the wedding requires transportation and overnight accommodations, the groom covers the costs for his immediate family.

✔ **Accommodations for the officiant and the wedding attendants:** If the location of the wedding requires overnight accommodations, the groom or his family customarily covers these costs for attendants and the officiant. If the attendants prefer to stay in separate rooms (as opposed to the shared rooms the groom's family typically reserves for them), they cover their own accommodations.

✔ **Honeymoon expenses:** Traditionally, the groom is responsible for covering the entire cost of the honeymoon; however, this rule of thumb is changing. Today some couples choose to set up a honeymoon registry where guests can contribute in lieu of a tangible gift.

Asking for cash for your honeymoon is rude, but if someone gives you money specifically for the honeymoon, feel free to accept it graciously.

Traditional Expenses for Members of the Wedding Party

You may have a vague idea that the wedding party is supposed to support the bride and groom in the months leading up to the big day and help organize a variety of activities. But you may not know the expenses that each member of the party is responsible for in detail.

Traditional expenses for the maid or matron of honor and bridesmaids include the following:

✔ **Personal wedding attire and accessories:** Without embarrassing anyone, the bride should choose a gown that everyone can afford. If you know someone may not be able to afford your selection, confidentially offer to help her.

✔ **Wedding shower:** The maid or matron of honor and the bridesmaids are typically responsible for this get-together, as I explain in Chapter 13. Traditionally, the bride and her immediate family members should never host the shower (although as far as family members are concerned, this rule may be changing).

✔ **Bachelorette party:** The bride should make these party plans together with her maid or matron of honor and bridesmaids. Having a general agreement on the locations and cost is a good idea. Never put pressure on guests to travel when they can't afford to.

✔ **Personal travel expenses to and from the wedding location:** Whether your attendants choose to drive, fly, or take the train to your wedding is entirely up to them, but, regardless of how they choose to arrive, they're responsible for all travel expenses. Make sure the bridal party members are aware of the wedding location as soon as possible so they can plan their travels well in advance.

✔ **Part of the cost of the bridesmaids' gift to the bride:** Traditionally, the bridesmaids get together and buy a gift for the bride. They may choose to jointly purchase one of the larger items from the gift registry or give the bride something more personal like a photograph of the entire group in an engraved frame.

However, considering that each attendant spends quite a bit to participate in the wedding and that most attendants like to give their own individual gifts to the bride, it's acceptable for the group to forgo this gift.

✔ **Personal gift to the bride and groom:** Each member of the bridal party usually gives her own gift to the wedding couple. Whether the bridesmaids choose to buy gifts from the registry or give something more personal, it's important for them to factor this cost into their overall expenses when they agree to be in the wedding party.

Traditional expenses for the best man and groomsmen include the following:

✔ **Wedding attire and rental fees:** The groomsmen are expected to cover the entire cost of their tuxedo rentals, as well as their shoes, socks, and belts. Some rentals include a shirt while others do not, so make it clear to the attendants what they need to buy separately. A typical tuxedo rental runs just shy of $100, and most tuxedo companies charge late fees if the whole suit isn't returned the day after the wedding (naturally, the groomsmen are responsible for any late fees they incur).

✔ **Bachelor party:** It's amazing to me how much bachelor parties can cost. Some groomsmen choose to take the groom on an elaborate trip while others opt for a night out at a ballgame. Whichever route the groom's attendants take, they're responsible for footing the bill. The groom's main job is to make sure this shin-dig doesn't conflict with any other prewedding festivities.

✔ **Personal travel expenses to and from the wedding location:** The groomsmen are responsible for getting themselves and the groom to the wedding. The travel expenses range all over the map — they depend greatly on the means for transportation and the distance.

✓ **Part of the cost of the groomsmen's gift to the groom:** Like the bridesmaids' gift to the bride, the groomsmen's group gift to the groom may be going out of style, but it's still a cost the groomsmen should factor in before accepting the invitation to be in your wedding. If a bachelor party is drawn out into a weekend-long event, the groomsmen may choose to cover the groom's travel expenses as their gift.

✓ **Personal gift to the bride and groom:** It's appropriate for each individual groomsman to give his own gift to the wedding couple. Groomsmen may choose to give something from the registry or something special from the wedding location — either option makes a lovely gift.

Staying on Budget (and Staying Engaged)

Before anyone writes a single check, both families should agree on who's paying for what. You may decide to stick to the division of costs outlined in the previous sections, or you may choose to split costs in a different way. No matter what, make sure that everyone is on the same page. In the following sections, I explain how to set a budget, how to discuss the division of costs with class, and how to keep track of expenses so that the planning process goes as smoothly as possible.

Establishing a budget

In general, the size of the wedding budget is up to the engaged couple (in other words, you!), but you do have to come up with a starting figure — and you have to do your best to stick to it as closely as possible throughout the planning process. How do you come up with this figure? Normally, it's a combination of any personal savings you want to use, plus your parents' contributions — this sum equals your budget. The tricky part is determining whether the wedding you want fits into that budget.

Who will contribute to the budget?

If you've already announced your engagement, chances are good that all the parents involved have already worked out their finances and figured out what they can contribute to your wedding. But keep in mind that you *never* want to pressure your parents into paying for something they can't afford. Simply ask whether they can help and make sure they understand that you welcome any contribution. Let them decide what they can afford. For example, say something like: "As we try to plan our wedding, Henry and I are hoping to find out how much of a contribution, if any, you can make to our budget." This request clearly states what you want to know, but it also takes off some of the pressure by letting your parents know you don't have an expected amount in mind.

Another option is to say something like: "Henry and I have been laying out our wedding budget and would really appreciate it if you could contribute $4,000 to help cover the costs of the reception site and catering." This second request works well when you're dealing with stepparents or extended family members with whom you may not be particularly close. Explaining how much you need and why gives them an opportunity to offer more, if they're able, or let you know they can pay only half of that particular fee. The section "Keeping the peace" has more advice on navigating sticky situations and avoiding disagreements.

Don't be disheartened if your parents aren't in a position to help. With a little imagination, good planning, and budgeting, you can still have a wedding to remember.

You and your spouse-to-be may have savings of your own you want to put toward your wedding expenses. Decide at the very beginning how much of this nest egg you want to spend on your big day. You may want to put some of it toward buying a home or paying bills while on your honeymoon.

However much — or little — money you decide to put toward your wedding, make the decision and stick with it; even put it in writing, if you feel it's necessary. Be honest with your spouse-to-be and explain your reasons for wanting to add to or subtract from your wedding budget. For example, before you set your budget, talk to each other about whether you're willing to put aside an additional $1,500 for unexpected expenses or whether you're okay with paring down other costs to keep from dipping into your own stash.

Does the wedding of your dreams fit into your budget?

First things first: As the engaged couple, you must agree on the style and scope of the wedding you want to have. Doing so allows you to make a first-pass estimate of the likely costs. Going hog wild is easy to do, but now's the time to be realistic and consider all your options, depending on your budget. Part II has information on different ceremony and reception styles to help you get started. You can also consult bridal magazines or the director of your reception site to get a better idea of what you and your spouse-to-be are looking for in your special day. Keep in mind that the smaller and simpler your wedding is, the less it costs.

Another one of the biggest impacts on the cost of your wedding is your guest list. Divide your guests into *must* invite, *should* invite, and *could* invite. Can your budget cover the musts? Traditionally, the bride's parents get one-third of guests, the groom's parents get one-third, and the happy couple get one-third. (See Chapter 10 for more information on assembling a guest list.)

Two more major cost-related considerations are the wedding location and the time of day, week, or year you pick for your wedding. For example, weddings near big cities may actually be less expensive than weddings in rural areas because there's greater competition among vendors and sites. Just scheduling your wedding in the "off-season" can bring huge savings, too. For example, early to mid-January and early fall tend to be slow times for travel and commerce, in general, which leave many vendors wanting to work (which brings prices down). Having the ceremony on a Friday or Sunday may also save you quite a bit of money any time of the year because so many couples choose Saturday instead.

If you simply can't stretch the dollars far enough to cover your dream wedding, you may have to get creative. It's perfectly fine to ask friends and family to contribute their talents and abilities to make your wedding vision come alive. For example, if your second cousin is a photographer on the weekends, ask him to photograph your wedding — he may just offer to do it free of charge as a gift! Focus on what you feel are the most important elements and make them happen first.

Deciding who pays for what

Conversations involving family and money are always difficult, and striking up a conversation about wedding expenses can be especially tough. In the following sections, I show you how to tactfully bring up the topic of who will pay for what, how to determine whether a less traditional division of costs is appropriate for your wedding, and how to recognize when culture plays a role in splitting expenses.

Conversations about wedding costs aren't the time for hidden agendas; use open and honest communication with all your family members.

Tactfully presenting and discussing your initial figures

Be prepared with all the facts and figures before you meet with your parents (both the bride's and the groom's at the same time, if possible) to determine who will pay for what. Have an outline of what expenses you foresee and how much each of them will likely cost: the ceremony site, the reception hall, rental chairs, catering costs, alcohol permits, and so on. You may even include low-end prices versus more expensive ones to give yourselves and your parents an idea of the options you have to consider. Your goal is to look organized and responsible so your parents feel confident you've given the budget a lot of thought.

If one set of parents says they can't give you an exact dollar amount but would like to pay for one specific item (the rehearsal dinner, for example), graciously accept their offer, but be prepared to have less input on that item than if you were paying for it yourself or dealing with a fixed price.

If it's impossible (or impractical) to speak with all your parents together, etiquette says to speak with the bride's primary parent (the parent with whom she has the closest relationship) first, then the bride's secondary parent, followed by the groom's primary parent, and, finally, the groom's secondary parent.

When you're meeting with only one of your parents at a time, you may want to mention only whether or not a particular parent has agreed to contribute; going into details or amounts is unnecessary and can make some parents feel bad about how much they can give.

Make sure you always ask your parents for specific solutions. For example, say something like: "Mom, I know you and Ted feel like you're contributing a lot more than Dad; would you like to cut back somewhere? Or is there something specific you'd like to see him pay for?" Keeping your questions concrete and specific is a good way to keep emotions from getting out of control.

Be open to hearing thoughts from all your parents; the conversation will go a lot more smoothly if you leave your options open. To keep disagreements at a minimum, share only "need to know" information with your parents. For example, if your dad asks, "How much did your mother chip in?" respond by saying, "Well, she's covering the bar bill and the rehearsal dinner." As long as you make it clear that you're not using one parent's contributions against the other, your parents should respect your boundaries.

Splitting costs in less traditional ways with class

With so many different family situations today, many couples have to deal with less traditional ways of splitting wedding costs. For example, couples with divorced parents can't just split the costs according to the guidelines I set out in the "Traditional Expenses for the Bride and Her Family" and "Traditional Expenses for the Groom and His Family" sections earlier in this chapter.

Unfortunately, etiquette doesn't lay out specific rules for how divorced parents should split wedding costs, though a good guideline to follow is how much custody a parent had when you were a child. For instance, if your parents had shared custody and saw you equally, it's reasonable of you to expect them to divide your weddings costs in half. If you lived mostly with your mom and saw your dad only on the occasional weekend or school holiday, an 80/20 split may be more appropriate. If you were raised by a single parent, be sure to consider all the other expenses your parent is responsible for (your siblings' college educations, for example), and never ask a parent to give more than he or she is able.

If all involved parties are agreeable and able, however, the simplest way to deal with your wedding costs is to do an even split. For example, you project the wedding costs to be $20,000 and you factor in an additional 10 percent for incidentals, which gives you a grand total of $22,000. Five parties are willing to contribute (you and your spouse-to-be, your mom and stepdad, your dad, your spouse-to-be's dad and stepmom, and your spouse-to-be's mom and stepdad), so each group's share is $4,400 each.

In the cases of second marriages or first marriages of couples who have been living independently of their families or who are in their 30s or older, the bride and groom often share in the cost of the wedding, or the groom pays for a significant amount, depending on the situation with the bride's family.

Keeping a record of who pays what

After everyone agrees on who's paying for what, put the division of expenses in writing, and make copies for both the bride's and the groom's families. Yes, your families love you, but a wedding is an emotional and stressful time, and things can easily be forgotten or overlooked.

I suggest creating a wedding budget worksheet like the one in Table 4-1. Make sure you include absolutely everything, from the cute monogrammed napkins you want to put on the cake table to the three-course meal you plan to serve to your 300 guests. Refer to the worksheet throughout the planning stages, and share the details with your wedding planner if you have one.

Table 4-1	Wedding Budget Worksheet
Item	*Cost*
Wedding planner	
Ceremony site	
Reception site (including all rentals)	
Catering	
Liquor and additional beverages	
Cake	
Photographer	
Videographer	
Wedding day transportation	
Bride and groom's travel expenses	
Bridal wardrobe	
Officiant's fees	
Payroll (valet attendants, bartenders, coat-check attendants, and so on)	
Insurance and permits	

The simplest way to keep track of who pays for what is to set up a wedding bank account and directly deposit all contributions into that account. Consider transferring a portion of your income into this account with every paycheck, too. You can then pay for all wedding services from this account.

You can set up the bank account with online access and share the password with multiple users so each person who has added money to the account can see what's being spent where and when. Doing so can help make your accounting a little bit easier, but, more importantly, it can minimize financial disagreements by keeping everyone who's contributing in the loop.

Keeping good records is important, but also remember that initial decisions on costs aren't set in stone. You can always change the budget as the planning progresses and new situations or circumstances arise. Agree ahead of time how changes to the budget should be handled. Do you and your spouse-to-be have the final say? Are you allowed to make changes up to a certain dollar amount? Can you simply e-mail everyone after you make a change, or do certain parties expect to be consulted ahead of time? You need to address all these questions as soon as you agree on the budget.

Giving Gratuities: Who Receives How Much?

Certain wedding vendors expect to receive a gratuity. Who's entitled to a tip, how much is appropriate, and when should you hand it over? Take a look at the following list for suggested guidelines.

Make sure that vendors and other paid support personnel do *not* place tip receptacles in their work areas during the wedding or reception. Seeing a jar labeled "Tips appreciated" next to the buffet line is just plain tacky!

- ✔ **Wedding planner:** A 10 percent tip is acceptable for a wedding planner, but if your wedding planner truly goes above and beyond, you may choose to offer a gratuity of up to 20 percent. Either way, you offer your tip when you make your final payment.

- ✔ **Officiant or pastor:** The officiant typically receives $25 to $50, but he or she may request a donation to a charity rather than a cash gratuity. If the officiant requests a donation to a specific charity in lieu of a fee or tip, you can deliver your check to the officiant ahead of time or at the ceremony. If your officiant isn't a member of the clergy or has been hired with a set fee, 15 percent is an appropriate tip and should be added to the final payment. However you choose to pay, the best man can give your officiant this payment after the ceremony. Just prepare a cash (or check) envelope in advance.

- ✔ **Ceremony musicians:** Each musician receives $25 to $30. The best man can pay a cash envelope at the end of the ceremony, or you can pay this tip in advance.

- ✔ **Florists, photographers, and bakers:** Thank-you cards and recommendations to friends are much-appreciated "tips" for these vendors. However, you should give each person who delivers or sets up flowers (if he or she isn't the florist who did the arranging) a $10 cash tip. If you choose to give a 15 to 20 percent gratuity to the florist for exceptional work, you may include it with the final payment.

- ✔ **Person providing transportation via limo, bus, and so on:** The driver receives 20 percent of the total cost, and you can add it to the final payment.

- ✔ **Valets and parking attendants:** Estimate the number of cars they will be parking based on your responses (a good rule of thumb is one car per "yes" reply card), and tip based on $1 to $2 per car. You should then divide the total amount (say, $100 for 50 cars) equally among the attendants, and you should prepay this tip.

  It's a good idea to have another $5 to $10 per attendant ready in envelopes in case they have to stay late or they end up going above and beyond their prior arranged duties.

- ✔ **Coat check and restroom attendants:** Each of these attendants should receive $1 to $2 per guest, based on the number of "yes" response cards you receive. The best man pays this tip at the beginning of the reception, in cash.

- ✔ **Reception/catering staff and servers:** The site manager and staff as a whole should receive an 18 to 20 percent tip after they clear everything away after the cake service and after they properly wrap up any leftovers.

- ✔ **Maitre d':** Each maitre d' receives a percentage of the reception cost. The father of the bride or the best man can pay this tip at the end of the reception. Prepare cash envelopes in advance.

- ✔ **Bartenders:** The bartenders receive $20 per person or 10 percent of the total bar tab and then split it. Make sure the bartenders aren't accepting tips from guests. The best man can pay this tip at the end of the reception. Prepare cash envelopes in advance.

- ✔ **DJ or musicians at reception:** Each DJ or musician receives $25 to $30. The best man can pay this tip at the end of the reception. Prepare cash envelopes in advance.

Some vendors add the gratuity into their contracts, so always read vendor contracts carefully to ensure that you aren't tipping twice. If a gratuity is included in the contract, you can always give an extra amount later for excellent service.

Before the ceremony, the best man (or other designated, responsible person) should have all gratuities ready in labeled envelopes for the various vendors. For the vendors who need to be prepaid (see specifics in the preceding list), the best man gives them their envelopes at the beginning of the reception. The best man can give the other vendors their payments at the end of the reception. He should give shared tips (for the bartenders, for example) to the lead attendant to be divided after the reception.

Putting Together a Planning Team

Planning a wedding usually isn't a one-couple job; you may find that you want the help of parents, relatives, friends, or even a wedding planner. In the following sections, I explain how to ask for the services of all these folks and how to keep the peace among them.

Whether you ask your family and friends to help or you decide to use the services of a wedding planner, basic etiquette requires you to allow an appropriate amount of time for each helper to complete his or her wedding tasks. For most weddings, you should allow at least six months to take care of all the details. If you have less time, you have to be willing to make certain changes to traditional expectations. For example, you may have to buy a wedding dress off the rack instead of ordering one and having a series of fittings. But don't be alarmed — you can certainly pull it off!

Deciding on your parents' level of involvement (and letting them know)

You need to handle asking your parents for planning help with extra sensitivity. Your parents may feel that they're entitled to a major say in the planning and decision making, especially when they're contributing large chunks of cash. But remember that you have the final say in deciding how much you want them to be involved.

Think about the skills and talents (or lack thereof) of each parent. Look for opportunities to match the talents of each parent with specific tasks. For example: Does your future mother-in-law have a passion for flowers? Wonderful! Give her the job of finding floral options, and then you can make the final decision. For example, say something like: "Helen, I've always admired your eye for flowers and would love some input on the arrangements and bouquets." Asking for help in this way makes it clear you're asking only for advice, not for someone to make the decisions for you.

Also consider each parent's physical location, health, and energy level. For example, a parent who lives on the other coast can't physically shop for wedding venues. In this case, say something like: "Mom, I know you can't fly into town this weekend just to see the venues, but if don't mind, can you call some of them for me to verify their fees and find out what permits I need to get?"

No matter how much help you decide to ask for, the key to making your parents feel comfortable with what they're doing is to ask for exactly the help you want and lay on the gratitude. You simply can't say "thank you" enough! For example, if your mother-in-law feels upset about her level of involvement, a great thing to say is: "Mary, your help has been amazing! I know you may feel like you can do a lot more than just polish up the guest list and gather addresses, but it would take me a really long time to get all this stuff done, and I really appreciate everything you're doing."

Asking friends and relatives for help

If you happen to be lucky enough to have willing and able friends and relatives, delegate wedding tasks to them, too. Let each of your friends or relatives know what your budget is and show them what you're looking for. Don't be afraid to offer a few suggestions and check in on them to see whether you can help out. And make sure you have the final say on all their decisions. Remember, though, that your family and friends are doing you a favor and aren't professionals, so you can't ask for your money back if you're unhappy with their choices.

Considering a wedding planner

If planning your wedding by yourself scares the living daylights out of you, or if you and your significant other have time-consuming jobs, poor planning abilities, or a lack of tolerance for stress, a wedding planner may fit the bill for you! A well-qualified planner can recommend and work with vendors, offer opinions on the style and design of the ceremony and reception, and provide etiquette advice.

Here are just a few of the benefits of hiring a wedding planner:

- **Time-saving:** Saves time in your busy schedule
- **Reliable:** Already has a list of reputable vendors and can schedule appointments for you
- **Experienced:** Has experience and knowledge of all parts of the planning process
- **Money-conscious:** Has access to preferred vendor rates
- **Objective:** Isn't emotionally involved with either family and can make objective decisions

Be aware that hiring a wedding planner does have some negative consequences, as well. Here are just a few to consider:

✔ You may feel a loss of control and authority.

✔ Your wedding planner's judgment and opinion may not always match yours.

✔ The fees may represent 10 percent or more of your total budget.

✔ The cost may be worth reducing some of the stress in the early planning stages, but the planner may not offer as much help with the smaller details as the big day approaches.

If you're convinced that you need a wedding planner, ask family and friends for recommendations. If you have a specific venue in mind, ask the person in charge of that venue whom he or she likes to work with. You're going to be spending a lot of time with your wedding planner, so invest some time upfront in thoroughly researching all your options. Ask for references, and follow up on them.

Schedule appointments with at least three different planners, and prepare a list of questions that are important to you and your spouse-to-be, including the following: Are you comfortable working within our strict budget? What are some common mistakes you see couples make? Can we see some examples of wedding day itineraries you've planned?

Don't forget to follow your instincts. Getting along with someone is based on personality, so make sure you feel completely comfortable with this person. (Need help? Flip to Chapter 17 for guidelines on getting along with your wedding planner.)

Wedding planner fees vary considerably, depending on the size of the wedding and the degree of involvement. Decide what you need from simply day-of-event services to a fully comprehensive package, including everything from securing the right location for your budget and guest list to hammering out all the details of your individual vendor contracts. You can estimate the fee to be about 10 to 15 percent of the event budget.

Keeping the peace

To keep the peace among all your helpers and your spouse-to-be, be prepared to compromise and pick your battles. You can make concessions on some details, but you really need to keep everyone on one side. Planning a wedding with as little stress as possible is all about communicating tactfully and gracefully and being sensitive to your helpers when you're delivering a message.

Your planning team members need to realize that their function is presenting you with good choices and that the final decision is always yours, unless you specifically say otherwise. So, how do you deflect an unwanted opinion or idea? Very carefully! For example, suppose your mother wants you to wear her grandmother's heirloom wedding gown, but you have your heart set on something sleek and modern. Be sensitive to her feelings and thank her for her offer, but make your decision clear: "Wearing your grandmother's dress would be such an honor for me, but I've been dreaming about what I want to wear for a very long time, and I really have a specific dress in mind. Thank you, though; I appreciate your kind offer."

If you plan to enlist the help of your future mother-in-law, making your spouse-to-be the ambassador for dealing with his mother is a good idea. Don't feel bad about delegating this task to him — after all, he knows her better than you do! Planning isn't a task that only the bride needs to handle, so if difficulties arise, always be honest and open in your discussions with your spouse-to-be. You can talk about someone's behavior without attacking him or her personally.

What should you do if fighting breaks out among your helpers? For instance, what if you're not getting along with your mother, your spouse-to-be is fighting with his parents, or several family members are arguing over wedding decisions? Always take the higher ground, and never respond to rudeness with rudeness. Easier said than done, right? But, truly, arguments are bound to surface, so you need to pick your battles carefully. You can reap the benefits by providing a greater sense of involvement for all your helpers and encounter less random interference by carefully planning early on. In the event that family members are arguing with each other, make it clear how upsetting their childish behavior is to you and your intended. And lay out ground rules for their future interactions so they don't have any question about what you expect from them.

Part II

The Main Event: Planning Your Ceremony and Reception

The 5th Wave   By Rich Tennant

"I don't know what table to seat the wolves at. We can't seat them with my side of the family, or have you forgotten what happened at the shower?"

In this part...

Get ready for a real etiquette workout because I cover everything from different ceremony styles to the basics of scheduling your ceremony in this part. I also give you a few notes on working with an officiant, personalizing your ceremony, and more.

But that's not all! I give you words of wisdom for picking the proper reception style and getting along with your reception manager, along with a strategic plan for putting together an appropriate seating chart. I finish off this part with some practical ways to ensure your reception is a success, such as picking out suitable favors and knowing when providing alcoholic beverages is appropriate.

Chapter 5

Checking Out Ceremony Styles

- -

In This Chapter

▶ Adhering to the etiquette of religious wedding ceremonies

▶ Looking at other types of wedding ceremonies

- -

*Y*our ceremony is the main event of your wedding day, and you have a ton of styles to choose from; for example, you can opt for a religious ceremony or one without the trappings of a particular faith. I cover the basics of different ceremony styles in this chapter, but keep in mind that because traditional rituals can be quite involved and complicated (not to mention numerous!), I don't go over their meanings and origins in great detail. Speak to your officiant or a family member who's knowledgeable in the traditions in your religion or culture for more details about your particular ceremony.

As you find out in this chapter, different ceremony styles have specific protocol and varying levels of formality (such as black tie, formal, semiformal, and informal), and conveying that information to your guests is important. To get the word out, post information about your ceremony's formality and any important rules your guests need to know beforehand on your wedding Web site (see Chapter 3) and include it in your program (see Chapter 6). You can also have your parents and members of the wedding party spread the word.

Surveying Different Religious Ceremonies

Being aware of religious customs when you're planning your wedding ceremony is extremely important. Appropriate etiquette calls for considering not only your own feelings about these traditions but also the expectations of your relatives and friends, particularly if they're very observant.

If your officiant is a member of the clergy from the religion that you and your partner adhere to, he or she will undoubtedly be one of the best sources of appropriate etiquette and protocol you can tap in to. When you meet with your officiant, he or she directs you in the traditions of the place of worship you've chosen for your ceremony and on the parts of the ceremony that you can choose, such as readings and hymns. (See Chapter 6 for details on working well with an officiant.)

Keep in mind that many shifts in etiquette have taken place within religious marriage ceremonies over the past few years. For example, the traditional vow that the woman takes to "obey" her husband is making its way out of style, except in conservative traditions. Today you may be able to write your own vows and still retain the traditional rituals of your faith. You also may be able to select your own readings and music.

To keep from surprising your guests with any unorthodox approaches, preparing your guests with written descriptions in your wedding program is a good idea. Always inform close family members of your ceremony plans beforehand, too. Chapter 6 has tips on putting together a wedding program and planning the other details of your ceremony.

In the following sections, I briefly describe the etiquette behind the marriage ceremonies of a variety of religions.

If any of your family members take a dim view of a religiously mixed marriage or are pressuring you for a particular religious ceremony, consider having two separate ceremonies, one for each of your faiths. This solution has become more common and can help maintain civility for both families — and provide some added peace for the bride and groom.

Catholic

In the Catholic Church, marriage is considered one of the seven sacraments believed to be channels of God's grace. The wedding is primarily a worship service (typically formal in terms of formality, although semiformal is acceptable) in which you and your spouse-to-be praise God for your coming together. The Church offers marriage as a sacred opportunity to have families and friends celebrate in the dedication of your marriage to God.

Catholic weddings are rich in tradition and liturgy. The ceremony has at least three biblical readings, a homily given by the priest (in which he focuses on the couple and marriage), the exchange of vows, the exchange of wedding rings, the Prayer of the Faithful, and the nuptial blessing. It also includes appropriate music for each of these elements. Your priest guides you through all the particulars because the service is fairly set; however, if you want to include some personal elements like lighting a unity candle or adding to the traditional vows, your priest can approve these changes.

The sacrament of marriage usually takes place during a Mass (called the *Nuptial Mass*) in the morning or early afternoon. However, Friday evening Nuptial Masses are becoming more common as people try to save money by having their weddings on Fridays rather than Saturdays.

Only Catholics are able to receive Holy Communion during the Nuptial Mass; however, some priests encourage everyone to come forward to receive a blessing.

If both you and your spouse-to-be are Catholic, the wedding must take place in a church for the marriage to be sanctified. It usually takes place in the parish church of the bride's family. Weddings don't take place on Holy Thursday, Good Friday, or Holy Saturday, and weddings aren't scheduled during the hours of Mass for the congregation at large.

Premarital preparation is very important and often required in most Catholic churches. The type of premarital preparation depends on the priest and the church, but most churches require engaged couples to attend premarital classes beginning six months before their weddings.

Some priests require weekly or monthly meetings with the couple, where they help the bride and groom understand the challenges of marriage and the sacredness of their commitment to each other. Some Catholic churches also offer weekend retreats for couples as part of the premarital preparation (and yes, separate rooms are a must!). With all these possibilities, you need to find out well in advance what premarital requirements your church has.

Interfaith weddings are allowed in some Catholic churches, though not all. The decision is normally up to the parish priest, who may require the non-Catholic bride or groom to take a few extra prep classes to better understand the Catholic faith.

Episcopal

Marriage is one of seven sacramental rites performed in the Episcopal Church, and Episcopal weddings tend to be less formal and can be held outside. A priest or a bishop normally presides at the wedding because he alone can pronounce the nuptial blessing and celebrate the Holy Eucharist. The ceremony normally lasts less than an hour and includes the declaration of consent, scripture reading, homily, exchange of vows and rings, signing of the register, and blessing of marriage.

A priest can help you choose the correct prayers and rituals for the wedding. For example, at Holy Communion, if included in the marriage ceremony, tradition calls for a specific liturgy followed by the Offertory (or offerings of bread and wine). The couple receives communion after the ministers. After the ceremony, the wedding party may leave the church as the congregation sings a hymn or psalm or as instrumental music is played.

In the Episcopal Church, at least one of the parties must be a baptized Christian, and the marriage must conform to the laws of the state and the canons of the Episcopal Church. But interfaith marriages are permitted, and most Episcopal priests will perform interfaith marriage ceremonies.

The Episcopalian Church usually requires three to four premarital counseling sessions, so it's important that you check in with your officiant in advance. The focus of the meetings is to help the couple explore their coming marriage relationship and the nature of Holy Matrimony more fully.

Mainstream Protestant

The term *Protestant* refers to Baptist, Lutheran, Methodist, and Presbyterian denominations or any denomination of Christian religions not of the Catholic or Eastern church. Marriage in the mainstream Protestant Church is considered holy but isn't thought of as a sacrament. Your ceremony may be formal or informal, but you want to discuss this issue with your minister to be sure that casual is acceptable.

You have quite a bit of say in how you organize and personalize your wedding in the mainstream Protestant Church. Most mainstream Protestant denominations allow you to marry outside of a house of worship, so you can be quite innovative with your location. However, no matter which denomination you're marrying in, you should talk to your officiant to make sure you observe all the correct traditions. For example:

- ✔ If you're marrying in a Methodist or Presbyterian church, you probably have to follow guidelines from the church's ceremony service book.

- ✔ If you're marrying in a Lutheran church, you can use your own ideas with the help of your officiant.

- ✔ If you're marrying in a Baptist church, the church will set the rules for the wedding for you.

A Protestant ceremony typically starts with a welcome from the minister, followed by readings and vows, which can both be either traditional or customized by the bride and groom. The officiant then blesses the rings before the bride and groom exchange them; many couples also choose to light a unity candle as a symbol of their marriage. The officiant concludes with a blessing, and, of course, the couple gets to finish with a nice, big kiss!

Depending on your particular church, you may not be able to schedule your wedding on certain days, such as any day during Holy Week. Check with your officiant for details.

Normally, couples receive three to four days of premarital counseling from the officiant as a part of their preparation for marriage. And most Protestant denominations allow interfaith marriages.

Eastern Orthodox

Like in the Catholic Church, marriage in the Eastern Orthodox Christian Church is a sacrament. The wedding ceremony (which is formal in nature) consists of the following two parts:

- ✔ **Service of betrothal:** During the betrothal, the priest blesses the bride and groom three times with their wedding rings in the name of the Father, the Son, and the Holy Spirit; the couple also exchanges the rings three times and places them on their right hands.

- ✔ **Ceremony of the sacrament of marriage:** During this part of the ceremony, the couple's religious sponsor crowns the bride and groom with wreaths three times to show that they're the king and queen of their union. The bride and groom also drink from a common cup and walk around a table in front of the altar as an expression of their joy; the priest removes their crowns at the end of the ceremony.

The sponsor must be of Orthodox faith, but other members of the bridal party may be non-Orthodox. The Eastern Orthodox Church allows interfaith marriages, but one partner must be Eastern Orthodox and the other partner must be a baptized Christian. Eastern Orthodox weddings can't take place outside a church or during special fasting periods throughout the year; talk to your officiant to make sure your wedding date doesn't fall during one of these periods.

Premarital counseling is required and is traditionally provided by the priest prior to the wedding. However, the couple may choose to consult with a professional premarital therapist as long as they inform the priest of their choice in advance.

Mormon

The Church of Jesus Christ of Latter-day Saints offers the following two types of wedding services:

- **Temple wedding:** A temple wedding is considered a marriage for all eternity and is held in one of the world's Holy Temples. You have to be of the Mormon faith and a member of the church as well as gain permission from several Mormon clergy before you can have a temple wedding (which is formal in nature). To gain permission, you and your spouse-to-be must satisfactorily answer specific questions in two main interviews with the local bishop. Only faithful members of the Church may attend a temple wedding and they, too, must receive an official "temple recommend" from a member of the Mormon clergy to enter the temple. The ceremony is considered sacred, and no floral arrangements or photographs are permitted.

- **Non-temple wedding:** This wedding service is open to anyone, whether you're Mormon or not. The ceremony is normally held in a home or church with a simple ceremony. A local bishop at any Mormon church can officiate this type of wedding (which may be informal, depending on the advice of the bishop officiating), but, according to the faith, a couple married this way is married only until death. To be married for eternity, a couple has to marry in a Holy Temple.

  After you're married in a civil or non-temple ceremony, you may be able to have a temple wedding later as long as you and your spouse-to-be have begun to practice appropriate Mormon precepts.

Quaker

Quaker (Religious Society of Friends) weddings are distinctly different from and much simpler than any of the others in this chapter. For example, Quaker weddings are made up of long periods of silence with no display of ceremonial rituals, such as music, giving away of the bride, or exchanging of rings.

Couples declare their desire to marry either in writing or by an announcement during a regular Quaker meeting. The meeting then appoints a clearness committee who meets with the couple to determine their readiness for marriage. After the clearness committee approves the couple for marriage, the committee makes a recommendation for the meeting to create another committee that helps the couple prepare for the wedding. The committee helps the bride and groom schedule events, create the Quaker marriage certificate, and find a premarital counselor.

Quakers don't generally register their marriages with local government; however, if a married couple ever needs proof of marriage, the Quaker certificate suffices. You should check the legal issues of this type of marriage document with a representative of the jurisdiction in which your wedding will take place and in the state in which you plan to reside just to be safe.

The Quaker wedding takes place during a worship meeting. The couple enters the meeting after everyone else has been seated. The couple then stands and exchanges their promises to each other after the required period of silence. The vows are usually very straightforward. No officiant is in charge, and the couple declares themselves married before God and then exchanges the rings.

The marriage certificate, which is much like the Ketubah of a Jewish wedding (see the following section), is written by a calligrapher on a large sheet of parchment paper. It contains the promises the bride and groom have exchanged and is signed by the couple and then the attendants, who include personal messages to the couple. Everyone in attendance then signs the document as witnesses.

In the traditional Quaker wedding, everyone — including the bride and groom — wears plain clothes, and no processional is held. However, today some couples are choosing to add a processional, and the bride may choose to wear a white dress.

To marry in a Quaker marriage ceremony, both the bride and the groom have to be Quakers or regularly attend monthly meetings. Couples who are registered as *attenders,* meaning they're not yet members of the Religious Society of Friends, are expected to attend meetings for a number of months before making an application for marriage. When one member of the couple isn't a Quaker, or is divorced, two adult members of the Society must give written permission before the marriage can take place.

Jewish

The Jewish faith has three main divisions. In order of the most observant and strict to the far less stringent, these divisions are Orthodox, Conservative, and Reform. Various wedding etiquette rules differ from one division to the other; however, some traditions are consistent with all three, including the following:

- Normally, Jewish weddings can't take place on the Sabbath, which lasts from sundown on Friday to sundown on Saturday, because no one is supposed to drive or work on the Sabbath. Plus, the Sabbath is considered a sacred observance, and having a wedding at the same time would interfere with that observance.

- The date of your wedding must avoid the major holidays, such as Rosh Hashanah, Yom Kippur, and Passover. The Orthodox and Conservative Jews also don't marry on the holidays of Shavuot and Sukkot or during the seven weeks between Passover and Shavuot. Reform rabbis, on the other hand, probably wouldn't object to these times.

- All Jewish weddings use a *chuppah,* or wedding canopy, as a symbol of a home. The bride, groom, and officiant stand under it during the ceremony, along with the parents of the bride and maybe the maid of honor and a bridesmaid if there's room. Who stands under the canopy also depends on the type of wedding and the officiant's requirements. The groom typically approaches the bride before she reaches the chuppah and escorts her to the canopy. This action symbolizes his bringing her into his house.

- The ceremony includes a blessing over wine, and the groom and bride both take sips of it. Then the groom gives the bride a ring, preferably a solid style with no stones. Only the groom gives the bride a ring in a traditional ceremony, but today some Orthodox rabbis allow the couples to have a double ring ceremony.

- A *Ketubah* is the traditional marriage contract. At one time, only the more traditional Jews used these contracts, but now Reform weddings often use them, as well. However, many couples today tend to veer away from the traditional Ketubah text and its implications and instead write their own version that expresses their hopes and expectations for their marriage. Generally, the contract needs to be signed by the officiant and two witnesses and is presented in the ceremony according to the officiant's desire.

✔ After the officiant pronounces the groom and bride husband and wife, the groom steps on a glass wrapped in cloth. This ritual has many meanings, but the most common and universal one is that it represents the destruction of the Temple in Jerusalem and the difficult times the Jews have had throughout history.

A rabbi almost always officiates Orthodox and Conservative weddings. The Reform Jews are more flexible on this tradition and sometimes employ a justice of the peace, a cantor (the musical director and soloist of a temple), or a community leader to conduct the ceremony.

A Jewish wedding can take place outside of a synagogue. Because the presence of the chuppah makes the place of the wedding a Jewish space, ceremonies can take place in backyards, in hotels, and on the beach. Selecting the location, venue, and level of formality is up to the bride, groom, and officiant.

Intermarriage isn't encouraged in the Jewish faith, especially by the Orthodox. However, it's much more common today for Reform rabbis to consent to officiate at interfaith weddings. Often the clergy member from the non-Jewish partner's church and the rabbi co-officiate.

Although the Jewish faith doesn't require formal marriage preparation, it does recommend some premarital counseling to give you and your spouse-to-be the chance to find out more about your relationship, your values, and your future together.

Muslim

According to Islam, the woman initially makes the offer of marriage, typically through a male relative. Then the couple creates the marriage contract. It includes a *meher,* or a formal statement or agreement specifying the monetary amount and other personal rights the groom will present to the bride. This contract is created before the marriage is agreed to. In addition to this contracted amount of money, the groom gives the bride a deferred gift of either a smaller amount of money, jewelry, land, or even an education, throughout her life.

Weddings that follow the contract signing can be held in a mosque, or they can take place in the home of bride. The marriage ceremony itself is very short, only about five minutes long, and is conducted by an imam, who reads from the Koran. Depending on how conservative the family is, the couple can either be separated in different rooms, or the bride and groom can be seated apart in the same room (in this case, the bride is heavily veiled). The imam asks the couple three times if they accept each other in marriage according to the terms of their traditional marriage contract. (Some couples also recite wedding vows.)

After the magistrate is satisfied with the answers the couple give, the contract — the only real requirement of a Muslim wedding — is signed, and the bride and groom are pronounced man and wife. One or two weeks later, several public celebrations are held in honor of the couple, and the groom and his family pay for them.

Muslim women must marry Muslim men, but Muslim men may marry non-Muslim women as long as their children are raised as Muslims.

Hindu

Hindu wedding ceremonies vary greatly from region to region. Traditional Hindu ceremonies in India can last for days and involve a lot of ritual performed in Sanskrit. In the United States, Hindu wedding ceremonies are standardized to avoid conflicts when the families of the bride and groom are from different Indian regions. This standard ceremony is much shorter and simpler than the traditional Indian ceremony and can take place in the bride's home.

Hindu weddings are considered semiformal, and no premarital counseling is required. Like many other religions today, Hinduism allows interfaith marriages.

Sikh

The Sikh marriage ceremony, which is normally quite elaborate, is considered a holy union between two souls that are joined in an equal, spiritual partnership. The whole event is informal, family-oriented, joyous, and festive.

Part of the wedding day is devoted to the religious ceremony, which normally takes place in a Sikh temple but can also be held in the bride's family's home if the holy scriptures of Guru Granth Sahib have been respectfully installed. Tradition doesn't mandate any time restrictions for the wedding, but Sikh weddings are usually performed in the morning and take a few hours to complete.

Both families meet at the bride's home for the Milni ceremony. They then sing devotional songs and recite prayers. The bride and groom circle around the holy scriptures and seek blessings. Then comes the Vidaai ceremony, during which the bride's family bids her a tearful farewell as she throws rice over her shoulders. Finally, the groom's family hosts a reception party to welcome the bride to the family and to formally introduce her to family and friends.

Sikh marriages are often arranged; however, in an attempt to move from ancient traditions, the Official Sikh Code of Conduct, called the *Reht Maryada,* specifies that no thought should be given to the perspective spouses in terms of caste, race, or lineage. The important issue is that both partners profess the Sikh faith and no other. To separate a wedding ceremony from any sort of business transaction, Sikh tradition doesn't allow dowry arrangements.

Buddhist

Buddhists believe that all people are equal and that life is a process of change, focused on increasing awareness, wisdom, and kindness through mindfulness and meditation. Buddhist practices and beliefs vary somewhat, and Buddhist matrimonial traditions aren't really based on religion, but rather on one's faith. Buddhists are allowed to marry a person of any faith, as long as the spouse respects the teachings of Buddhism.

To be considered legal, the Buddhist wedding ceremony, which is known for its simplicity as reflected in the Buddhist religion, must be performed by a person who is legally registered to conduct weddings; otherwise, the couple has to also have a civil ceremony (which I discuss later in this chapter).

Having no religious tangles or mandatory rules and regulations, the entire Buddhist marriage ceremony is treated as a social affair. It can be performed in a home or in a temple. Keep in mind, however, that a Buddhist wedding conducted in a temple that caters to a specific culture is quite different from a ceremony that a western Zen teacher officiates outside a temple.

Some couples prefer to follow strict Buddhist religious rites and customs, while other couples choose to compose their own vows that acknowledge all the Buddhist elements. The bride and groom are required to make a sincere commitment to each other to create a harmonious relationship. Blessings and marriage advice are normally included in the ceremony.

In some Buddhist communities, the bride and groom traditionally visit a monk that has taken a vow of poverty on the morning of the wedding. The couple offers food to the monk in exchange for his blessing.

Unitarian

Unitarian Universalism is a liberal, non-Christian denomination known for its scholarly and pluralistic approach to religion. A Unitarian wedding can include many different traditions and can be extremely creative as long it's based on the spirituality and personal integrity of the couple. There's no set liturgy or format for Unitarian weddings; rather each ceremony is a collaboration between the couple and the lay chaplain that incorporates elements that are meaningful to those involved.

A Unitarian wedding may be the right choice for you if you want to be married by a minister but don't want the event to be a full religious ceremony. The flexibility of most Unitarian ministers is a bonus when you're planning to have your ceremony outside a house of worship, such as in a museum or a home.

Meet with your minister at least two months before your wedding so that you can give him an idea of what you're looking for. Couples who decide to marry in a Unitarian ceremony are welcome to explore the Unitarian Fellowship of Fredericton, but attendance at services isn't a prerequisite for having a Unitarian wedding ceremony.

 To find a Unitarian Universalist minister in your area, go to the Unitarian Universalist Association of Congregations' Web site (www.uua.org).

Examining Other Types of Ceremonies

Even with the growing number of nonreligious or otherwise unconventional weddings occurring nowadays, most ceremonies are still conducted with some tradition. Having a good understanding of the etiquette rules of any of the following ceremony styles can help you make sure you carry out every detail properly.

Secular ceremonies

Secular ceremonies are similar to civil ceremonies (see the next section) in that little or no religion is involved and they take place outside a house of worship, although most couples choose to share their spiritual beliefs by incorporating them into their wedding vows, special readings, or personal affirmations. Anyone — a justice of the peace or a friend or family member, for example — can conduct a secular ceremony as long as he or she fulfills the legal requirements for conducting weddings. Secular weddings have become popular with interfaith couples and can be anything from a conservative, formal, traditional white wedding to a casual, imaginative, unconventional ceremony.

The typical secular service has a structure similar to a religious one. The officiant begins the ceremony by making an introduction; next, the couple recites their vows and any special readings and then exchanges their wedding rings.

 If one of you prefers a religious ceremony in a house of worship and the other wants a service in a secular setting — try to compromise by designing a ceremony that both of you can live with. Often, you can have a religious ceremony in a secular location (such as a park or museum) with a minister or other religious officiate, or you can hold a nonreligious ceremony in a nondenominational church.

Civil ceremonies

 To have a civil wedding ceremony, your officiant must be an official of the state, hold one of the following civil titles, and sign your marriage certificate:

- ✔ County clerk
- ✔ Court clerk
- ✔ Judge
- ✔ Magistrate
- ✔ Mayor
- ✔ Justice of the peace
- ✔ Notary
- ✔ Celebrant/minister

Laws for civil ceremonies vary from state to state, but all states require that you obtain a marriage license at least six days before the ceremony. In most states you can obtain your license at the county clerk's office at the county court house. To qualify for the license, you and your spouse-to-be must meet requirements set by the particular state issuing the license.

The ceremony venue is up to you; it can be romantic or themed, in a location that's meaningful to you both (such as on a cruise ship with the captain officiating or on a secluded beach), or in a place as simple as a judge's chambers or an attorney's office. You also can personalize the ceremony's formality and customize your vows as you wish.

Military ceremonies

A U.S. military wedding ceremony has many similarities to a traditional civilian wedding. Normally, the ceremony is a religious one. The main differences in a military service are the pageantry and the various military traditions used.

The formal attire (full dress uniform) of a military wedding sets the tone. Each branch of the military wears specific uniforms and attire. For example:

- ✔ If the groom is an officer, he wears his full dress uniform. If the bride is an officer, she may choose to wear either her dress uniform or a traditional wedding gown.

- ✔ The bridal party may or may not be in the military. Enlisted personnel wear uniforms in accordance with the formality of the wedding and seasonal military regulations. Officers wear their evening dress (Mess dress) uniforms for formal ceremonies that call for civilian white tie and tails or black tie; they wear their Class A uniforms for more casual ceremonies that call for civilian business attire.

- ✔ As for the active duty or retired military guests, they can choose to wear their military uniform or civilian attire.

One big difference from a traditional civilian wedding is that members of the military — whether they're grooms, brides, groomsmen, bridesmaids, or honored guests — never wear boutonnieres or other flower accents with their military uniforms.

Other military traditions include the presentation of flags, the arch of swords, and the seating of commanding officers. During the ceremony, both the American flag and the bride or groom's unit flag are presented. And immediately following the ceremony, the couple walks through the arch of swords. The bride or groom's commanding officer and spouse may sit in the front pew if the parents aren't present, or the commanding officer may sit near or with the family. General officers are customarily seated just behind the two families.

A military chaplain performs the service, usually in the base chapel. The couple needs to consult with the chaplain beforehand to discuss other details of the wedding ceremony. No premarital prep is mandatory for military weddings.

Destination weddings

Planning and executing a wedding somewhere other than your own locale can be particularly challenging, especially when you choose a place abroad. You not only have to consider specific etiquette and protocol for the wedding and wedding guests, but you have to follow international etiquette, as well.

Using common courtesy for your guests is important in the planning stages of a destination wedding (which can be anywhere from extremely formal to very casual). For instance, you need to provide your guests with as much information about the destination as early as possible. You can post the following information to your wedding Web site (see Chapter 3) or send it in the form of a save-the-date announcement:

- ✔ Air and ground travel and costs

- ✔ Lodging and reservations

- ✔ Maps, addresses, and phone numbers of all locations of pre- and postwedding activities and events

- ✔ Necessary medical and travel documents, passports, and visas

- ✔ Information on the destination's weather at the time of year of the wedding

- ✔ Details on the local food, culture, customs, and language of the destination

- ✔ Appropriate attire and other personal necessities, such as sunscreen and bug spray

- ✔ Daily agendas with planned events and activities, as well as a list of activities your guests can do during their free time

- ✔ Locations of the local hospitals and medical clinics

- ✔ Information on extending their stay

Legal requirements from state to state and country to country vary greatly, so do your research on the laws of the location where you plan to marry (and your own country) before you plan your destination wedding.

Remember to send wedding announcements to the friends and family who can't attend the wedding. Having a belated reception or get-together is a great way to celebrate with them when you get back from your honeymoon. (Check out 11 for more on wedding announcements.)

For more in-depth information about planning a destination wedding, see *Destination Weddings For Dummies* by Susan Breslow Sardone (Wiley).

Commitment ceremonies

The commitment ceremony of a gay or lesbian couple is similar to other wedding ceremonies. The main difference is that the ceremony isn't legally binding. The details of the ceremony depend on the personal preferences of the couple; it can be either religious or secular, and it can have any level of formality. The only difference from a wedding ceremony is that you don't have a marriage license.

Basically, you can make the ceremony whatever you want it to be — from a very public affirmation of commitment to an intimate union with rituals and blessings. You can follow the structure of a religious ceremony, using prayers, readings, vows, an exchange of rings, and a final declaration, and you can choose to do so in a secular location. You can also choose to hold the ceremony in a house of worship with traditional wedding attire; just make sure you check with your officiant to find out whether you can have a commitment ceremony in your preferred house of worship.

In some states, gay and lesbian couples can legally marry, so check with your state to see whether you can have a traditional wedding or you need to have a commitment ceremony instead.

Chapter 6

Nailing Down the Basics of Ceremony Protocol

. . . .

In This Chapter

▶ Choosing a proper site, date, and time for your ceremony

▶ Getting the information you need from your officiant

▶ Adding personal touches to your ceremony

▶ Handling a few other ceremony-related tasks with grace

. . . .

*A*fter you've decided on a ceremony style (see Chapter 5), it's time to get down to the nitty-gritty of ceremony planning. First up: Selecting a location, date, and time to match your ceremony style, followed by working with an officiant. Then you need to decide on personal touches and make plans for programs and more. This chapter gives you the scoop on the etiquette involved in ceremony planning. (For info on how to set up your processional, whom to seat where, and how to properly use a reception line, all of which occur on the big day itself, check out Chapter 14.)

Scheduling Your Ceremony

The date of your ceremony depends almost entirely on the location you select for your ceremony (as well as the one you choose for your reception; see Chapter 7), so be prepared to be a bit flexible when you try to set a date. The most popular wedding sites fill up long in advance, and you may find yourself going down a long list of possible places and dates before you find a site that can accommodate all your wants and needs — even when you're looking a year or more into the future. For many couples, the availability of sites for the ceremony and reception creates a large footprint on the entire wedding.

The following sections provide guidance on finding a ceremony site and selecting your ceremony's date and time. (Keep in mind that in some instances — particularly when you're planning a religious ceremony — finding a ceremony site goes hand in hand with finding an officiant and discussing specific ceremony details. I provide guidance on these issues later in this chapter.)

Choosing a ceremony site the right way

In real estate, the golden rule is location, location, location! Well, this rule also holds true when you're looking for a wedding ceremony site; selecting the venue is the most important decision you have to make for your ceremony. What type of venue is right for you *and* your guests? What amenities and services do you need?

The most traditional and popular sites for weddings have always been churches, synagogues, banquet facilities, hotels, and homes. (In fact, if you've chosen a particular type of religious ceremony, you may be limited to a house of worship as your ceremony site; see Chapter 5 for details.) However, many couples today choose more unconventional locations if their preferred ceremony styles allow it. You may consider a location with a historical significance or one with a particularly special meaning to you and your spouse-to-be. For instance, weddings today take place in museums, art galleries, wineries, country clubs, resorts, on yachts, in public parks, on the beach, or in other natural settings. These locations make beautiful venues, but each one presents its own challenges.

Whether you want a traditional or more unconventional site, your first consideration is to choose your location with respect to the size of your guest list. Imagine a tiny room crammed full of friends and relatives. On the flip side, picture your small wedding party and fifty guests in the middle of a gigantic room with the officiant shouting to be heard. Memorable, yes — but not for the right reasons.

After you've narrowed down your list to a few choices for your ceremony based only on general size, it's time to go and have a look. If you're not working with a wedding planner, you want to prepare questions for the officiant or ceremony site manager in advance. (A wedding planner usually has a standard list of questions prepared for every ceremony he or she arranges.) Here are a few questions that can help you make a final decision:

- ✔ What dates and times are available for your chosen month?
- ✔ Exactly how many people (including vendors and attendants) can the location accommodate comfortably?
- ✔ Is the facility in a location that will limit the number of guests who will be able to attend (size of facility, destination venue, and so on)?

✔ What security concerns or restrictions does the venue have? Will guests need to be on a list or show identification to enter the venue?

✔ Does the location have restrooms and preparation areas available?

✔ Does the venue charge a rental fee, and, if it does, what's included (an aisle runner and tables and chairs, for example)?

✔ Does the venue offer a discount for booking an off-season date or weekday?

✔ What are the restrictions on food/beverage services?

✔ Are outside vendors allowed?

✔ Are any religious items available (altar candles, chuppah, and lecterns, for example), or does the couple have to provide them?

✔ Does the venue book other weddings or events into the same space on the same day?

✔ Does the venue have any restrictions on photography, recorded or live music, flowers, or other decorations in the facility?

✔ How early (before the event) can you access the space, and who will let you in?

✔ Is there sufficient parking? Will guests need to be shuttled?

✔ Is valet parking permitted/recommended?

✔ Are receiving lines allowed?

✔ Is the facility accessible for people with disabilities or mobility devices?

✔ Does the venue have suitable backdrops for wedding photos after the ceremony, both inside and outside?

✔ What's the cancellation refund policy?

Visit as many locations in person as possible; photos of venues online can be deceiving.

The key is to select a location that you and your spouse-to-be really want — a venue that reflects your style and personalities and that fits within your budget. Yet, you also want to think of your guests and be extra courteous. Is the site easy to find and easy to navigate? Are there too many stairs to climb? Is the lighting good? Is it drafty? Is the seating comfortable? (For example, if your Catholic ceremony includes a full Mass, you don't want your guests to be sitting on hard pews for an hour and a half.)

Depending on the circumstances, you may want to consult with your parents or other family members to get ideas from different points of view, particularly from those who are contributing to the cost of the venue. But, in the end, you should base your decision on what feels right for the two of you. Remember that the wedding is for you first — and then for your family and friends.

Picture this: You have visions of a restaurant on the top floor of a downtown hotel for your ceremony, but your parents think the old house on the lake you rented every summer growing up is just perfect! How do you come to a happy resolution, especially when your parents are footing the bill? Start by looking at the numbers. Does having the wedding at the old lake house really save that much money? If the numbers aren't much different, you may be able to bring your parents to your side without much of a fight. If the numbers aren't on your side, however, explain how your vision for your wedding comes together in your chosen location. If your heart is set on a certain place, your parents may have a hard time saying no; just be prepared to compromise somewhere else down the line.

You may find that you and your parents share the perfect venue in mind; your spouse-to-be, on the other hand, is picturing something very different. You and your spouse-to-be need to discuss both of your visions for the wedding and reception. Find out which elements of your respective venues will best contribute to the overall wedding theme. After the two of you have hashed out the details, you should be able to come to the conclusion that works best for your wedding. If you happen to choose the location that doesn't match that of your parents' imaginations, go to your parents together, and, as a united front, explain why you've changed your mind.

Agreeing on a date and time

After you and your beloved have chosen a ceremony site, it's time to select the precise date and time of your nuptials. I provide pointers on how to do so in the following sections.

Many religions require premarital counseling, which can take anywhere from six weeks to six months. Be sure to discuss this topic with your officiant before choosing the date.

As soon as you mutually and *amicably* agree on a date and time, make reservations for the site. This booking is especially critical if your wedding date is during popular wedding months, such as June, when venues fill up quickly.

The date

The first thing you have to do after you choose a site is select a few dates that are available at that site. Make sure you choose dates that you know work well with both of your work schedules and also with close family and friends. The obvious goal is to avoid any conflicts, if possible. But don't forget to check for particular religious or secular holidays, recurring weather patterns, local celebrations that can impact traffic, or availability of overnight accommodations, all of which can have an impact on the scheduling.

The location and catering will probably be the most expensive elements of your wedding. Often, having a wedding on a Friday or Sunday, as opposed to a Saturday, can save a lot of money and allow you to adjust your budget for other expenses; however, doing so may not be convenient for some guests.

If you and your spouse-to-be are having trouble deciding on a date, first take a look at your calendars. Do your families have any big birthdays or graduations to celebrate this year? Are any of your friends or family getting married? If your calendars are totally free, ask yourselves what you want your anniversaries to look like down the road — summer vacations to the beach or winter escapades to a ski resort? Try to take into account your wedding style, too. If you've always pictured heavy, floor-length bridesmaids' dresses, you may want to go with a fall or winter wedding, for example. Whatever date you decide on, just make sure you do so together.

The time

Wedding ceremonies can take place in the late morning, afternoon, or early evening. Here are some etiquette considerations to keep in mind for each time:

- ✔ A morning wedding and a brunch reception is a great idea for small intimate weddings. Don't start too early, though. Somewhere between 9:30 a.m. and 11:00 a.m. is good for most guests, as well as vendors, who may be able to go to another event after yours.

- ✔ Afternoon ceremonies are the most popular choice for any style of wedding except the most formal. A ceremony between 4 p.m. and 5 p.m. keeps the majority of your guests happy. (If your ceremony takes place in a house of worship, make sure an afternoon wedding doesn't conflict with any weekly congregational services.)

- ✔ An evening or sunset wedding can seem like a very romantic option, but consider your guest list. Children may not be able to attend, and older people may wish to leave early. Also note that evening weddings tend to be the most formal.

Establishing a schedule for the big day

Etiquette calls for you to allow a reasonable amount of time for completing tasks on the day of your wedding to enable everyone involved in the wedding (from attendants to vendors) to do their jobs properly. The best strategy is to give everyone a little extra time so no one feels rushed — doing so also shows that you're courteous and considerate.

Most wedding planners have master schedules they use, so you don't have too much to worry about. However, if you're not using a planner, you can find a number of scheduling software programs and templates online (such as at www.onewed.com or www.frugalbride.com). The programs have helpful worksheets for scheduling every task that needs to happen on the big day.

When you're trying to map out all the wedding day activities, a good rule of thumb to follow is to work backward. How long will it take for you, your spouse-to-be, and the wedding party to get ready? Consider time for meals, hair, makeup, and getting dressed. How long will photos before the ceremony take? Factor in plenty of travel time to the ceremony location as well — and don't forget about traffic!

You or your wedding planner will want to make copies of the schedule for everyone involved in the wedding planning, including the officiant, wedding party, and all vendors. Each time you change the schedule, be sure that everyone receives an updated version. Communicating this schedule via e-mail is the most reliable way so that you and your wedding team have it in writing in case an issue comes up, but always follow up with a phone call.

The schedule needs to be as precise as possible. Being organized not only keeps everyone on the same page but also helps avoid conflicts and disagreements with vendors and others in the planning stages. After all, the goal is to keep the process running smoothly and on schedule, while also maintaining civility.

If you and your spouse-to-be can't agree on the time for your wedding, consider how formal you want your event to be and what events you have taking place the next day. For example, if you plan to leave on the 7:00 a.m. flight for Fiji, you may not want to stay up until 2 a.m. dancing at your reception.

A time slot for your ceremony includes the time it takes to set up and dismantle. Make sure you know exactly how long you have the space reserved for.

Working Well with an Officiant

As a couple, you should feel like you have some control over the ceremony, but you can't argue about one fact: You need someone to

perform it! You can have either a religious official (such as a minister or rabbi) or a secular leader (such as a justice of the peace) perform the ceremony. In the following sections, I explain how to find
an officiant, describe the importance of making appointments for
every meeting, and list a few crucial questions to ask.

Unless your officiant has said otherwise, be sure you (and your
spouse-to-be and all your parents) always address the person
performing your wedding by his or her title. Whether your officiant goes by Father, Rabbi, Reverend, or any other variation, you
need to respect the position he or she has earned. If the officiant is
an old family friend, you should still introduce him or her by title
and give the officiant the choice whether to have others use a first
name only.

Finding potential officiants

If you regularly attend a house of worship, you may want the affili-
ated officiant to perform your ceremony. Keep in mind that many
houses of worship set up their calendars up to a year in advance,
so call the office to get details about availability. If you don't attend
a house of worship regularly, or if you want to have a secular or
civil ceremony, speak to your friends and family; perhaps they can
recommend someone. If you come up dry and can't find anyone in
the phone book, you can have any friend or family member serve
as your officiant with just a little bit of planning. Some counties
require only that your officiant be older than 18 and pay a small fee
to obtain a one-day license allowing him or her to perform civil ceremonies. Just make sure the license applies to the county where
the ceremony is being performed!

Some religious officiants have strict rules about whom they marry;
for instance, they may only marry members of their own house of
worship. Other officiants welcome any denomination. If you want
to have a wedding outside a house of worship, you can choose a
religious officiant who doesn't mind providing such a ceremony, or
you can arrange a civil wedding at your local city hall (see Chapter
5 for information on civil weddings).

Whatever you decide, *always* check references before meeting with
your potential officiant for the first time. See whether the officiant
has a Web site so you can find out more about his or her services
and experience. If you can't find any references there, just ask the
officiant — he or she should be glad to share them with you. After
all, having a beautiful ceremony in a beautiful location with an
unorganized or poorly conducted ceremony can ruin your big day,
so you must choose your officiant wisely.

Making appointments to meet

If you and your spouse-to-be have very busy schedules, you have to plan and schedule appointments with your officiant carefully. However, being busy doesn't excuse you from being mannerly. Checking with the officiant's schedule first and working around it is the polite thing to do. You'll almost certainly have to meet more than once, so map out a timeline with a clear purpose for each meeting. After you confirm dates and times, be sure that the scheduled appointments give you enough time to go over all the details, as well as any issues or concerns you may have.

Officiants are usually happy to meet at their offices or houses of worship. Some may travel a short distance to meet at a location convenient for everyone, such as a coffee shop. But keep in mind that you're using their time, so don't expect them to travel too far for free.

The chances of having to cancel an appointment are high because you're working with a number of vendors and other people involved in the wedding planning. And you can't forget the possibility of an emergency. Here are a few etiquette pointers to keep in mind when you have to cancel a meeting with your officiant (or anyone else, for that matter):

- ✓ Never wait until the last minute. Canceling an appointment affects another person's entire day, so if you must cancel, do so as soon as possible.

- ✓ Don't *just* send an e-mail (or a text message) to cancel a meeting — you never know whether the officiant will check e-mail in time. Making a phone call is best. If you leave a voicemail, call again to be sure your officiant received the message.

- ✓ Apologize for the inconvenience.

- ✓ Ask what works best for the officiant when you reschedule the appointment. In other words, you should work around the other person's schedule.

Even though you're in the throes of planning one of the most important events in your life, you're not the only one with a packed calendar! Chances are good that your officiant has a slew of other weddings and events to worry about, too.

Asking important questions

In this section, I tell you which questions to ask to get the answers you need regarding both your officiant and your ceremony.

Getting a sense of the officiant's background and style

When you meet an officiant for the first time, be sure to ask about his or her wedding ceremony experience, training, and education. Other qualities to keep in mind are trust and reliability. And, as with most relationships, you want your personalities to *click!*

If you're planning a laid-back, informal ceremony in an outdoor setting, having an officiant who has a more formal or polished presence obviously isn't the best choice. You may want to look for someone who's more casual and upbeat and who uses some humor.

You don't have to make up your mind about an officiant immediately. In cases in which you meet with more than one officiant, you and your spouse-to-be should discuss what you liked (and maybe didn't like) most about each candidate. You want to choose the person who meets most of your requirements and the person you both feel the most comfortable with.

Digging for ceremony-related details

The officiant has likely heard just about every imaginable question about wedding ceremonies, so be as candid and open as possible during your meeting. You want to feel free to ask the questions that you're really curious about; now's not the time to be shy. Here are a few typical ceremony-related questions you may want to consider:

- Is the officiant available on the date and at the time you most prefer?

- Can you use your own vows, poems, or music?

- Does the officiant recommend any particular untraditional approach or unique feature to make the ceremony truly your own?

- Will the officiant perform the ceremony if you have circumstances that are unique — such as an interfaith marriage, a pregnant bride, or a same-sex marriage?

- To what degree is the officiant involved in the wedding planning?

- Will the officiant allow special readings by family members or others?

- Will the officiant allow you to add elements to the ceremony, such as a rose ceremony, the lighting of candles, or cultural traditions?

- Can children be included in the ceremony?

✔ Do you have final approval of the script?

✔ When will the officiant arrive at the ceremony?

✔ Can the officiant guide you on appropriate music for the ceremony?

✔ What are the requirements (premarital counseling, for example) for being married by this officiant?

✔ Is the officiant willing to allow other clergy to participate (as in the case of an interfaith marriage)?

✔ Is the officiant available for a rehearsal the day or evening before the ceremony?

✔ Does the officiant conduct the rehearsal or look to the couple to choreograph it?

✔ Does the officiant want to attend the rehearsal dinner after the rehearsal and the reception following the ceremony?

✔ What is the officiant's fee, and do you have to sign a contract?

✔ Can you or the officiant break the contract for any reason?

After you've asked the officiant these questions, you and your spouse-to-be need to ask yourselves whether you like the sound and tone of the officiant's voice. Is the officiant's voice pleasant sounding? Will your guests be able to hear it clearly? You certainly don't want to hire someone who has a shrill or nasal tone or a dull, ponderous voice that completely puts people to sleep. (Your guests will thank you for choosing a nice-sounding officiant!)

Finally, you should ask what the officiant wears to the ceremony to make sure it coordinates with the level of formality you and your guests will display. Officiants normally wear plain dark suits or dark robes. Some officiants give you a choice of colors and styles. If you decide to get married in Las Vegas, you may even find an officiant who'll be happy to wear a costume to your theme wedding!

Making your officiant and ceremony match

After interviewing several different officiants and picking the one you like best, you have to take a look at how well the officiant and your ceremony style match up. In the best of circumstances, the officiant and the ceremony style (namely, the location) click together without issue. But if your officiant of choice and your ceremony dreams don't go well together (you've chosen a religious officiant who doesn't hold outdoor ceremonies but you really want a ceremony on your parents' lake, for example), be ready to make some tough decisions. All in all, you and your spouse-to-be have to decide whether the person or the place is the deal breaker.

Properly Personalizing Your Ceremony

Some officiants require you to stick to the traditional wedding rituals and wording associated with their religion, but others are happy to work with you to personalize the ceremony. In the following sections, I describe several meaningful ways to add your own touch to your wedding ceremony.

Etiquette is all about respecting others and making them feel comfortable. But respecting others doesn't mean you have to sacrifice who you are or change your plans to please your family or friends. You can tastefully personalize your ceremony to reflect your own personalities, beliefs, and cultural customs. Just be reasonable on the amount of changes you ask for so you don't make the ceremony completely unrecognizable or unfamiliar. It's also a good idea to warn any members of your family who may be shocked or displeased with the changes you've made so they can have time to prepare themselves before the big day.

Picking your music

Music is one of the most important components of your ceremony because it sets the mood for your special day. I may be beating a dead horse here, but, as I state throughout this book, etiquette changes with the times. So, if playing a recording of "Here Comes the Bride" when you're walking down the aisle isn't your style, choosing something more contemporary is perfectly appropriate.

If you're having a nonreligious ceremony, your music options are endless. Even if you follow a traditional format, you can still add personal touches — through your music selections — to create a memorable ceremony. But if you're having a religious ceremony in a house of worship, be sure to clear your music selections with your officiant; some houses of worship don't allow secular music and have limited options for what you can play.

Here are a few other etiquette tips to keep in mind when you're choosing your ceremony music:

- ✔ **Try to keep the music within the framework of the style and formality of the wedding.** Although a church wedding doesn't dictate that all the music must be religious, you want to be respectful of your location and the event taking place. In church weddings, popular music fits well during the prelude to the ceremony. And smaller, informal weddings lend themselves to a wider variety of music choices than the large, white-tie-and-tails affairs.

Don't forget to mention the titles of the songs and music on your program to give your guests a heads up of what's to come. (See the "Putting together appropriate wedding programs" section later in this chapter for more on programs.)

✔ **Check with the officiant or the person in charge of your ceremony location to find out whether you need to work with a particular music coordinator or use a particular musician or singer.** For example, some churches have music ministers and pianists whom they recommend to brides and grooms.

✔ **Keep your religious and cultural backgrounds in mind when selecting your music.** After all, you want your parents and other family members to feel comfortable, too. For example, if your grandmother is an immigrant, you may choose to play a song in her native language. Your officiant can guide you on acceptable selections.

Featuring special readings

So you've always loved poems by Kahlil Gibran or the lines from the classic "Sunrise, Sunset" from the *Fiddler on the Roof* musical. If these selections are meaningful to both you and your spouse-to-be, why not include them in your ceremony?

Select poems or passages that reflect your journey as a couple or your hopes for the future. Look for items written by someone you both admire. But whatever you choose, *always* check with your officiant before adding a reading. Certain religions don't allow for much (if any) deviation from their own liturgical texts.

If you have a particular passage you just can't bear to cut out of the day, consider printing it in the program or sharing it before the meal at the reception.

Writing your own vows

The words you recite on your wedding day are some of the most important words you'll ever say in public, and you may choose to write your own vows (if your officiant and/or your house of worship allow you to do so, of course). As you write your vows, you probably visualize your partner and want to express your undying love. How romantic!

Remember that people of all ages — including many folks you don't know very well — will be listening very closely to this part of the ceremony. So, you want to keep a few key points in mind as you write your vows:

✔ **Don't get carried away.** You must consider the comfort levels of your guests at hearing the personal words you share. So try not to get too carried away with your thoughts and emotions — not too intimate, funny, or sarcastic.

Remember that you're setting the tone for the true essence of the whole wedding during your vows, so attempt to express your beliefs and desires for your life with your partner in a meaningful and succinct way.

✔ **Don't forget to include promises.** If your officiant isn't going to be an active part in your vows, remember to include the basic promises to be true to each other in sickness and in health, in good times and bad, and to love and honor each other. Guests expect to hear these words, and your partner probably does, too!

✔ **Do make sure your officiant is comfortable with the words you choose.** Some couples choose to say their own vows and then have the officiant finish with the official promises. If you choose to do it this way, make sure your officiant is comfortable with what you want to say in your vows *before* the ceremony.

If you don't check in before the wedding, your officiant's discomfort at your words will be obvious to your guests and may create unnecessary tension.

If you and your spouse-to-be come from two different cultures or religions, mentioning in your vows how your marriage will help to bridge your differences and create a blend of both backgrounds is a nice touch.

You may be a talented writer and have some specific ideas of how you want to compose your vows. If you don't have a particular penchant for writing, however, many sources are available to help you write your vows. Check out bible.org for samples of religious vows, or take a look at myweddingvows.com for a wide variety of traditional and modern wording (including interfaith vows and vows for those getting remarried). You may even be able to get some help from your officiant.

Honoring the deceased

Remembering loved ones who played important roles in your life is a lovely thing to do at your wedding. Honoring parents or grandparents who are deceased is especially appropriate.

You can honor your deceased loved ones by mentioning their names at some point during the ceremony, lighting a candle in their honor, printing a short tribute to them in your programs, or simply wearing something that belonged to them — whatever you're most comfortable with. Just make sure that any acknowledgements are brief and in keeping with the joyful tone of the day.

 If a loved one died close to the time of the wedding, a moment of silence in that person's honor may be appropriate. In this case, you don't want to dwell on the person's death because doing so can bring a feeling of sadness into the festivities, not only for you but for many of your guests, as well. Before the wedding, you should discuss with the family members closest to the deceased how they would like you to honor the loved one (if they want to do so at all).

Other Etiquette Guidelines for Planning Your Ceremony

Not only do you have to think about the rituals of the ceremony itself, but you also have to consider the etiquette behind some items related to the ceremony, such as programs for your guests, transportation to and from the ceremony for important folks, and entertainment for guests after the ceremony (but before the reception). I explain what you need to know in this section.

Putting together appropriate wedding programs

Your wedding program is a wonderful way to showcase your personalities while also setting the stage for your ceremony. Of course, your program will be a lovely keepsake after the wedding, but it should also include important information and details to help put your guests at ease. For example, a wedding program should outline the order of the ceremony so that guests know what to expect next. It can also remind people to turn off their cellphones or inform them that photographs aren't allowed in the sanctuary. And, finally, the program can include a map and directions to your wedding reception venue on the back.

Wedding programs are particularly useful at cross-cultural and interfaith wedding ceremonies. They can help explain some of the unfamiliar rituals and traditions that the officiant performs and the bride and groom participate in during the ceremony.

Using the right style and wording

Normally, wedding programs are printed in a style that matches the style of the wedding invitation, which means you want to use similar fonts and lettering. Like your invitation, the design you choose for your program should reflect the overall style of your wedding. For example, you want to use a more elegant font and lettering for a more formal wedding. You can hire a professional graphic artist and printer, or you can design and print programs on your own. If you do it yourself, use a laser printer for a more professional look.

In terms of wording, a program should be brief, employ proper grammar, and have a more formal tone than your everyday writing (such as using full names instead of abbreviations — Charles instead of Chuck). To follow etiquette rules, you should *not* include advertisements for wedding service providers.

Laying out the information correctly

Your program contains the following information, all of which you should run by the officiant for accuracy (see Figure 6-1):

- ✔ The elements and highlights of each stage of the ceremony
- ✔ The titles of songs, readings, and dedications
- ✔ The names of all the participants and their roles in the ceremony

You can ask either your ushers or a few children to hand out programs as the guests arrive. Or, you can place them in pews, on chairs, in baskets, or in some other nice containers next to the entry door for guests to pick up themselves.

Planning for transportation to and from the ceremony

If you provide transportation for the wedding party to the ceremony and to the reception, make sure you provide enough vehicles (or one vehicle large enough) so that everyone has enough room. If you're not hiring a driver to take the bride and groom to the reception, the best man is responsible for driving them.

The Wedding Ceremony
of
Harriet Henshaw and Randolph Smith

July 17, 2010
St. Catherine Church
Vail, Colorado

~ Celebrant ~
The Reverend Philip Wilson

The Wedding Party

Parents of the Bride	Christopher and Jennifer Henshaw
Parents of the Groom	Steven and Cynthia Smith
Matron of Honor	Claudia Allen
Bridesmaids	Phyllis Smith Jessica Jones Val Baldwin
Best Man	Peter Porcini
Groomsmen	Stanley Logue August Webb Kevin Decker
Readers	Charlotte Vaughn Candice Nichols
Organist	Wallace Tuttle

Figure 6-1: An appropriate wedding program.

Generally, you should provide the following transportation to and from the ceremony:

To the ceremony

✔ A car for the bride and her father (or other escort down the aisle)

✔ A car for the bride's mother or both parents plus the children who are in the wedding party

Order of Service

Prelude
        Canon in D   Johann Pachelbel
        Air (Orchestral Suite No. III in D Major, S. 1068)   Johann Sebastian Bach

Processional
        Trumpet Voluntary   Jeremiah Clarke
        Grand Triumphal Chorus   Alexandre Guilmant

Call to Worship

Prayer

Presentation of the Bride

Interval
        Parzival   Wolfram Von Eschenbach

Scripture Reading   Romans 12:1-2, 9-18

Meditation

Marriage Vows

Exchange of Rings

Reading
        Sonnet 116   William Shakespeare

Pastoral Prayer & The Lord's Prayer

Declaration of Marriage

Reading
        Apache Wedding Poem

Benediction

Recessional
        Wedding March   Felix Mendelssohn
        (From A Midsummer Night's Dream)

Figure 6-1: *(continued)*

- A car or limo for the rest of the bride's attendants
- A car or limo for the groom and groomsmen
- A car for the groom's parents and siblings

To the reception

- A car for the bride and groom
- A car or limo for the rest of the wedding party

If you provide transportation for any special guests, such as grand-parents or other family members, you need additional vehicles. These cars should be waiting at the entrance of the ceremony site. To avoid any miscommunications, carefully coordinate these plans ahead of time. It's also considerate to provide transportation to the post-ceremony celebration for out-of-town guests.

Setting up activities for your guests between the ceremony and reception

Many ceremony venues offer only limited time slots for weddings, which can create dilemmas with the timing between the ceremony and reception. What do you do when you and your spouse-to-be both have your hearts set on a ceremony in the family church — which allows only 2 p.m. ceremonies — and a dinner reception? What do you do with your guests during the block of time in between? Planning the reception directly after the wedding makes more sense, but if there's absolutely no way around having a lot of time between the two events, you have to provide some activities for your guests.

If most of your guests happen to be from out of town and have hotel rooms near the ceremony or reception location, you can let the guests know that they have enough time to relax or freshen up before the reception. You can do so by making a note in the program or having the officiant make an announcement after the processional. If there's a lot of time to spare, you can also arrange for some sightseeing tours of the city.

 One popular way to handle this space of time is to have the recep-tion venue set up with a cocktail reception and light appetizers. Just don't provide too much alcohol, or your guests may become too intoxicated before the real festivities even begin. You can also have music and other entertainment, put out photos albums for your guests to look at, and designate someone to introduce guests who haven't met each other. In addition, you can have the guest book available at the venue's entrance and designate someone to encourage guests to sign it. This downtime also provides the per-fect opportunity for the videographer to interview your guests.

 If you only need time for photos after the ceremony, remember that etiquette requires you not to keep your wedding guests wait-ing more than one hour between the ceremony and reception.

Chapter 7

Perfecting Your Reception Plans

*A*fter you've had the beautiful and moving wedding ceremony of your dreams, with a charismatic officiant and beautiful words from your spouse that you'll remember forever, you probably want to celebrate for the rest of the day and night with your family and friends. Making the choices that surround the reception festivities requires time, energy, and lots of forethought. In this chapter, I describe the etiquette that goes into choosing your reception's style and site; working well with reception managers and caterers; and providing refreshments, proper seating, and favors for all your guests.

 The key to any successful event is *planning*. Planning well in advance is the best way to ensure that you'll be able to handle the inevitable unexpected glitches with grace — and that's what etiquette's all about.

The Essentials of a Proper Reception Style and Site

When you're in the throes of planning your wedding reception, take a moment or two to think back to weddings you've attended in the past and those you've seen on TV or in films. Did any of the receptions seem to be too "over the top" or too casual in relation to the ceremony? Which locations were unforgettable? And, which ones did you feel weren't so great? If you had certain misgivings about some of the wedding receptions you attended, chances are other guests did, too.

In the following sections, I explain the etiquette behind choosing the right style and site for your reception. (See the later section "Getting the Info You Need from Site Managers and Caterers" for details on how to narrow down your choices.)

Deciding on the level of formality

When you're planning your reception, the first thing you need to do is decide how formal you want it to be. The level of formality is usually dictated by the time of day of your wedding and the style of your ceremony (see Chapter 9 for more on formality). For example:

- ✔ **If you have your heart set on a morning wedding ceremony and early afternoon reception, your reception is most likely an informal or semiformal event.** Appropriate reception choices include a brunch, a luncheon, or a tea. At an informal reception, the food (often smaller portions and finger foods) is usually set out on tables throughout the venue. Seating is open and may be composed of small groupings of chairs. If you have tables, you don't set them elaborately, and guests collect their own utensils according to the food they pick up.

- ✔ **If you're having an early afternoon wedding and a late afternoon or early evening reception, your reception is typically semiformal or formal.** Appropriate reception choices include a tea, a cocktail party, or a sit-down dinner. Semiformal receptions can range from deli platters and finger foods to multi-station buffets. Guests are expected to sit for the meal, and the tables are set with glasses and utensils. You may choose to have open or assigned seating, but all guests should have a place card. The wait staff primarily fills water glasses and pours the champagne for the toast (if you choose to serve it); each waiter probably serves two or three tables.

- ✔ **If you plan an evening affair, your reception is expected to be formal or black tie (ultra formal).** Dinner is certainly a must, and you also may choose to include dessert and champagne. The meal at a formal reception is served, and the tables are elaborately set with at least one server per table. And each guest should be assigned a seat at a specific table.

The most important etiquette rule to follow here is making sure your reception matches the formality of your ceremony. That means all the details (from attire to invitations and more; see Part III) must fall in line. Imagine your guests' confusion if you have a formal evening church wedding followed by a super-casual back-yard barbecue reception!

Selecting a comfortable, appropriate site

There's no question you want to find the perfect venue for your reception, but you also want to be considerate of all your guests and their comfort — that's the meaning of good etiquette! Here are a few important suggestions for choosing a reception site that fits all your guests' needs (see the later section "Asking the right questions" for a list of additional considerations):

✔ Find a reception site that isn't too far from the location of your ceremony; after all, you don't want to lose guests who aren't willing to drive the distance. Anything more than 30 to 35 minutes away is too far.

✔ Look for a venue that can hold the number of guests you plan to invite. You don't want your 300 guests crammed into a venue suited for only 100 people!

✔ Make getting from the church to the reception site easy for your guests. If access to the reception site is difficult because of limited parking or security restrictions, for instance, you may want to provide hired cars, limousines, minivans, or buses to take guests to and from the site. Likewise, if the site's parking lot is enormous, you may want to provide valet parking or a shuttle so that guests don't have to walk a long distance in heels or bad weather. Your guests won't be too much fun if they're worn out from the trek from their cars to your reception.

✔ Make sure the site allows for easy access to entrances of the main room and restrooms, especially for children, the elderly, and people with disabilities.

✔ If you know many of your guests smoke, you can try to accommodate them. First, check with your venue to see whether smoking is even allowed on site. You may have to provide your own receptacles and fire extinguishers, and some sites may require additional insurance coverage. If smoking is forbidden at the site, you should mention the fact in the invitation. Say, for example, "Reception immediately following at the Seaside Inn (a smoke-free venue)." Or you can put a note on the directions to the site.

In addition to finding a site that offers convenience and comfort to your guests, you need to match your site to the level of formality you've chosen for your big day (see the preceding section). Depending on how formal your event is, you can ask the whole gang back to your place for a casual afternoon barbecue; you can use a small social hall for an informal late afternoon reception featuring hors d'oeuvres and nonalcoholic beverages; or you can invite guests to an evening cocktail reception and a fancy sit-down banquet with dancing at the best hotel in town.

A few questions to ask yourself when trying to determine whether or not a venue matches the level of formality you've chosen for your ceremony are

- ✔ How many guests can fit in the space?
- ✔ Is the wait staff big enough to serve the kind of meal you plan to have?
- ✔ Is the space big (or small) enough for the type of seating plan you envision?

Getting the Info You Need from Site Managers and Caterers

Your working relationship with the reception site manager starts at your first tour of the venue. When you choose your site, the manager is part of the package (which means you don't interview site managers as you do officiants, a topic I discuss in Chapter 6), so if you don't hit it off with a particular site manager when you do your tour, keep in mind you'll have to work closely with that person during the course of planning your wedding.

The site manager is the person who finalizes all the details of your event (date and time), as well as your contract. Many venues (hotels and banquet halls, for example) have on-site catering services you must use. If you have to bring in your own vendors, though, the site manager should be able to give you some good references (and you can always ask your friends and family for ideas).

In the following sections, I explain how to get in touch with your site managers and what questions to ask them to get the answers you need.

Making appointments as a matter of course

Although e-mail or other means of communication can be effective, in-person meetings with site managers and caterers allow for direct eye contact, clear body language, and opportunities to ask plenty of questions. But don't just show up at a site and expect instant service — you'll get better treatment and a clearer focus from the manager or caterer if you make an appointment first. Plus, giving the vendor a heads up that you're coming is the courteous thing to do!

Be prompt for all meetings with managers and caterers (and anyone else, for that matter!), and if you know you'll be late, it's polite to call to let the person you're meeting know. Yes, you're planning the most important day of your life, but more than likely, the manager has other clients with scheduled appointments and important events, too. Don't assume he will be available when you arrive late. Also, if you need to reschedule a meeting, call the manager immediately, apologize, and let him choose the day and time of the rescheduled appointment.

If you have a major concern or issue, try to make an appointment to discuss it face to face, but if you just have some basic questions, try to communicate via e-mail and voice mail. That way you don't drive your site manager crazy by showing up every 15 minutes!

Asking the right questions

When you meet with a site manager or caterer, you need to have clear communication — period. Just discussing your wishes may not be enough, so make sure you have all your expectations written down. Know that you can never ask too many questions during an initial meeting with a reception site manager or caterer, and the person you're meeting with should be more than happy to respond. This isn't the time to be coy or shy.

Making a list of questions before the meeting is a great idea. Doing so helps you not to forget anything at the meeting; plus, you can keep adding to it as you think of new questions. Here's a sampling of the questions you definitely want to ask when you're touring reception sites and meeting with caterers:

- ✔ Are menus set, or do you have some flexibility? Can you customize your own menu or use a family recipe?
- ✔ What are their most popular dishes?

✔ Can you see photos of other wedding receptions at the site?

✔ Can you review the standard contract?

✔ Do you have to pay a deposit to hold the date? If so, how much is it and what does it cover?

✔ What's the cancellation policy? Is the deposit refundable?

✔ Do the reception/catering staff and servers receive a flat gratuity? Is this number in the contract?

✔ Does the cost cover just the food, or does it include linens, utensils, dishes, and glassware rental, too?

✔ Does the per-person cost include the service staff and cleanup?

✔ Are sales taxes included in the contract?

✔ If you provide your own wedding cake (and groom's cake if you have one), do you have to pay the servers an additional fee for cutting and serving the cake?

✔ Can you arrange for a tasting at which you try some options for each course of the meal, the cake (if you're getting it from the same vendor), and the wine and champagne?

✔ Can they accommodate dietary restrictions if guests have any?

✔ Do they require any special kitchen arrangements? (For example, does the kitchen come with enough refrigeration? Is there sufficient heating available to keep the food warm? Can it accommodate the necessary staff? Will the food be cooked elsewhere and brought in from another kitchen?)

✔ Do they have any other events or weddings the same day or weekend?

✔ For how long is the site available, and is there a minimum time requirement? Do you have to pay an extra fee if the reception runs long?

✔ Do they provide a children's meal? If so, is there a reduced cost per person?

✔ Do they provide a less expensive meal option for the band, DJ, photographers, and videographers?

✔ Do they have a liquor license, and, if so, do they provide brand-name liquors? Can you purchase your own? What are the prices for a cash bar? Is there a corkage fee for bringing your own wine or champagne? If so, how much is the fee?

✔ Can they provide a bartender? If so, what are the charges?

✔ Do they have insurance? If so, what does the insurance cover? Does the insurance cover china, crystal breakage, and, heaven forbid, food poisoning? Is the insurance included in the final contract price? Ask to get a copy of the insurance policy to review.

✔ Will a catering manager be on site during the reception? If so, do they charge an additional fee?

✔ Can they give you a final per-person estimate if they know details of the reception, such as the time of day, location, style, theme, and number of guests?

✔ If you have a list of certain foods you absolutely don't want (peanut oil, for example), can the caterer comply?

✔ Is there an additional fee for staff overtime?

✔ What are the shapes of the tables, and how many people can sit comfortably at each?

✔ What's the ratio of servers to guests?

✔ Are any types of decoration forbidden?

✔ Is there dedicated space for the bridal party either for pictures or for freshening up before the party?

There is such a thing as "polite assertiveness." It's not rude to ask the manager or caterer if she has a good understanding of what you and your spouse-to-be have in mind; just say something like: "A few of your suggestions don't really match our ideas for our wedding. How do you see these items contributing to our overall theme?"

You don't have to be railroaded into menus or decorating suggestions that don't fulfill your wishes. Stand your ground, and if you think you may have difficulties getting what you want or being understood, find another caterer or maybe another site altogether.

Negotiating on the price is common, but it's not a game. Work with your manager or caterer to reach a compromise you're both happy with. Avoid making condescending or negative comments, such as "You know you can do better than that," and keep the exchange as positive as possible.

Providing the Right Food and Drinks for Your Guests

Your menu can be as simple or as elaborate as you want it to be, depending on your budget and the style of your reception. You may want to stick to simpler dishes for an informal reception and more gourmet treats for a more formal reception. In the following sections, I explore the option of offering an entrée choice and help you determine whether alcohol is appropriate to serve and whether you should feed your vendors.

Offering an entrée choice for seated meals

Having a set meal for a large reception is very difficult because it's almost impossible to accommodate everyone's tastes, but if you choose a set menu for the main course of your sit-down reception, make sure you have some sort of variety on the plate. For instance, if you serve a meat for the entrée, consider a meat-free risotto or pasta as the side dish in case any of your guests are vegetarian. Also, try not to make the food too spicy; many people have a low tolerance for hot food.

It's considerate to think of the palates of your guests, so if your budget can handle it, you may want to provide a choice of entrée, typically two or three choices (any combination of red meat, white meat, fish, and vegetarian). Offering a choice doesn't necessarily mean the meal will be more expensive, depending on the choices you provide. Offering lobster and steak, for example, will obviously cost more than chicken and steak. Caterers normally have set menus, with a choice of entrées, although you can ask for suggestions for alternatives if you're not happy with some of the choices.

Before you decide on your entrée choices, you definitely want to try all of them. Make sure you have a nice variety of dishes to accommodate all your guests. For example, having a vegetarian dish for the guests who don't eat meat is considerate. And don't forget the little ones; children (and their parents) always appreciate having a special kid-friendly food, such as ravioli.

If you're more adventurous and want to serve a favorite ethnic dish that goes along with the theme of your wedding, or if you select a menu based on your culture, go for it! But, if it's a really spicy dish, make sure you have an alternate choice for those guests who can't handle food with a bite!

Whatever meal choices you choose, make sure you deliver them to the reception site manager or the caterer by the deadline you established in your contract, and try not to keep changing your mind! Doing so causes a lot of frustration and problems for the catering staff.

It's acceptable to include a place for guests to state their preference of entrée on the response card (see Chapter 11 for examples of the correct wording to use). If you have a wedding Web site, you can set up a way for guests to make their meal choice via the site or e-mail. As soon as you have a final head count and the number of each entrée to order, let the reception site manager or caterer know so he or she can get to work promptly.

Determining whether alcohol is appropriate

Alcohol or no alcohol? What a dilemma. Having an open bar can be an expensive proposition, but, on the flip side, asking people to join your wedding celebration and then making them pay for their own cocktails at a cash bar isn't the best etiquette and isn't recommended.

For cocktail and dinner receptions, alcohol is typically expected, but you can choose several different serving options. For example, if you crunch the budget numbers and the cost is too high for an open bar, you can consider having champagne served as the guests arrive at the reception, wine with the meal, and beer, wine, and a couple of specialty drinks after the meal. If this plan is still over your budget, you may consider serving a punch that contains some alcohol instead. Or you can serve pre-purchased beer, wine, and specialty drinks at the meal, during the toasts, and at the bar. After the alcohol's gone, the bar can serve water and other nonalcoholic beverages.

For weddings taking place early in the day (brunch or lunch) you may choose to leave out alcohol completely. However, it's appropriate to have a champagne toast or serve other "morning" cocktails, such as mimosas and bloody marys.

 If you know that some guests may be prone to drink too much and may cause discomfort, embarrassment, or danger to other guests, you may want to avoid having an open bar — doing so can help lessen the chances for that potential problem. However, if you're set on hosting an open bar, ask a close friend or family member (who doesn't drink) to watch over the guests who may cause problems.

To help everyone leave the venue on time, you may want to close the bar before the end of the reception. A good time to stop alcohol service is about an hour before the band or DJ closes up shop. (Note that you don't necessarily need to make an announcement that the bar is closing.) If you do leave it open later, however, it's a polite gesture to provide some additional snacks for the late crowd.

Some cultures and religions prohibit alcoholic consumption. Also, certain guests may just prefer that it not be served (especially folks who are recovering alcoholics). So, if it's important to you and your partner that you have some alcohol at your reception, by all means, have it — just make sure you also serve nonalcoholic beverages for the guests who don't want to imbibe.

If a few people challenge your choice to serve alcohol, kindly remind them that it's your wedding and you hope they'll be respectful of the celebration you've planned. You don't have to justify yourself for the decision you made, but if you think doing so will help, say something like: "We knew the majority of our guests would enjoy being served alcoholic beverages."

Knowing whether to feed vendors

Providing meals for hired vendors, such as videographers, DJs, photographers, and musicians, is appropriate and appreciated. They'll be at the reception for the majority of the event, so they often expect breaks for refreshments and meals.

Discuss details of meals with all your vendors beforehand, and review their contracts so you're aware of their requirements and expectations. You can probably negotiate a better per-person price with the catering service because it doesn't have to provide the same amount or level of service it does for your guests.

Putting Together an Appropriate Seating Chart

You want all your guests to feel special and know that they were invited to your wedding because they have a special place in your life. One way of making your guests feel special and comfortable is giving a lot of thought to the seating plan. As with most other elements of wedding planning, there's a degree of protocol involved in this process.

If you're having a very small, informal gathering (say, fewer than 30 people), you have the option of having open seating, but in most cases, a seating chart is a necessity for a large reception for several reasons. For one, seating charts cut down on wasted space and ensure that traffic runs smoothly. They allow you to make your guests feel more comfortable by sitting them next to people they may get along with (or far away from people they don't get along with). Seating charts also get the guests to their seats faster, which keeps the whole reception on schedule.

Here are a few important seating rules you need to know upfront:

- As the engaged couple, you always have the final say on seating, but you should take into consideration any requests from family members.

- Don't use the space near the DJ or band, next to the kitchen, or in front of any exit doors for seating guests.

- Try to make sure everyone can clearly see the head table. (But don't sweat it if this isn't possible because of the room or table setup.)

In the following sections, I explain where to seat the bridal party, close family members, friends, and children; I also provide pointers on using place cards to politely inform your guests of where to sit.

Seating the bridal party and close family

Today you don't have to follow any hard-and-fast rules for table shapes and arrangements or for who sits where, but you do have several traditional seating options to choose from.

One option is this: When sitting at the head table, the groom sits to the bride's right, the best man sits to her left (with the grooms-men sitting to his left), and the maid of honor sits to the groom's right (with the bridesmaids sitting to her right). Any child attendants should sit with their families at a table near the head table. Sometimes the bride and groom sit at a round table with the rest of the bridal party rather than a rectangular one, but the order is basically the same.

When bridal parties are very large (more than six attendants on each side, for example), an acceptable option is to use two large, round tables instead of one big rectangular one. Round tables make mingling a little easier. In this seating arrangement, the bride and groom sit with the maid of honor and best man. The other members of the bridal party sit at the second round table. This seating arrangement is acceptable for a reception of any formality level.

It's becoming more and more common for couples to opt for another seating arrangement altogether, which is to have no bridal party table at all. Typically, the bride and groom sit by themselves at what's called a *sweetheart table;* the rest of the bridal party sits at tables near the bridal couple. This choice is also acceptable for receptions of all formality levels.

So where do the parents and close family members of the happy couple sit? Typically, it helps to have two parents' tables, one for the groom's family and one for the bride's family, although it's acceptable to seat both sets of parents at the same table. Having two parents' tables allows you to accommodate a larger number of important people (close family and friends, for example) at both tables. Whether you choose one or two tables is purely at the discretion of you and your families. (Figure 7-1 shows the traditional setup of the head table and the parents' tables.)

If either or both sets of parents have been divorced, you need to put a lot of thought into deciding how comfortable the divorced couple will be sitting together, even if they seem to get along well. You want to do this planning carefully to ensure a tension-free celebration for everyone in attendance. If you don't want to seat your divorced parents together, you can seat the parent who raised you at the same table with the parent or parents who raised your spouse-to-be. Or, you can let your divorced parents host their own tables with their closest relatives sitting with them. Basically, you have many options to choose from based on your particular circumstances.

Figure 7-1: Seating the bridal party and close family members.

You may want to double-check with all divorced parents before you confirm the seating chart. Although it's your wedding day, it's a gracious gesture to make sure your family and friends are comfortable. After all, etiquette's all about making others comfortable.

Assigning seating for other guests

As you assemble your seating chart, you want to consider sitting friends and family you know mix well together next to each other and be sensitive to those friends and family you know may not mix well. The aim of any sit-down meal is polite conversation that's interesting, stimulating, and upbeat. Keep in mind that interesting conversations will be the ultimate memory for your guests. Here are a few suggestions to help you give all your guests an evening of fun and laughs:

- ✔ Think about whether the dates of the bridal party would be more comfortable sitting together at one table or sitting at different tables throughout the room with folks they already know.

- ✔ Seat vendors (such as the photographer, the DJ, and so on) together at one table.

- ✔ Give some thought to the personalities of the people you're sitting together. You don't want two overly chatty people — or two introverts — next to each other. The dream seating arrangement is to seat introverts next to extroverts, with other people clustering in the middle. In other words, you want the people you think are the most social, comfortable, and outgoing to bring out the people who are shy and quiet.

- ✔ Consult with your friends and family if you have any doubt about seating certain guests next to other ones. For example, if your friends Ken and Carol had a perfectly amicable divorce and are now happily remarried to new mates, you may think they'll have no problem sitting at the same table. However, if you're not completely positive, call your friends and ask them how they feel about your seating options.

- ✔ Don't seat one stranger with a group of friends who know one another well — doing so isn't considerate to the lone guest. If this situation is unavoidable, be sure to speak to a couple of the guests who know each other before the reception and give them a little information about the person they don't know, and vice versa. Normally, at least one outgoing person at the table can make the stranger feel comfortable.

    If possible, try to mingle and make introductions beforehand, too, remembering to give everyone at the table a little bit of information to help them start a conversation. Something as simple as mentioning that you're childhood friends can help generate conversation because most of your guests probably know something about your childhood.

You can also ask individuals you know well to serve as the unofficial hosts at their tables to facilitate introductions and conversation — it helps to keep things moving along smoothly.

✔ Make sure to seat similar age groups together at the same table. Teenagers usually enjoy being seated together, and, although a couple in their eighties may enjoy sitting at a table of teenagers, they'd most likely have a better time with guests near their age.

After you decide who will sit with whom, you need to decide where to put the actual tables. The parents' tables are closest to the head table with relatives' tables close behind. Beyond that, you're free to arrange tables according to your preference. Just make sure you consider issues, such as accessibility to the restrooms or lobby.

As you try different seating configurations, draw up the correct number of tables and use sticky notes with guests' names written on them to arrange (and rearrange) your chart. Figure 7-2 shows you what I mean.

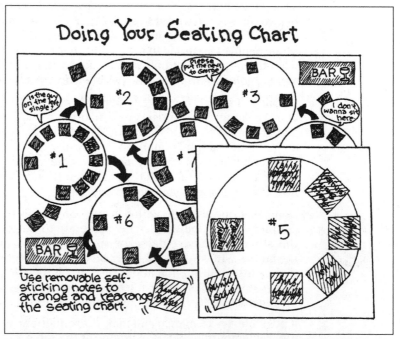

Figure 7-2: Sticky notes are a great tool in arranging your seating chart.

Making special arrangements for children

Seating children with their parents usually works best for everybody concerned, except in the case of teenagers who usually prefer to sit together. Depending on the children's ages, you can also seat the little ones at a table together — within view of their moms and dads, of course. Run the idea by all the parents beforehand to see how they feel about this arrangement; they may have a child who's especially shy and prefers to be with his or her parents.

If prominent members of the bridal party have children but will be busy tending to traditional bridal-party tasks during the meal, you can seat their children with other family members or close friends. In some cases, these bridal party members choose not to sit with the rest of the bridal party so they can sit with their children.

Unsupervised children can ruin a wonderful celebration. If you're going to have a sizeable group of kids at your reception, consider having a special children's buffet or another room available where you can set up a variety of activities to keep the kids occupied until the real party's over. The bridal couple may even benefit from hiring a babysitter or nanny to watch over the group.

Keeping everything straight with place cards

Traditional protocol requires you to set up a table (or tables) for place cards, usually by the entrance to the reception room. The place cards are alphabetized by the last names of the guests, and each card has a table number on it that corresponds to the table where that particular guest is seated. Be sure that the writing on the cards is legible and large, and ask the reception site manager to have the tables ordered numerically so guests can easily find their seats.

Today more and more couples are using themes rather than numbers to identify the tables at their receptions. For instance: When my son, Stephen Fox, was married, he and his wife used the "Fox" (the animal) as a theme. The tables had a variety of names or sayings related to a fox, such as "The Fox Den," and "Sly like a Fox." Another creative idea is to use different years and corresponding pictures of the couple (some of them together and some separate) to identify the tables. Other couples choose to name tables after favorite destinations, films, or books.

What do you do if some guests switch tables? Unfortunately, I've heard of this happening — and at some formal wedding receptions. If the change is discovered in time to remedy it, explain to the offenders that you prefer they remain at the table to which they were originally assigned. If it's too late to make the change, ignore the ill-mannered folks who moved their place cards to another table, but check on the other guests who got bumped to make sure they're comfortable at the tables where they ended up. If they didn't notice the change, you don't need to say anything; if they did notice, apologize. Don't respond to rudeness with rudeness.

Selecting and Presenting Appropriate Favors

Many couples choose to give their guests a little gift (one placed at each table setting) to remember their special day. These gifts can be as simple as specially engraved place cards and napkins. If you set aside money for a more elaborate gift, you have countless options.

Talk to your wedding planner, reception site manager, or caterer for recommendations. Or try an Internet search — you'll find numerous Web sites that specialize in wedding favors of all kinds. The following list offers suggestions for tasteful and meaningful favors:

- ✔ A small silver frame put at each place setting, which can hold the wedding date and names, the menu, or a photo of the wedding couple
- ✔ Engraved champagne flutes, which can either be presented at the beginning of the reception on a table at the entrance to the dining room or brought to the guests with champagne for the toasts
- ✔ A bottle of wine with a special label
- ✔ Scented candles in a glass container
- ✔ An elegant box of chocolates

Your favors should be based on your personal taste and budget and can be specific to the theme of your wedding. Just make sure they're tasteful — nothing of a sexual or offensive nature.

 If the theme of the wedding represents your culture, you can choose culture-specific favors, such as a small replica of the German marriage cup, an Irish horseshoe, or traditional Jordan almonds wrapped in tulle at Greek weddings.

It's perfectly acceptable to include only the couple's name and wedding date with the favor. But if you chose to include a little note of thanks with each favor, you still must send a proper thank-you note to each guest after the wedding.

You may choose to donate money to a charity of personal significance in lieu of a favor. For example, if you've lost a parent to cancer, you may choose to donate money to the American Cancer Society. In this case, each guest should receive a small card explaining the details of the donation; however, never include the specific dollar amount.

Regardless of what you give your guests to thank them for coming to your wedding, give all your guests the same favor. No playing favorites!

Part III

Working on Wedding Details with Your Manners Intact

The 5th Wave

By Rich Tennant

I love a ceremony that has some tradition in it.

In this part...

I start this part by helping you tackle one of the biggest etiquette challenges: Selecting your wedding party. I set you on the right path with suggestions on the appropriate number of attendants and cover the responsibilities of all your bridal party members. Then I help you understand the various levels of wedding formality and give you tips on choosing tasteful attire for all the main players.

In this part, you can explore tactics for assembling the guest list while avoiding arguments, and you can get advice on exactly whom to invite. You can also find out what you need to know about composing, assembling, addressing, and mailing your wedding invitations.

Hold on — there's more! I walk you through the nuts and bolts of your wedding gift registry and explain how to appropriately present gifts to your wedding party and other loved ones. I close this part with the etiquette involved in festivities before the big day, such as showers and the rehearsal dinner.

Chapter 8

Putting Together Your Wedding Party

● ●

In This Chapter

▶ Figuring out how many attendants to have

▶ Understanding the traditional roles of the wedding party

▶ Discarding old rules when it comes to selecting attendants

▶ Dealing with sticky situations

▶ Working well with your wedding party

● ●

Although you may have a vague idea that your wedding party is supposed to support you and your spouse-to-be, help organize showers, and host the bachelor and bachelorette parties, you may not know the details of each member's responsibilities to you and your spouse-to-be. This chapter gives you the scoop on wedding party duties, as well as a few tips on dealing with potential pitfalls and working with your wedding party courteously and respectfully.

Determining an Appropriate Number of Attendants

The custom of having bridesmaids and groomsmen stand by your side as you say, "I do," may have originated in ancient Roman times when the bride and groom were required to have ten attendants at the altar to confuse evil spirits. Today, however, choosing bridal attendants is just a way to honor the people most important to you and to share your special day with them.

You want to choose your attendants from your closest friends and family; however, doing so may not always be easy. For instance, what do you do when you have four brothers, your spouse-to-be has one sister, and you both have dozens of cousins, college

buddies, and devoted childhood friends? And don't forget your unwavering co-workers! How *do* you keep your entourage under a baker's dozen — without hurting anyone's feelings? Here are a few etiquette tips to help you resolve your wedding-party dilemmas:

- ✔ No set rule tells you how many bridesmaids or groomsmen you *have* to have. With this fact in mind, consider your budget before making any decisions. The more attendants you have, the more flowers, gifts, and meals you have to pay for. (See Chapter 4 for wedding budget basics.)

- ✔ The number of attendants should be suitable for the size and style of your ceremony. For example, if you plan a small, intimate ceremony and reception with 50 guests, having ten bridesmaids, a maid of honor, ten groomsmen, and a best man isn't appropriate. A good rule of thumb to follow is one groomsman for every fifty guests.

- ✔ Traditionally speaking, the numbers of bridesmaids and groomsmen should be equal. However, in this day and age, etiquette doesn't dictate this equality. In the case of unequal numbers, bridesmaids may walk in pairs or alone, or each groomsman may escort two bridesmaids.

You and your spouse-to-be should each make a list of the people you want in your party. If the number isn't even and you want it to be, you can assign some of the people to other jobs, such as ushers or readers. (I describe these extra jobs and others in the "Let's Get Together: Your Wedding Attendants" section later in this chapter.)

Disagreements can arise between the bride and groom about the selection of certain attendants. Handling the situation with grace — especially remaining respectful of each other — is important. Your goal is to listen to and understand your spouse-to-be's point of view without considering how it stacks up against yours. The bottom line is: If asking a certain someone to be in the wedding party makes one of you uncomfortable, not asking that person is best.

Like a Rock: The Maid or Matron of Honor

The maid of honor (or *matron* of honor, if she's married) is clearly an essential element for the success of any wedding. She must be a rock! The maid or matron of honor needs to be completely supportive of the bride, and she has to remain levelheaded and calm throughout the emotional roller coaster of planning the wedding. She's traditionally someone the bride is extremely close to — her sister, a close friend, or even her mother. In the following sections, I describe the duties of the maid or matron of honor and provide etiquette pointers on how to select your own.

Note: In some religions, the maid or matron of honor (or best man) must be of the same faith as the bride and groom and will have to receive some coaching from the officiant.

The responsibilities of the maid or matron of honor

The maid or matron of honor has a number of major responsibilities — above and beyond the call of duty! I describe these responsibilities in the following sections.

Managing the bridesmaids

The traditional role of the maid of honor is to lead and manage the other bridal attendants, including the bridesmaids and flower girls. For example, she must keep a close eye out for potential conflicts or concerns that may arise (such as disagreements over accessories or what to serve at the bachelorette party) so that the bride doesn't have to worry about little details that the maid of honor is more than capable of handling — the bride has enough on her plate already! With this in mind, the bride must consider a maid or matron of honor she knows will get along well with the other attendants.

What if the maid of honor doesn't know any or some of the other attendants? Although this kind of situation can make managing the duties of the wedding party a bit challenging, don't count your best friend or your sister out of the running for maid of honor just because she doesn't know your three college friends. Simply make sure all the attendants have the right contact information for one another (phone numbers and e-mail addresses, for example), and take the time to make introductions early. Make special arrangements for all the attendants to get together before any of the wedding functions are scheduled to give them all an opportunity to get to know one another. Doing so gives the maid or matron of honor a chance to get to know the girls she's in charge of keeping in line during the weeks leading up to the wedding.

If the maid or matron of honor and attendants don't know each other well, the bride may choose to write a small bio on each attendant, sharing stories of their friendship. If you and your spouse-to-be set up a wedding Web site (as I suggest in Chapter 3), don't forget to include all this information there, as well!

If the bride is concerned that there may be personality conflicts among the attendants, she needs to let everyone know upfront that the maid of honor is in charge. The bride can do so in a subtle and polite manner. For example, the bride can send an upbeat e-mail asking for the attendants' commitment and support (saying something like, "I've chosen Amelia as my maid of honor. She's going to help me with all the planning for the wedding, and I look forward to you all being able to work together as we prepare for the big day"), or she can speak to each attendant individually. Letting the ladies know that you don't want any bickering or squabbling is absolutely acceptable!

The duty of managing all the bridesmaids includes dealing with the expenses associated with being in the wedding party (see Chapter 4 for a list). A great first step is for the maid or matron of honor to create a list with cost estimates for the various expenses the bridal attendants need to cover. Such a list may include the following: a gift for the couple ($300, $50 each) and the bachelorette party, including transportation, lodging, and meals ($2,500, $416 each). Creating this list and then sharing it with the other bridesmaids gives all the girls an opportunity to say where they want to trim costs or to specify exactly how much they can afford to contribute. The maid or matron of honor and attendants should work together *amicably* to come up with a budget they can all agree on.

Fulfilling other traditional duties

In addition to managing the bridal attendants, the maid or matron of honor traditionally has a few other responsibilities before, during, and after the wedding. These duties include the following:

- ✓ Oversee the prewedding expenses for the attendants and keep excellent records of them.
- ✓ Help the bride with shopping for the wedding day wardrobe, bridesmaids' dresses, groom's gift, decorations, and favors.
- ✓ Coordinate and manage appointments for all the attendants' dress fittings.
- ✓ Be available to help address wedding announcements and invitations.
- ✓ Arrange and host the bridal shower.
- ✓ Organize and plan the bachelorette party.
- ✓ Organize and purchase the bridesmaids' gift to the bride.
- ✓ Pay for an individual gift to the bride and groom, as well as her own wardrobe and travel expenses.
- ✓ Attend all prewedding functions, including the rehearsal and rehearsal dinner.

✔ Help the bride pack for the honeymoon.

✔ Be sure the bridal attendants get to the ceremony on time.

✔ Assist with the bride's general appearance on the wedding day: Help her dress before the ceremony, adjust her hair, and help her with her wedding veil, gown, and train during the ceremony.

✔ Work with the photographer and organize the bridesmaids for photos (as well as pose for photos).

✔ Assist the flower girl with her duties.

✔ Walk in the processional and recessional.

✔ Hold the bride's floral bouquet during the ring exchange.

✔ Hold the groom's wedding ring during the ceremony.

✔ Stand in the receiving line if the bride asks her to.

✔ Sign the wedding certificate.

✔ Give a toast at the rehearsal dinner or the reception.

✔ Dance with the best man during the wedding party dance at the reception.

✔ With help from the best man, transport wedding gifts from the reception.

✔ Attend the postwedding brunch or send-off party.

✔ Take care of the bride's wedding gown after the wedding by taking the gown to the bride's home or her parent's home.

✔ And, of course, fulfill any other request the bride may have!

Selecting your maid or matron of honor

Throughout the course of planning your wedding, you spend a lot of time with your maid or matron of honor. You need someone you can rely on for organizational and emotional support, someone who will be there when you need her. For these reasons, many brides choose their sisters, mothers, or best friends for the role, but if your best friend just had a baby or started medical school, she may not have the time to be the maid or matron of honor you need. But don't worry — you can still ask her to be a bridesmaid! You just have to look elsewhere for a maid or matron of honor.

As you begin to consider someone for this all-important position, ask yourself the following questions: Will this person be able to attend the wedding? Will she be able to help pick out and prepare the site? Can I count on her to answer the phone when I call and help calm me down when things get overwhelming? If you decide that a certain man in your life fulfills this job description better than any women you know, don't worry about breaking the rules — ask him! (See the "Breaking Old Rules" section for more advice.)

If you plan to have a large, extravagant wedding or a destination wedding, or you can't bear to choose between two sisters (or your sister and your best friend), it's perfectly acceptable to have two maids of honor or a maid of honor and a matron of honor, though the maid of honor takes precedent (in other words, she stands immediately next to you in the ceremony and gives the first speech at the reception). Keep in mind, though, that you need to be very specific about the duties of each honored attendant so you can avoid any misunderstandings. Lay out ahead of time, possibly even in writing, who will be in charge of what tasks.

The Groom's Right-Hand Guy: The Best Man

During ancient times, the best man's key responsibility was to protect the bride from abductors and angry family members. Luckily, the job isn't quite as risky today. Much like the maid or matron of honor, the best man is the groom's right-hand man. I describe the best man's duties and provide some etiquette tips on choosing a best man in the following sections.

The best man's responsibilities

The best man has an assortment of responsibilities before and during the wedding, and he should be ready to run any last-minute errands or offer assistance to anyone who needs it at the wedding — from the mother of the bride to a guest who may be unwell. Note that it's the groom's responsibility to clearly set the expectations for the best man. A best man's roles include the following:

✔ Coordinate the tuxedo fittings for the groomsmen and ushers.

✔ Organize the bachelor party with the help of the other groomsmen (and make sure the groom makes it through the evening in one piece!).

✔ Attend the rehearsal and rehearsal dinner, as well as any co-ed showers.

✔ Orchestrate the toasts at the rehearsal dinner and make the initial toast at the reception.

✔ Provide general camaraderie and support for the groom and groomsmen in the time leading up to the wedding and the day of the wedding.

✔ Drive the groom to the ceremony, making sure, of course, that the groom gets to the venue on time.

✔ Walk in the processional (if asked) and the recessional.

✔ Hold the bride's wedding ring in his pocket during the ceremony.

✔ Give the payment check to the officiant either just before or just after the ceremony (the groom's family traditionally pays for this expense). (For more on who pays for what, check out Chapter 4.)

✔ Give payment to the service providers, such as chauffeurs and reception coordinators, as outlined in Chapter 4.

✔ Sign the marriage certificate after the wedding.

✔ Organize the groom's attendants and pose for pictures.

✔ Dance with the maid or matron of honor during the wedding party dance at the reception.

✔ Decorate the getaway car with the groomsmen.

✔ Help the maid or matron of honor transport gifts from the reception site.

✔ Drive the bridal couple to their post-reception location (if they don't hire a car).

✔ Coordinate the groomsmen's gift to the groom.

✔ Attend the postwedding brunch or send-off party.

✔ Pay for his own tuxedo rental and travel expenses.

✔ Return the groom's attire if the groom rented it.

✔ Confirm the couple's honeymoon reservations the day before the honeymoon.

The best man should also keep an eye out for any potential mishaps at the bachelor party, rehearsal dinner, and reception. He should be prepared to deal with the unexpected and do what he can to try to avoid any embarrassing moments for the bride and groom. For example, if he knows the groom's college buddy is known to drink too much, he should make sure that particular friend doesn't give a toast at the rehearsal dinner or reception. He should also give a list of the people who are giving toasts to the MC or DJ and make sure no one else gets hold of the microphone!

Choosing your best man

Normally, the groom asks his brother, best friend, or father to be his best man; it makes no difference whether the best man is single or married. Though the best man may have fewer duties than the maid of honor, his duties are just as important, so think "reliable" and choose your best man wisely!

If you're lucky enough to have two men you want as best men, it's perfectly acceptable to give them both the title. Many grooms are close to their fathers but don't know how to honor them at the wedding; having your father stand as one of your best men is a great way to include him in the ceremony. You may also have a hard time deciding between two brothers or a brother and a best friend. Both men may be equally responsible and available, so putting them both in the position works out well. As soon as you can, make sure you clearly define who will be in charge of which tasks.

If you have a favorite sister or another special woman in your life, feel free to ask her to be your best man if you're closer to her than any other man. (See the "Breaking Old Rules" section for more advice on this topic.)

Let's Get Together: Your Wedding Attendants

As you're deciding whom to ask to be in your wedding party, you may wonder about each member's actual responsibilities. In the following sections, I describe the main players and their duties so you can figure out who's up for the job.

A great way to keep all your wedding party members informed of their responsibilities is to post information (details like times and locations for all the events) on your wedding Web site (see Chapter 3). Folks will be very appreciative (and probably relieved!) to know exactly what you expect of them.

Bridesmaids

Normally the bride selects some of her trusted friends and relatives and those of the groom to fill the roles of bridesmaids. The bridesmaids have many traditional duties, including the following:

✔ Help with wedding planning and prewedding activities, such as addressing invitations.

✔ Help pick out the bridesmaids' dresses and accessories.

✔ Help the maid or matron of honor plan and host a bridal shower (or at least attend the shower if someone else hosts it). (See Chapter 13 for more on bridal shower etiquette.)

✔ Help the maid or matron of honor arrange the bachelorette party.

✔ Share the costs of the bridesmaids' gift to the bride.

✔ Buy an individual gift for the couple and pay for their own dresses, accessories, and travel expenses.

✔ Attend the rehearsal and rehearsal dinner.

✔ Assist the bride with dressing and primping on the wedding day.

✔ Help the mother of the bride with whatever needs to be done, and be gracious to all the wedding guests.

✔ Walk in the processional and the recessional.

✔ Participate in the receiving line, if asked.

✔ Offer the bride any other help she may need — calming her nerves and providing emotional support, for example.

✔ Take the role of co-host at the reception and ensure that it runs smoothly.

✔ Pose for photos and participate in the reception activities (dancing and the bouquet toss, for example).

✔ Attend the postwedding brunch or send-off party.

If you're having trouble incorporating a young lady into your wedding, asking her to be a *junior bridesmaid* may be the perfect solution. Junior bridesmaids are usually between the ages of 9 and 14; they may be your cousins, nieces, daughters, or any other young girls who hold special places in your life. Junior bridesmaids participate in the shopping outings for the wedding, help mail invitations, help put together wedding favors, and, basically, help with any other age-appropriate activities. She doesn't attend (or contribute to) the bachelorette party, though you may want to plan a special one-on-one luncheon or tea for the two of you.

Groomsmen

The groom usually asks male relatives or close friends to stand as his groomsmen at the wedding. He may also choose to ask the spouse or significant other of one of the bridesmaids if he and his bride spend a lot of time with them as a couple.

Here are the traditional duties of the groomsmen:

- ✔ Attend any co-ed bridal showers.
- ✔ Help the best man plan and pay for the bachelor party.
- ✔ Share the costs of the groomsmen's gift to the groom.
- ✔ Buy an individual gift for the couple and pay for their own tuxedo rentals (or other attire-related expenses) and travel expenses.
- ✔ Attend the rehearsal and rehearsal dinner.
- ✔ Provide support, reinforcement, and camaraderie for the groom before the wedding.
- ✔ Be ready to help anyone who needs help the day of the wedding, especially with last-minute errands, and be sure to greet all the wedding guests graciously.
- ✔ Walk in the processional and the recessional.
- ✔ Take the role of co-host at the reception and ensure that it runs smoothly.
- ✔ Decorate the getaway car.
- ✔ Participate in the receiving line if asked.
- ✔ Attend the postwedding brunch or send-off party.

 Another male attendant is the *junior groomsman,* who's traditionally between the ages of 9 and 14. During the ceremony, he stands at the front of the aisle with the groom; he doesn't walk down the aisle with the flower girl. The junior groomsman is expected to be at most of the events that the rest of the wedding party attends, but he doesn't participate in or contribute to the bachelor party. If you have a junior bridesmaid, too, whether or not your junior groomsman walks with her during the recessional or dances with her at the reception depends entirely on their comfort levels.

Ushers

Ushers are typically male, but modern protocol doesn't dictate that they have to be. The greatest distinction between ushers and groomsmen is the fact that ushers sit in the pews during the ceremony instead of standing on the altar with the groom. Many couples choose to have their groomsmen also serve as ushers, but they can be two separate positions. The traditional duties of ushers are

- Arrive at the ceremony location before the groom and tend to any last-minute tasks, such as lighting candles, tying bows on reserved rows, and the like.

- Find out where the restrooms are; at least one guest will certainly want to know.

- Greet all guests as they arrive, and direct them to the appropriate seats (see Chapter 14 for more on seating guests properly).

- Escort immediate family members to the front and direct late guests quietly to seats at the rear of the venue.

- Inform guests about any venue restrictions against taking photographs or throwing confetti.

- Take a designated place at the back of the venue before the bride arrives.

- Stay at the ceremony venue until the last guest has left and ensure that no one has forgotten anything after the ceremony.

- Attend prewedding events, including the rehearsal dinner.

- Participate in tuxedo shopping and fittings.

- Attend co-ed bridal showers.

- Roll out the aisle runner.

- Help decorate the getaway car.

- Help transport the wedding gifts from the reception site.

- Attend the postwedding brunch or send-off party.

 Assigning usher duties is a good way to include those friends or family members who didn't make the groomsmen list, particularly younger members of the family who aren't ready for the debauchery of the bachelor party.

Flower girls

In ancient times, the children in the wedding party had the responsibility of sprinkling herbs in the bride's walkway to encourage her fertility — which is one reason why today's weddings traditionally incorporate at least one flower girl into the ceremony (although etiquette doesn't require you to have one).

Flower girls are typically younger relatives of the couple, but if neither you nor your spouse-to-be have any young female family members, you can ask friends whether their daughters would like to volunteer. Although you may have as many flower girls as you like, remember you have to buy them all flowers, get them all to the ceremony on time, and provide for them at the reception, so having more than four may be difficult to accommodate.

Traditionally, the flower girl walks down the aisle just before the ring bearer or before the bride, depending on your ceremony style (see Chapter 14 for more information). She carries a decorated basket filled with rose petals and sprinkles them on the floor to give the bride a fragrant carpet to walk on.

Check with your venue about the use of flower petals during the ceremony; some churches and other venues don't allow flower petals because they stain the carpet (or for a variety of other reasons). However, you may be able to overcome the ban on flower petals by having the child hand out flowers to guests as she walks down the aisle or sprinkle silk rose petals instead of real ones.

Even though she's just a child, the flower girl has several duties to fulfill as a member of the wedding party. She should attend the bridal shower (bringing a gift, of course), the rehearsal, and the reception, but she doesn't have to attend the rehearsal dinner. The flower girl walks in the processional and recessional with the ring bearer and poses for pictures before and after the ceremony, but she doesn't stand in the receiving line. She also can attend any morning-after gatherings, such as a brunch. Her mother should be invited to all the events the flower girl is expected to attend.

The parents of the flower girl are responsible for the cost of her outfit, and they should be close by before and during the ceremony to help with nerves. (Chapter 9 has more on the flower girl's attire.)

The ring bearer

A ring bearer is a sort of page with the special responsibility of carrying the rings down the aisle to the altar. Usually, the bride and groom choose a nephew or godson between the ages of 4 and 8 to fulfill this role, but you may also choose the child of a very close friend, or even your (or your spouse-to-be's) own son.

Make his role symbolic by having him carry imitation rings sewn onto a satin pillow. That way the real rings can remain safely (you hope!) in the care of the honor attendants. If you want the ring bearer to carry the real rings, consider a decorative box with a lid rather than the traditional pillow. It's a much safer option.

In addition to processing in with the bridal party and carrying the rings, the ring bearer is expected to attend the prewedding festivities (co-ed showers and rehearsal, for example), give the couple a gift, walk in the recessional with the flower girl, and take part in the bridal party photos. You should invite the boy's parents to all the events you invite him to (including the reception).

Additional helpers

In addition to all the folks in the previous sections, you may choose to have a few other additional helpers, including the following:

✔ **Guest book attendant:** To make sure you get a complete record of everyone who attended your wedding, you may want to assign a young friend or family member the job of getting all your guests to sign your guest book at the ceremony and/or reception. The best candidate for this attendant is a preteen or teenager who isn't too shy. To be sure all guests sign the book, ask your greeter at the entrance (or your ushers) to direct the guests toward the table with the guest book. (Find out more about greeters in Chapter 14.)

To make sure no guests are skipped, it's a good idea to have the guest book (and attendant) at both the ceremony and reception.

✔ **Readers:** Many couples choose to have someone read scripture, poems, or literary passages during the wedding ceremony. You can ask a member of the wedding party (a bridesmaid or groomsman) to do these readings, or you can ask a close friend or family member you want to include in the ceremony but didn't have room for in the bridal party.

✔ **Postceremony greeter:** To help your guests with the wedding-to-reception transition, designate a person to round up the guests, make sure they have directions to the reception site, and encourage them to take some light refreshments before the wedding party's arrival. This job is a great way to include a friend or family member who didn't make the bridal party cut.

Breaking Old Rules

You should choose your attendants from your closest family and friends, whether or not they fit the traditional image of a wedding party. Read on to find out how modern brides and grooms are breaking some old rules of choosing attendants — oh so politely, of course!

Attendants of the opposite sex

Modern protocol allows you to choose attendants of the opposite sex. Although you may see a few raised eyebrows at very traditional weddings, your closest friends are worthy of consideration no matter which sex they are.

If you're having a religious ceremony, check in with your officiant before the big day so you don't create a fuss at the rehearsal. You want to make sure the tradition you're marrying in allows attendants of the opposite sex before you start asking friends and family.

Follow these simple rules when trying to decide what to call a male maid of honor or a female best man:

- ✔ If you have a woman take the best man role, refer to her as "the groom's honor attendant."

- ✔ If you have a man take the maid of honor role, refer to him as "the bride's honor attendant."

In either case, simply refer to the rest of the group as bride's attendants or groom's attendants rather than bridesmaids or groomsmen; do the same when you choose to have a male equivalent to a bridesmaid or a female equivalent to a groomsman.

In general, when the honor attendants are of mixed genders (a man on the bride's side or a woman on the groom's side), it's best to have the attendants walk out single file for the recessional.

When you have a woman among the groom's attendants, make sure her outfit coordinates with the male attendants' attire. Some modifications are of course appropriate, such as the female attendant wearing a dress rather than a tux and having a corsage in place of a boutonnière. Similar rules apply for male attendants on the bride's side. Take care to coordinate the man's suit to the style and color of the bridesmaid's dresses. The man should also wear a boutonnière instead of carrying a bouquet.

If a man is filling the position of the bride's honor attendant, the next bridesmaid in line should hold the bride's bouquet during the ring exchange, and she should help the bride with her dress and train when required. Also, female attendants on the groom's side aren't expected to serve as ushers or help guests to their seats.

The male attendant in the bride's party appears in the photos with the female attendants. The same rules apply for a female attendant in the groom's party. Tell the photographer before the day of the wedding that you have a member of the opposite sex among either or both of the attendant groups.

If you don't have a young gentleman among your family or friends to be your ring bearer, you can choose to have a female ring bearer instead. She should wear a dress similar to the flower girls' dresses, but she should stand on the same side as the groom, not with the flower girls on the bride's side (unless she's very young, in which case, she should sit with her parents during the ceremony). It's acceptable, however, to omit the position of ring bearer altogether.

Pregnant attendants

Traditionally, a pregnant attendant at a wedding was considered embarrassing or even disgraceful. A lot has changed since the old days, though. In fact, today it would be bad manners to leave a friend out of your wedding just because she's pregnant.

 Accommodate your attendant's pregnancy by ensuring that she has an appropriate dress for the stage of pregnancy she'll be in during your wedding. Remember that she will get bigger, so you may want to leave her dress alterations until closer to the wedding date. Be prepared for your pregnant attendant to request a completely different dress in a matching or coordinating color. (See Chapter 9 for more information on proper attire for pregnant attendants.)

Assign a trusted friend or family member to be available to help your pregnant attendant if she needs it the day of the wedding. For example, make sure you put a chair near the place where she'll stand during the ceremony in case she needs to sit down, and have transportation available from the reception in case she wants to leave early. You should also have a contingency plan in place and discuss it with the attendant in question just in case she's unable to be at your wedding. Two options to consider are: having an alternate attendant on standby or being prepared to have an uneven number of attendants on your wedding day.

Handling Sensitive Situations

Emotions usually run wild around weddings. There's so much excitement and so many expectations of everyone involved that you're bound to run into some sticky situations. The key is to handle those moments of discontent with grace and remember that you want the people involved in your wedding to be around to help celebrate your anniversaries.

Feeling pressured to ask someone to be an attendant

Your wedding is one time when you can rightfully say, "It's my day, and I'm going to do what I want." It's critical that you have attendants who make you happy (and make the day run smoothly). Etiquette doesn't require you to add extra attendants out of guilt or pressure. In fact, etiquette says not to do so! If someone pressures you to be in your wedding, explain to that person that the attendants hold a meaningful and special place in your wedding and that you want the choice to be left to you and your spouse-to-be.

For example, if your parents demand that you include your long-lost cousin Brenda as a bridesmaid, explain that you've made your selections already by saying something like: "We've already finalized the list of attendants and everyone has agreed; there really isn't space for anyone else."

Always be respectful when you discuss whom to include in your wedding, whether you're talking to your parents, other family members, your friends, or your spouse-to-be. Sometimes you may find a way to compromise. For example, maybe you have another role in the wedding for Cousin Brenda (to say the blessing before the meal, for example). Just don't forget how your cousin (or anyone else, for that matter) would feel if she sensed friction in the family because of her.

Staying cool when someone turns you down or drops out later

At the end of the day, don't lose sleep over someone who doesn't want to be in your wedding. After all, a reluctant attendant won't be any help to you on the big day. On the other hand, if you're really disappointed that someone has turned you down and it means a lot to you to have that person be an attendant, try to find out why he or she doesn't want to join in. The person may be secretly and painfully shy in social situations or possibly unable to afford the expenses of being a wedding attendant. Although just being asked is a special honor, being in a wedding involves many responsibilities and often a considerable financial cost.

If you have your heart set on inviting someone whom you think may have trouble meeting the costs, you'd be kind to offer to cover some expenses, such as the person's lodging or plane fare. Say something like: "My parents want to include your travel expenses in the wedding budget; we'll keep that between us, of course. But if you still don't feel comfortable saying yes, I'd love to have you deliver a reading at the ceremony." Use your best judgment, and don't make someone incur a hardship out of guilt or loyalty.

If someone still doesn't want to be part of your wedding, let the situation be and reassure that person that you're not upset. It's inconsiderate and disrespectful to pressure anyone who doesn't want to participate in your wedding.

If a person has to drop out because of an unforeseen event (death in the family, illness, or some other event) and you have time to ask an alternate to step in, you may be able to arrange for the alternate attendant to reimburse the original attendant for some of the costs. For example, the new attendant may buy or rent the dress or tux from the original attendant and have it altered. If such a solution isn't reasonable, it isn't your responsibility to reimburse any costs, though you may try to arrange a return with the bridal store.

If an attendant simply bails because he or she doesn't have enough time or energy to devote to your wedding or drops out at the last minute for some other reason, you really aren't obligated to help the attendant in any way; however, you may want to find another attendant to step in — if you have time.

Removing an attendant

Weddings can bring out some not-so-positive aspects of a person's personality. If you find that one of your bridesmaids has turned into an overbearing diva or that one of your groomsmen has dropped off the face of the earth and won't return phone calls or e-mails, you and your spouse-to-be may have to make a difficult decision. Think carefully and consider the source of the issue; possibly the attendant has some jealousy issues or time restraints that may pass with time.

Solicit input from your other close friends or family members to make sure you have a clear perspective of the situation and aren't being oversensitive. At the same time, however, don't turn the situation into a poll with the rest of the bridesmaids or groomsmen. After you've heard a few trusted opinions, talk directly to your attendant (no phone calls or e-mails are allowed in this situation), and take the time to really listen to his or her side of the story.

If you genuinely believe your attendant will modify his or her behavior, give the attendant another chance. If your gut feeling is that you're going to see more of the same, quickly and politely tell the attendant that you're removing him or her from the wedding party. As difficult as it may be, let the attendant know (graciously) that you've made your decision to save your friendship. It's often best to be practical, not emotional, in situations like these. Say something like: "Clarissa, I appreciate the fact that you agreed to be in our wedding, but you haven't made it to any fittings, contacted the maid of honor about dates for the bridal shower, or confirmed your travel arrangements for the wedding. I think it'd be best to find someone else to take your place. Of course, we'd still like to have you share in our day as a guest, if it fits into your schedule."

You're not expected to reimburse this person for any of the costs he or she has already incurred. Though, if you know the expenses created a financial hardship, offering aid would be gracious.

Treating the Wedding Party Respectfully

Be considerate of everyone who has a role in your wedding; your attendants all have lives of their own and probably aren't thinking about your wedding 24/7. It may consume much of your life, but it shouldn't consume the lives of your wedding party members. Even though it's "your day," it's polite to focus on "we" rather than "me." Here are some general etiquette guidelines to follow when you're dealing with your attendants:

- Give your attendants plenty of time to check their schedules when you want to plan a meeting or other event with them. Remember that not everything is an emergency.

- Avoid calling and e-mailing your attendants at work.

- Keep appointments with your attendants, and be on time.

- Delegate tasks in a kind and appreciative manner, whether it's through e-mail, on the phone, or in person. Using your pleases and thank-yous is a must.

- Avoid micromanaging your attendants, but know that calling or e-mailing someone who hasn't come through on a task is okay when a deadline is approaching.

- Pick your battles carefully, and don't sweat the small stuff. Does it really matter if all your bridesmaids have exactly the same makeup? A good rule is no more than five must-haves for your attendants; any more than that and you'll come off looking like a spoiled brat.

✔ Always try to understand your attendants' points of view, and even when you don't agree with them, listen to what they have to say. Remember that showing respect for your attendants' opinions is more than just biting your tongue on witty putdowns.

✔ Always practice patience!

Hopefully, your wedding day will be absolutely perfect, but chances are something will go awry. Yes, you're stressed beyond belief, but you need to keep that inner drill sergeant locked up during the wedding planning and on the big day. Keep in mind that it's a wedding, not a military operation. Don't intimidate people, throw orders around, or expect miracles. Maintain your sense of humor from the start of the planning, and you'll be much happier.

If you find you're on the verge of responding in a less-than-polite manner to anyone in your wedding party (or anyone involved with the wedding, period), take control, count to ten, and maintain your composure. You gain nothing by responding to rudeness with rudeness. Keep in mind that people are much more inclined to cooperate with people they see as considerate and courteous than they are with people they see as rude and obnoxious.

If you inadvertently behaved rudely, made a mistake, blundered, or said the wrong thing, apologize immediately! The longer you wait to express your regrets, the less effective your gestures will be. If you don't think the verbal apology is enough, follow up with a handwritten apology or card.

Chapter 9

Choosing Appropriate Wedding Attire and Doing So with Grace

*W*hat should I wear to my own wedding? All eyes are really going to be on me!" This thought can be enough to completely overwhelm many brides. After all, every bride wants to look beautiful on her special day, but what should she wear and where will she find it?

And what about the groom? All eyes will be on him, too! You may think that all the groom has to do is show up in a tuxedo (or maybe a suit) and hopefully remember the ring — but etiquette dictates the groom's wardrobe, too.

In this chapter, I help alleviate some of your angst when it comes to selecting and purchasing appropriate wedding attire for yourself and your wedding party. I also clear up some of the confusion concerning different levels of formality.

Wedding attire should definitely reflect the personality of the couple as they say, "I do," but it needs to be appropriate as well as creative. The key to picking a proper wedding wardrobe is not to choose anything that fits too tightly or too loosely, shows too much cleavage, or otherwise calls too much negative attention to you or your wedding party. Save these extreme outfits for evenings out on your honeymoon!

Recognizing Different Levels of Formality

As you find out in Chapters 5 and 7, different types of wedding ceremonies and receptions have different levels of formality: black tie, formal, semiformal, and informal. What you, your spouse-to-be, and your wedding party wear hinges on your wedding's overall level of formality. (Your invitations reflect this level of formality, too; see Chapter 11 for details.)

If you and your partner are usually more on the casual side, having a black tie wedding may not be fitting for you, and the idea of an extra formal affair may make you uncomfortable. But, on the flip side, this is one time in your life when you may want to splurge and spice up the formality a bit! In the following sections, I describe different levels of formality and the basics on appropriate attire for each level.

By selecting all the elements of your wedding to have the same levels of formality, you ensure that your entire day will flow with ease and style. The connectivity between the ceremony, the reception, and the wedding attire help make your family and friends feel comfortable throughout the event.

Whatever your style and level of formality, it's always best to remain tasteful. Don't forget you'll have the photos to look back on for years to come! Also, be sure to check with your officiant on any wardrobe restrictions, especially if you're having a religious ceremony in a house of worship. For example, some churches don't allow you or your wedding party to wear strapless dresses unless you also wear sweaters that cover the shoulders. (See Chapter 6 for general guidelines on working with an officiant.)

Black tie

Traditionally, black tie attire marks a very formal wedding — one that takes place in a house of worship or an upscale hotel, has an elaborate sit-down dinner at the reception, and features at least 200 guests and a large wedding party (as many as 12 attendants for the bride and 12 for the groom!). Choosing a black tie wedding gives you the opportunity to take not only the attire, but the entire ambiance of the day to the highest level of elegance. Black tie weddings don't necessarily have to be in the evening; your wedding can begin in the late afternoon and still be very formal.

The bride at a black tie wedding wears an elegant full-length gown with a train and a veil. The groom wears a full-dress tuxedo with a black tailcoat, matching black pants, white shirt, white vest, and white ascot tie. The bridesmaids wear full-length gowns, matching shoes, and sometimes gloves (if the bride so chooses). The groomsmen wear black tailcoats and pants with white stiff shirts, white ascot ties, and black socks and shoes.

If you're having a black tie wedding, you must make a note on the invitation by stating *black tie* so that your guests know what they're expected to wear. Not all male guests own tuxedos or have the budget to rent them, though, so some of your guests may wear dark suits instead. Female guests wear long or dressy short ensembles with beads, sequins, and so on.

Formal

A formal wedding is typically held in a house of worship or a hotel, starts in the afternoon or evening, has a sit-down dinner or buffet at the reception, and features at least 100 guests. Also, the bride and the groom each traditionally have between three and six attendants.

The bride in a formal wedding traditionally wears a full-length gown with a sweep or chapel train and a fingertip veil; the groom wears a black coat, black pants, white shirt, black vest, and black tie. The bridesmaids wear matching full-length dresses, and the groomsmen wear tuxedos that match the groom's.

Stating *formal dress* on your invitation tells your guests that they're expected to wear formal eveningwear, which is very dressy by American standards, but the invitation note isn't necessary. For formal weddings, male guests typically wear suits and ties, and female guests wear short dressy or longer-length cocktail attire.

Semiformal

A semiformal wedding can be held in a house of worship, but you can also have one in a home, an outdoor location, or another spot. It traditionally starts in the afternoon, has a simple meal or refreshments at the reception, and features fewer than 100 guests. The bride and groom each have between one and three attendants.

The bride in a semiformal wedding wears a full-length or cocktail-length gown (falling between the knee and the floor) with a fingertip veil; the dress either has a short train or none at all. The groom wears a tuxedo or a dark suit with a tie. The bridesmaids wear matching full-length or cocktail-length dresses, and the groomsmen wear tuxedos that match the groom's or dark suits with ties.

For semiformal weddings, you don't need to add any notation to the invitation. Guests dress according to preference, usually wearing cocktail attire.

Informal

An informal wedding is usually held during the day in a home or another spot that isn't a house of worship. It has a simple meal or refreshments at the reception and features fewer than 50 guests. The bride and groom traditionally each have one attendant.

Informal wedding attire can be just about anything you can think of. The bride can still wear a wedding dress (but no veil); it just has to be cocktail or knee length. If you and your spouse-to-be are thinking even more casual, the bride can wear a classic pantsuit with a soft blouse or a fun cotton or linen sundress rather than an actual wedding dress.

Informal attire for the groom can be a dark suit with a tie or a dark jacket with nice slacks and a button-down shirt (no tie). Again, if you and your spouse-to-be are going for something even more informal, the groom can wear khaki pants paired with a plain polo shirt, a long-sleeved button-down shirt, or a short-sleeved button-down shirt. In tropical weather or for beach weddings, all the men in the wedding (and the male guests) can wear linen shirts and linen slacks or, even more casual, Hawaiian shirts, Bermuda shorts, and flip-flops!

 If you're having a wedding set in a tropical climate, consider wearing clothing that fits in with the locale. Traditional cultural attire never goes out of style and can give an informal wedding more of a formal feel. For example, at casual or outdoor weddings in Hawaii, the bride can wear a traditional floral Hawaiian dress (normally cotton and floor length) and the groom can wear slacks and a traditional white Hawaiian wedding shirt, normally made of light, soft poplin cotton with a white-on-white embroidered design, sewn with authentic coconut buttons.

A bridesmaid in an informal wedding can wear a knee-length dress, and a groomsman can wear a suit, a jacket with slacks, or another ensemble matching the formality of the groom's attire.

 For informal weddings, you don't need to add any notation to the invitation. Telling guests what to wear is appropriate only for black tie and formal weddings.

Dressing the Women in the Wedding

Just a few steps into a bridal store can leave your head spinning with all the possibilities of what to wear at a wedding! Fear not! In this section, I describe the proper attire for the women in a wedding, including the bride, her bridesmaids, her flower girl, and the mothers of the happy couple.

As you're outfitting the women in your wedding, keep in mind that the season in which you're getting married dictates the fabrics and styles you can choose from (a bridal store consultant can help you choose options that fit your wedding's season). Think about it: You don't want to wear a long-sleeved satin gown for your July wedding, and strapless silk gowns may leave bridesmaids in a December wedding feeling a little chilly. Most importantly, you want your bridal party to be comfortable in whatever you select.

The bride

"Here comes the bride!" Your wedding dress may be the single most important clothing purchase of your life. (Now if that statement doesn't put on the pressure, I don't know what will!)

As with many of the other aspects you plan for your wedding, the level of formality for your wedding helps you choose the type of dress and coordinating accessories (check out the earlier "Recognizing Different Levels of Formality" section for more info). Even so, whether you're planning an elaborate church wedding or an informal, intimate affair, your gown should also reflect your personality, taste, and style. In the following sections, I discuss how the style and color of wedding dresses, along with trains and veils, relate to your wedding's formality.

The style and color of dress

Has everyone asked you about your dress, yet? Will it be a sheath dress? A mermaid style? Princess cut? Empire waist? Who knew you had so many styles to choose from! Before you get too overwhelmed, take a deep breathe, let it out slowly . . . now you can begin to understand the following styles and how they relate to the formality of your wedding:

✔ **Ball gown or ballerina:** The most formal style, this type of gown is often a popular choice for brides who envision a fairy tale wedding. It pairs a fitted bodice with a full skirt. The ball gown is most appropriate for large, traditional weddings that are black tie or formal, but today's wedding fashion choices offer a wide selection of this traditional style that makes it appropriate for semiformal weddings, too.

✔ **A-line or princess cut:** This classic and simple style of gown is fitted around the bodice and typically flows to the ground, resembling the outline of an uppercase *A*. It flatters most body types and is appropriate for anything from a garden wedding to a traditional church ceremony that's formal or semiformal.

The princess cut is the most striking variation of the A-line dress. It's slightly flared to accentuate the waist without hugging the body and is appropriate for formal or semiformal weddings. Its short version is appropriate for informal weddings.

✔ **Slip, column, or sheath:** Each of these similar styles has a narrow fit that's straight from top to bottom. This style (with long and short versions) is very appropriate for semiformal or informal weddings, especially for brides getting married on the beach.

✔ **Empire waist:** If you want to feel like a Roman Goddess, this style is for you! It has a raised waistline that gathers under your bust line with a long, flowing skirt. This design is loose and non-form-fitting; it's meant to elongate the body and can be found in both long and short styles. It's appropriate for all levels of formality because it can be dressed up with the right embellishments or made less formal depending on the type of fabric.

✔ **Mermaid and trumpet:** These sexy, modern styles contour to your body, giving you a dramatic look. They're extra fitted through the bodice and hips and flare at the knee. These styles are suitable for formal or semiformal weddings.

The preceding style descriptions are good guidelines to follow, but you may want to try on a dress in each style to find out which one fits your body type the best. You just never know — you may end up choosing the complete opposite of what you imagined at first. The perfect dress should give you a sense of added self-confidence, and it should be fairly comfortable — remember you'll be wearing it for a whole day!

Brides have many decisions to make about color for their weddings — and not just for the bridesmaids' dresses. Bridal gowns come in a variety of shades from white to ivory, and some even incorporate splashes of color to match the wedding colors. In today's weddings, all these colors are appropriate for bridal gowns.

No matter which style and color you choose for your wedding dress, make sure your final choice is both tasteful and classy. Believe it or not, your wedding dress will leave the first and last impressions on your guests. A shockingly low neckline or a completely backless style likely isn't what you want your guests to remember when they leave your reception, and it's never proper, no matter how informal your wedding is.

The train

Not only do you have to match the style and color of your dress to the formality of your wedding, but you also have to consider the train on your dress. Each of the following styles relates to different levels of formality:

- ✔ **Sweep train:** A short train that just brushes the floor, it's appropriate for semiformal weddings.

- ✔ **Chapel train:** Usually extending 1.3 yards from the natural waist, this train is most suitable for formal or semiformal weddings.

- ✔ **Cathedral train:** Typically extending 3 yards from the natural waist, this train is most appropriate for black tie and formal weddings.

The veil

Not surprisingly, formality also plays a role in which veil a bride chooses to wear. Here are the main veil types, along with their levels of formality:

- ✔ **Blusher veil:** Short in length and usually covering the bride's face, this veil is perfect for semiformal and some informal weddings, depending on the location.

- ✔ **Fingertip veil:** Measuring 36 inches long and reaching the bride's fingertips when her hands are at her sides, this veil is most appropriate for formal or semiformal weddings.

- ✔ **Full-length veil:** Extending onto the floor at least 6 inches beyond the train, this veil offers a very dramatic look. It's most appropriate for formal weddings.

Be certain to discuss veils and other head coverings with your officiant. Certain religions require specific attire.

Pulling a dress switcheroo

Some brides choose to change out of their wedding gowns before their receptions. If you choose to make this change, you should do so only after the formal photos have been taken. It's the bridesmaids' responsibility to make sure your second outfit is ready to go and any accessories make it to the changing area.

Personally, I think a bride should choose a wedding dress that's comfortable for both the ceremony and the reception. However, some cultures or traditions dictate a wardrobe change, and if you're marrying in one of them, changing your dress can be a great addition to your day. You may even want to explain its significance in your wedding program.

Bridesmaids

Before you choose what your bridesmaids are going to wear on your special day, you need to consider the following rules of etiquette concerning the level of formality and the color of your bridesmaids' dresses:

- ✓ A bridesmaid's dress should complement the bride's gown in terms of formality. For example, if you're wearing a knee-length dress to your informal wedding, your bridesmaids shouldn't wear full-length dresses, no matter how casual they may look.

- ✓ The color of a bridesmaid's dress should coordinate with the season of the wedding. In general, lighter colors are for spring and summer, and darker colors are for fall and winter. Your bridal store representative can help you choose an appropriate color.

 A popular trend today is for the bride to let her bridesmaids choose their own styles of dress from the same color and fabric. Some bridesmaids may choose to have the same dress, or they may all choose something different, but either way they'll look similar, thanks to the fabric. I've seen this trend in action at a few weddings, and, believe me, it's a beautiful look. It's creative and shows a little part of each bridesmaid's personality. And, more importantly, because you let your girls pick out their own styles, you have a happier, more comfortable bridal party. It's a win-win situation.

If your mind is set on having the same dress for all your brides-maids, consider a dress that flatters most figures, such as an A-line or princess-cut style (which I describe earlier in "The bride" section). Just be prepared for at least one not-so-happy bridesmaid who asks you over and over if you're sure this is the dress you want because it looks hideous on her. Be respectful of her feelings and reassure her that you took her opinion into consideration but felt this particular dress was best for all your bridesmaids and your special occasion. (For more about receiving dress input from your bridesmaids, see the "Simplifying shopping and decision making" section later in this chapter.)

Friendships always come first. When you look back on your wedding in five years, you won't care too much about what your bridesmaids wore, but you will care whether you're still best friends with them.

Junior bridesmaids' attire can be the same color and style as the bridesmaids' attire as long as it's age appropriate. However, you can also have the junior bridesmaids stand out a little from the others by selecting a coordinating color and style that complements the bridal party.

Some couples today choose to have a male bridesmaid or maid of honor (the brother or close male friend of the bride, for example). For more information about this attendant's attire, check out Chapter 8.

Pregnant attendants

You can find many bridesmaids' dresses that can accommodate a pregnant bridesmaid. An empire-waist style (which I describe earlier in "The bride" section) usually works the best, and with good alterations, your mommy-to-be bridesmaid will fit right in, literally. Seeking professional advice from a dressmaker or bridal salon may give you additional ideas on styles that work for pregnant attendants.

Be sure to order more material or encourage your pregnant brides-maid to order a larger size of the dress. After all, it's always easier to take in than to let out.

Consider choosing one color and fabric for your bridesmaids' dresses and then letting your pregnant bridesmaid choose a maternity dress in the same color and fabric. You may be surprised to see the wide array of stylish maternity dresses available today, and your bridesmaid will surely be more comfortable, which is important if you want to have a happy bridesmaid.

Flower girls

Flower girls always steal the show — it's *so* true! Dressing a flower girl may seem like a fairly easy and super fun job, but hold on! Don't forget about her mom. Most moms are more than happy to let the bride run the show, but you absolutely must have Mom's approval when selecting the flower girl's dress.

Little girls look adorable in white or ivory dresses that are age appropriate and well coordinated with the bride's and bridesmaids' dresses. Longer-length styles with short sleeves and coordinating satin bows are favorite choices among today's brides. Matching tights and patent leather shoes are a nice touch, too. You may also consider adding a halo of delicate flowers in your flower girl's hair and offering her a colorful floral basket of rose petals to complete her ensemble. Can you hear your guests oohing and aahing as she skips down the aisle?

If you're in a position to pay for the flower girl's dress and accessories, doing so is a nice gesture. If her parents are paying for her dress and accessories, be considerate of the cost. Almost all bridal stores carry a large selection of dresses for flower girls, so you can find something in every price range.

Mothers of the couple

The infamous "what dress will the moms wear" discussion can be a sensitive part of your wedding planning. Yet, contrary to popular belief, it's not a competition — in fact, it can be a fun bonding experience for both mothers to talk about what to wear.

Every mother of the bride or mother of the groom I've talked to asks, "Do I have to color coordinate with the bridesmaids?" I always suggest that it's best to talk to the bride first about color. Some brides like the moms to be in the same color (or at least a coordinating color) as the bridesmaids. For example, picture this: Bridesmaids are in a rich navy, the mother of the bride is wearing a beautiful light blue, and the mother of the groom is wearing a perfect silver. The different colors look stunning together, especially in the photos.

Colors to avoid are of course white, ivory, beige, and red. A white or ivory dress obviously competes with the bride's for attention. And tradition says that red can be too flashy and may send a not-so-nice message from the mother of the groom to her son's bride.

It's tradition that the mother of the bride should choose her dress first and then call the mother of the groom. The mother of the bride should try her best to sound friendly and nonterritorial: "Susan, I am so excited, I thought you'd like to be the first to know I found the perfect dress for Jeremy and Kate's wedding. I chose a lovely bronze cocktail style with a jacket." Calling the groom's mother isn't a requirement, but chances are the groom's mom wants to know about the bride's mom's dress because she, too, is thinking about what to wear.

Moms certainly don't have to look frumpy, but a low-cut dress isn't suitable, either. The best advice I can give to mothers of the couple is not to try to outshine the bride; doing so won't go over well and may strain a relationship. What's most important is that everyone feels comfortable and beautiful.

Dressing the Men in the Wedding

Outfitting the men in a wedding may be much simpler than outfitting the women, but you still have some etiquette guidelines to follow. In this section, I explain how to dress the groom, the groomsmen, the ushers, the ring bearer, and the fathers of the couple.

The groom

I know what you're thinking: Grooms have it easy when it comes to dressing for their weddings. Well, for the most part, you're right. What the groom wears depends entirely on the type of wedding:

- Classic tuxedos are a safe bet for black tie and formal weddings, and they can make any groom look like Clark Gable or Fred Astaire. The tuxedo should include a jacket, matching pants, stiff shirt, vest, bow tie or tie, shoes (and socks, of course), and cuff links. If your wedding is black tie or ultra formal, the tuxes may include a tuxedo coat with tails, wing-collar shirt, and white bow tie.

- For semiformal or informal weddings, a nice alternative to a tuxedo is a dark suit. Purchasing a nice-looking suit is a good investment because the groom will surely find a time to wear it again. Wearing a suit also allows the groom to get a little creative by adding a colorful tie, but he should always run this bit of color by his bride — or better yet, let her pick it out!

- The most informal weddings allow grooms to wear casual attire (which is why many people refer to these grooms as "the lucky ones"). For example: For a beach wedding in Hawaii, a groom may wear linen khakis, a silk Hawaiian shirt, and flip-flops. Must be nice!

Wearing shorts when you're getting married on a beach or some other warm locale may seem favorable to you, but seeing overly hairy, extra white bare legs in wedding photos with a gorgeous sunset in the background doesn't look so pretty.

Because the groomsmen and ushers wear tuxes or suits to match the groom's, you can select something different for the groom's attire to make him stand out. A noticeably different boutonniere, vest, or shirt can help the man of the day feel as important as he is!

Groomsmen and ushers

Picking out what your groomsmen and ushers wear is quite simple. Their outfits should be similar to the groom's ensemble, but they can also deviate a bit. Making slight color changes in the boutonniere, shirt, vest, or tie is an excellent way to separate the groomsmen from the ushers.

For example, if the groom is wearing a classic tuxedo with an ivory shirt, ivory vest, and ascot tie, the groomsmen can wear the same tuxedo and the same shirt but with a black vest and tie. The ushers may wear the same style as the groomsmen or maybe a different style tie, such as a bow tie.

The junior groomsmen's attire should coordinate with the groomsmen's jackets, pants, shirts, vests, and ties. You can vary the boutonniere slightly; just make sure it coordinates with the other men's flowers and is age appropriate.

Today some couples choose to have a female groomsman or best man (the sister or childhood female friend of the groom, for example). For more information about this attendant's attire, check out Chapter 8.

The ring bearer

Can't you just picture how adorable a little boy looks with a bow tie on? In essence, ring bearers should be dressed in attire that's similar to that of the groomsmen and ushers, depending on the formality of the wedding, of course. Here are a few guidelines to follow:

  ✔ If your wedding is black tie or formal, the ring bearer should be in a tuxedo with a bow tie. Keep the tuxedo simple and age appropriate.

✔ If your wedding is semiformal or informal, the ring bearer may wear a suit or sport coat, dress shirt, and nice slacks. Picking attire in the style and color of the groomsmen's is always a safe choice. If your ring bearer is very young (under 5 years old), you may want to consult your tuxedo shop for alternate choices.

Most likely, the ring bearer will have his jacket and tie off as soon as he gets his hands on it. How do you keep them on? Bribe the little guy! An acceptable accessory for a ring bearer is a small toy that he can carry with him to distract him from the itchy dress shirt.

Be sure to discuss all outfit options with the ring bearer's parents and, if your budget allows, pay for the ring bearer's outfit. If your budget is tight, keep the cost of the ring bearer's outfit in mind out of respect for his parents.

Fathers of the couple

Unlike dressing the mothers of the happy couple (which I discuss in the "Mothers of the couple" section), dressing the dads doesn't require a phone call to each other because they traditionally dress similarly to the groom and groomsmen, no matter the level of the wedding's formality. Whether your wedding calls for formal tuxedos or beach attire, fathers of the bride and groom should look sophisticated and important.

One of the nicest ways to honor the fathers is by selecting boutonnieres that are totally different from those of the groom and groomsmen.

Dads may have their own tuxedos that they've had stowed away for the past ten years. Perhaps not surprisingly, they may not fit as perfectly as they once did. Talk directly to your own dad about the issue, and enlist your spouse-to-be's help to talk to his or her father about it. Any dad would rather listen to his own son or daughter tell him that he needs to go out and rent a more stylish tuxedo or suit than receive the information from the person his beloved child is about to marry. Some dads are very attached to the idea of wearing their own tuxedos or suits, so tread lightly if you hope to change their minds.

The Etiquette of Shopping for Attire

After you have a solid idea of what everyone in your wedding should wear, it's time to take action! In this section, I explain the protocol behind shopping for formalwear.

Simplifying shopping and decision making

The processes of shopping and deciding exactly what the women and the men in a wedding should wear are slightly different, as you find out in the following sections.

The women

From the bride's point of view, the most important outfit she needs to pick out is her wedding dress, and, naturally, she doesn't want to shop for this alone. In many cases, it's almost a rite of passage for the mother of the bride to go shopping with her daughter to find that special dress. Or sometimes an aunt or other female role model comes along with the bride's mother or in place of her. The bride can also invite her maid or matron of honor or another bridesmaid if she lives close by.

It isn't necessary to have an entourage of ladies accompany you during your hunt for the perfect dress. In fact, having a large group with you is often an inconvenience for bridal stores to accommodate. Not to mention, the more opinions you receive, the more confused you'll be about your final decision.

Whomever you decide to ask to join you, be sure to ask them several weeks in advance; however, be prepared to accept that they may not have the time to shop — as much as they'd love to. Make sure you show your appreciation to anyone who can come along, and be gracious for their willingness to spend this special time with you (for instance, you can treat everyone to lunch or coffee after the shopping is over).

Visiting a bridal boutique requires an appointment, during which time you receive personal attention from a bridal consultant. If you have an idea of a particular style, or have a photo of a gown you saw in a bridal magazine, show it to your consultant at the beginning of your appointment so she has an idea of your personal choices. Always be mindful of your appointment time, and listen to

the consultant's recommendations, whether you agree with them
or not. After all, she knows much more about the store's stock
and the styles that may flatter you and any bridesmaids who have
accompanied you than you may think. Always show your appreciation for the consultant's advice, and be thankful for her time. You
may go back to that store, so you don't want all the consultants to
run to the back room when you return.

It's the bride's privilege to select the bridesmaids' dresses, but
the bridesmaids can provide input. Before you go shopping, sit
down with some or all of your bridesmaids and show them photos
of dresses you like from bridal magazines, or e-mail them links to
photos you find online. Doing so gives you a chance to gauge their
general opinions on style and color. Be sure to consider the bridesmaids' personal styles, color preferences, figure types, comfort,
and budgets, but keep in mind that it's ultimately your choice, no
matter how much one bridesmaid pushes for a particular dress
while you're out shopping.

If you feel confused and overwhelmed from all the selections you
see during your first trip to a bridal boutique, apologize to the consultant and ask whether you can make another appointment in the
near future to start the process again. Maybe you'll have a better
idea of the style you want for yourself and your bridesmaids after
you have more time to think about it.

Everyone will have an opinion of what looks best on you; be sure
to thank them graciously for their input, but, ultimately, which
dress you wear on your wedding day is *your* decision.

The men

When you're choosing the type of tuxedo for the groom and the
other men in the wedding party, you and your spouse-to-be should
visit the tuxedo rental place together. Usually the bride and groom
pick out the tuxedos and then show the groomsmen and ushers
the selections, but it's always considerate to keep costs in mind
when choosing the men's attire.

If the groom decides to have the groomsmen and ushers wear
darker suits, he needs to let the men know about the choice and
ask them what color suits they have in their wardrobes. In most
cases, each groomsman and usher has a suit that's close enough to
the color of the others' suits. If one or two of the groomsmen have
to purchase suits, they can likely find some that don't exceed the
cost of tuxedo rentals.

Grooms, your brides may have been thinking about your weddings since they were 5 years old. Try to be patient and understanding. If your choice of the tuxedo is different from your bride's, why not compromise and work it out? Ah, the first true test of what married life is all about!

Keeping cost in mind

It's easy for you and your spouse-to-be to get caught up in the excitement of your upcoming wedding. However, your wedding party is surely on a budget. Be considerate of everyone's financial situation as you select all formalwear, and *never* expect your attendants to pay for more than they can afford. Be honest and sincere with all the members of your wedding party when you're trying to determine what they can and cannot afford. Discuss this issue with each party member sooner rather than later to avoid uncomfortable situations that may arise.

The couple can offer to pay for their wedding party's attire if their budget allows, but doing so certainly isn't mandatory. Let your wedding party members know the approximate financial responsibilities to expect before they accept your invitation to be in the wedding. Financial disputes often lead to strained relationships — and you definitely don't want any of those! For more on who pays for what, head to Chapter 4.

As the big day gets closer, some of your bridal party members may find that they're not in the position to pay for the necessary wedding attire items. In situations like this, you definitely want to talk to them and try to work out a reasonable solution. Assuming the cost yourself for one person can be difficult to keep a secret and may cause hard feelings with other bridal party members if they find out. So, if you choose to pay for one attendant's attire, you may want to consider doing something additional for the other bridal party members to keep their feelings and your kindness in balance.

Chapter 10

Assembling the Guest List

. . . .

In This Chapter

▶ Beginning the process of building your guest list

▶ Understanding the best way to handle sticky situations

▶ Being considerate when cutting the guest list

. . . .

Compiling your guest list can be an extremely stressful part of the wedding planning. It's also a time when you need to be extra tactful and sympathetic to the feelings of others. Above all, you need patience and understanding to avoid conflicts and hurt feelings. In this chapter, I show you how to handle the process of building — and potentially trimming — your guest list with your manners intact.

The First Steps of Figuring Out Who Attends the Festivities

Putting together your wedding guest list begins with two important tasks: reviewing your budget to determine how many people you can invite and working with your parents to figure out who those lucky folks will be. I get you started with these tasks in this section; the later section "Keeping in Mind Guidelines for Specific Groups" has additional pointers for polishing your list.

Considering your budget before you begin

After you know what kind of wedding you want and how much money you have to spend (see Chapter 4 for budget advice), you can use that information to decide how many guests you can invite. Keep in mind that the head count at your reception is the biggest expense in your wedding budget. The head count determines the size of your venue, which figures into the per person costs. (If you select your reception venue before assembling your guest list, the size of the venue determines the number of guests.) Your head count also determines how much food and drink you need to provide at the reception, which are two of your most pricey expenses. So find out how much money you can spend per guest, and use that amount to determine the number of guests you can have.

You can make assembling and managing your guest list a piece of cake by using one of the following programs:

- ✔ www.theorganizedwedding.com
- ✔ www.mystylewedding.com
- ✔ www.rsvpprogram.com
- ✔ www.wedding-assistant.com
- ✔ www.weddingwire.com

Building a master guest list

To ensure equanimity, set a maximum number of guests and then divide that number evenly among the bride's parents, the groom's parents, and the bride and groom. You may need to make adjustments when one of the families is much larger than the other.

Before you or your parents officially throw any names into the hat, you and your spouse-to-be need to decide on the level of input you're willing to accept from your respective parents' guest lists. If either of you is concerned that your parents will go overboard with their guest list, try your best to cool their jets before they draft their part of the guest list. You can say something like: "We really appreciate your love and support, but please remember that it's our day. We want to be fair in this process, but we hope you understand that we may have to make changes, which may mean cutting some of your guests."

Give both sets of parents a number to start with (in addition to an estimated cost per person), and ask them to prioritize their guests. If you have to make cuts later, you can start from the bottom.

Even when one set of parents is paying for the majority of the wedding, you still need to speak to them about the number of guests they plan to invite. If Mom and Dad become upset over not being able to invite more people, talk about the issue, listen to their concerns, and, if there's room to compromise, do so. But unless your parents are willing to cover the additional expenses for extra guests, find a way to negotiate. Just make sure you remain respectful toward all the parents involved.

After your parents and you and your spouse-to-be complete your lists, compare notes to check for duplicates, particularly if you and your spouse-to-be are from the same hometown. These lists form the master guest list, which you then need to prioritize. To do so, first identify the *must* invites, second, the *should* invites, and third, the *could* invites. Does your budget cover all the *must* invites? If so, move on to the *should* invites and then to the *could* invites. By using this system, you ensure that the people who are most important to you, your spouse-to-be, and your families make the cut.

Depending on your reception venue and its policy, you may have to include the band members, photographer, videographer, and wedding planner in your final head count, which means you have to include the cost of their meals in your budget.

Keeping in Mind Guidelines for Specific Groups

Unfortunately, you can't always invite everyone you want to your wedding because of either budget constraints or the size of your venue. After close family and friends make the list, the bride and groom have to think about the remaining spots. Do you want to invite only those folks you're very close to, or do you want to include acquaintances, as well? What about your co-workers or all those people you were once friends with but haven't talked to in ages? Where do you start?

In the following sections, I explain how to polish your guest list with a few guidelines for several different groups of people.

Knowing that shower guests are a must

Traditionally speaking, a bridal shower is a fun gathering of female family members, your bridal party, and your close girlfriends. Today many couples have co-ed showers, too, which provide a great way for family and friends of the bride and groom to meet before the wedding.

Even as you finalize your guest list for the wedding, be certain of the people you plan to invite to your shower (no matter the style or how many you have). In most cases, everyone invited to your shower should be invited to your wedding — period. The following is a general guide of whom you should invite to your shower:

- Mothers of the bride and groom
- Grandmothers of the bride and groom
- Sisters of the bride and groom
- Aunts of the bride and groom
- Cousins of the bride and groom
- Bridesmaids
- Wives of groomsmen — if you're close to them
- Close girlfriends

Including stepmothers is also a nice gesture, assuming that Mom and Stepmom get along. If they don't get along, talk to them in person and ask them to put aside their differences for the day.

Keep in mind that not all women invited to your wedding need to be invited to your bridal shower. Flip to Chapter 13 for the full scoop on bridal showers and other festivities before the wedding.

Determining whether single guests can bring dates

The date-or-no-date discussion always seems to come up at some point during the guest list assembly. Picture this: The groom wants to invite his single buddies to bring dates, but the thought of whom they may bring just isn't going over well in the bride's mind. What should they do?

The good news is that inviting a date with every single friend isn't a requirement. Your budget dictates whether inviting *any* dates with single friends is even a possibility. But when you invite single folks (in particular, close family members and friends who are unattached), be sure to follow these guidelines:

- As a rule of thumb, if any single friend or family member is in a long-term relationship, you should invite that friend or family member with his or her significant other (by name) even though they aren't married.
- If your budget allows, single members of the wedding party and any single family members should have the option of bringing a guest.
- If you're inviting a single friend who doesn't know anyone else at the wedding, consider inviting him or her with a guest.

If your budget doesn't allow for each single guest to bring a date —
and many couples' budgets don't — be sure to address the invitation appropriately. Don't include "and guest" in the hopes that
they won't bring one because they probably will.

If your guest list has similar numbers of single women and single
men, problem solved! However, if your wedding is a more intimate
affair and you have only one or two single friends, you may want to
consider including "and guest" on their invitations.

If you receive calls from guests asking to bring someone else along,
graciously explain the reasoning behind your decision not to invite
dates and do your best not to cave in to pressure.

Deciding whether to invite work colleagues

What's interesting about co-workers and bosses is that you
spend more time with them than you do with your own families!
However, you aren't obligated to invite co-workers or your boss
to your wedding.

Deciding whether you should invite co-workers, bosses, and other
business acquaintances can be a really difficult decision for you
and your spouse-to-be to make. For example, you may be close
to your co-workers and want to invite them, but your spouse-to-
be may work in a law firm where people traditionally invite their
immediate bosses to their weddings even though they don't inter-
act much with them.

Your budget helps you make this difficult decision. If your budget
allows, you can follow the unwritten rule that says to invite the co-
workers and business acquaintances you socialize with outside of
work. However, inviting everyone on your team except one person
isn't appropriate.

If you decide to invite co-workers but simply can't include their
spouses because of budget constraints, inviting them without their
spouses is appropriate. Just make sure you talk to them about the
situation so they understand that their spouses aren't invited (and
expect one or two of them to decline the invitation because they
can't bring their spouses).

If your budget is limited, not inviting the people you work with is
perfectly acceptable, too (even if your spouse-to-be invites a few
close co-workers). It's okay to mention to your co-workers that
your wedding is small and that if things were different, you'd love

to have them there. Most bosses and co-workers understand and are still supportive. In fact, don't be surprised if your office surprises you with a shower! (Don't worry; this is an exception to the you-must-invite-everyone-who-attends-your-shower-to-the-wedding rule.) Show your colleagues your appreciation by sending each person a thank-you note.

Handling sticky situations

Nothing in life is perfect, so don't be surprised if you have to deal with a few messy situations as you build your guest list. I explain how to deal with divorced parents, estranged family members and friends, and exes in the following sections.

Divorced parents

Okay, take deep breaths as you embark on the journey of dealing with divorced parents. Hopefully, both parents put their differences aside for this one special day and make it all about you and your future spouse. If you anticipate tension or charged emotions, take some time to talk to each of your parents sincerely and bring your spouse-to-be along with you. Express that you love them and want them to be a part of your wedding and that it wouldn't be the same without them both there. Remain respectful to all your parents, and if you have any specific concerns, address them politely. Be compassionate, but be firm.

Suppose that during your conversation with your father, he says, "Of course, I'll be respectful toward your mother, but do you mind if I bring my new girlfriend?" Oh dear, pick up your jaw from the floor and try to figure this out! If you and your spouse-to-be are uncomfortable with this situation, or if your dad's bringing a date would make your mother too upset, politely explain to your dad that your wedding isn't the right place for him to introduce his girlfriend — but let him know that you'd like to meet her after you return from your honeymoon. Hopefully your dad will understand and respect your wishes. (Naturally, the same solution applies if your mom wants to bring her new boyfriend to your big day.)

What if both Mom and Dad are in new relationships? Although this is a tough situation, as long as no one has any legitimate objections with Mom or Dad bringing their new partners, it's a nice gesture to invite them. If the significant others are stepparents, you must invite them. Your relationship with your stepparents may not be the best, but they're family.

Sometimes the resentment is just too much, and one parent can't overcome the past. The "I'm not going if he's going" syndrome can be very hurtful to you and your spouse-to-be. Unfortunately, when this kind of situation happens, you likely have to make some very tough decisions. Talk to your parents about your thoughts on the subject, and tell them how important it is to you that they both be there.

You should never have to choose between Mom and Dad, so don't. Invite both parents if you're on good terms with them, and let them make their own decisions about what to do. You can't control what your parents say or do — or don't do. Remember that you've expressed your wishes respectfully and diplomatically and you've taken their feelings into consideration — now enjoy your day!

If you aren't on good terms with one of your parents, discuss the issue with your spouse-to-be. Evaluate the situation and be sure not to set any expectations for yourself. If you think it'll make you feel better to reach out to your parent, do so, but keep in mind that your parent may not give you the reaction you were hoping for. If you feel the need to apologize for any reason, do so, but again don't expect immediate effects. You may decide to extend an invitation to your estranged parent knowing he or she may not come — if it makes you feel better, go for it. If you're certain that your parent will cause a scene or do or say something to hurt someone's feelings, it may be better not to invite this parent.

Estranged relationships

So, you've finally finalized your guest list, and you're still wondering about Uncle Joe and Aunt Betty whom you haven't seen in years? Inviting estranged family members or friends is deeply personal. Carefully thinking through this kind of situation is very important; talk to your spouse-to-be and your family members and/or friends who may be opposed to seeing the estranged relative for good reason. Including an estranged relative or friend may seem like the gracious thing to do — after all, weddings are about the coming together of family and friends. However, as gracious as it may seem, you simply don't have to invite someone who hurt you or offended you some time ago. And, as harsh as it may be, this goes for estranged parents as well.

Your wedding isn't the right venue to mend a broken relationship, so be sure to resolve your differences first. But keep in mind that even if you successfully resolve your differences or at least agree to disagree, your relationship may not prosper after your wedding.

Exes and former spouses

How *ex* is your ex? If the bride wants to invite her ex-boyfriend because they're still friends and there's no love connection, she still needs to ask her groom about it — his answer may be very different from hers. So, if you're considering adding your ex to the guest list, don't do so quite yet.

You can find some very extreme opinions on this topic. Some people take the view that you shouldn't invite an ex to your wedding under any circumstances. However, some couples who have been able to carry on platonic, mature friendships with their exes disagree.

First and foremost, think this situation over carefully and be respectful of your spouse-to-be's wishes. If having your ex attend your wedding is going to upset your spouse-to-be in any way, the discussion is over. Don't push the subject because doing so may signal that you still have feelings for your ex, and, if that's the case, you have bigger issues to address.

What if you've been married before? Should you invite your former spouse to watch you walk down the aisle again? Well, are you and your ex like Demi Moore and Bruce Willis — getting along beautifully even though you're both in new relationships? If so, then inviting your ex is perfectly okay, especially when children are involved. Letting your children see that Mom and Dad have a respectable friendship and can continue to support each other even when they love and marry another person can be very healthy for both your kids and you.

On the other hand, you may choose not to invite your ex because doing so may confuse your children. After all, it's important for children to see that Mom and Dad are still the parents but no longer connected and that there's a new family unit. Before you decide whether to invite your ex or not, it's a good idea to have an honest conversation with your children to find out how they feel about your new relationship and how they feel about your ex being at the wedding.

A few things to pay attention to when you and your spouse-to-be are in agreement about inviting an ex-boyfriend, an ex-girlfriend, and/or a former spouse include the following:

- ✔ Invite the ex with a guest.
- ✔ Greet the ex at your wedding as you would any other guest, but don't spend a lot of time chatting with him or her.
- ✔ Introduce your ex as the mother or father of your children or as an old friend, not as your ex.
- ✔ Be respectful of your guests, as well; some guests may feel uncomfortable being around you and your ex. Therefore, don't say or do anything that makes your ex stand out. For instance, dancing with him or her right after your first dance is a major no-no.

The big dilemma — Kids or no kids?

You and your soon-to-be spouse are standing on the altar exchang-ing your wedding vows; it's a moment you'll never forget, and, all of a sudden, little Billy announces to the congregation, "Hey, Mommy, why is that lady's hair blue?" Grandma just had her hair done and the coloring is a tad overdone, and, lucky for you, Billy took note. Your guests start laughing, and your unforgettable moment is interrupted. Some couples roll with interruptions like this one and welcome the laughter; however, others are offended by them.

Determining whether to invite children can be tough when you're planning your guest list. Before you make the decision, consider the type of wedding you're having. If it's a black tie affair and your reception begins in the evening, you may have to deal with a few meltdowns as children become tired. If you're having a casual, garden wedding in the early afternoon and your motto is the more the merrier, by all means, invite children.

Children count toward your final number, and, if space is limited at your reception, you may have an easier time making your decision. Keep in mind, though, your flower girl and ring bearer are part of your wedding party, so you should invite them, of course. If either you or your spouse-to-be has children, you should absolutely include them, too. If either of you has children in your immediate family (that is, brothers or sisters), you should invite them, as well.

If you and your spouse-to-be have quite a few children in your families, think about hiring a babysitter or a teenage family member to watch the children during the ceremony and recep-tion. Many churches have separate rooms that can accommodate a large group of children. Usually, older children would rather be in charge of the younger children than sit through your ceremony anyway.

If you decide to include children, it's a nice gesture to provide coloring books, crayons, games, and other quiet entertainment to keep them occupied at both the ceremony and the reception. Also, be sure to order meals for the children — they don't need what the adults eat, but they do need something because hungry children are sure to let you know they're hungry by their loud screams!

Questions regarding the attendance of children at formal catered occasions have triggered legendary family feuds, so think about the implications of not including children on the guest list. Be aware, too, that not inviting children may cause their parents to turn down the invitation.

If you decide not to invite children and you anticipate that some of your guests may have a problem with that decision, be sure that you're crystal clear on whom you address the invitations to. For example, you need to write "Mr. and Mrs. John Anderson" on both the outside and inside envelopes. Don't write "The Anderson Family." You may also want to put a note on the reception card of your invitation that says "adult reception." (See Chapter 11 for details on addressing your invitations properly.)

Be prepared — no matter how clearly you announce that you're not inviting children to your wedding, at least one or two guests will call you to ask whether they can bring their children. Always be polite and sympathize with their predicament, but simply explain that you and your spouse-to-be have made the decision not to have children other than immediate family at your wedding.

Whether you decide to have children or not, stick to that decision. Don't make exceptions for some guests and not others. Doing so is a sure way to hurt feelings.

Cutting Back the Guest List

No matter how much careful planning you do, you'll most likely have to confront the dreaded task of cutting back the guest list. You can count on some disagreements — and maybe even a few tears. But remember one thing: You and your spouse-to-be have to remain respectful to each other and be understanding to each other's feelings about making tough decisions. In the following sections, I walk you through the process of deciding whom to cut, I show you how to deal with any fights that arise, and I explain how to communicate graciously to folks who aren't invited.

Deciding whom to cut

Few couples come in under the allotted number for their guest list. Figuring out exactly whom to cut is never fun, but it has to be done. After you compile the guest lists from you, your spouse-to-be, and your parents, you need to get out the marker and criss-cross. Follow these steps to whittle down your list:

1. **Review the list, and, if you don't recognize a name, check with your parents or future in-laws and politely ask them whether you can remove that person from the list.**

2. **Next, look at your co-workers, bosses, and business acquaintances.**

If you must make cuts, this group is probably the safest place to start after eliminating the unrecognizable names. Your colleagues should understand that you want to keep it to just family and close friends.

3. **Still need to downsize? Look at your friends and your spouse-to-be's friends. Ask yourself, do you see them regularly? Or at least talk to them often? Do you see yourselves keeping in touch with them long after your wedding?**

   If you hesitate in the least bit, cut 'em. Just because you attended your friends' wedding years ago doesn't automatically extend them an invitation to yours. In fact, anyone who has planned a wedding before should certainly understand what it feels like to have to remove people from the guest list to reach a manageable number.

4. **Finally, look at distant relatives whom you haven't seen or heard from in a few years.**

   After checking with your parents (especially if they're footing the bill), take them off the list. They may be appreciative that they don't have to travel and buy a gift!

Anyone you invite to the ceremony *must* be invited to the reception, too, so don't try to meet your budget by cutting people from the reception guest list. If finances are truly tight, consider limiting the number of guests to both the ceremony and the reception.

You may feel a bit of relief mixed with guilt after cutting down your list. These feelings are completely normal, so feel confident with your decisions.

Avoiding arguments about cuts

Welcome to the world of give and take. If you can master this technique during your wedding planning, you're well on your way to a successful marriage!

As I mention earlier in this chapter, the guest list is one of the most difficult parts of the planning process. Building your guest list often leads to arguments with your spouse-to-be and even more so with your parents and in-laws. So what can you do to avoid, or at least minimize, arguments? First of all, always remind yourself to be polite and respectful of yourself and whomever you're speaking with. After all, raising your voice to make a point usually doesn't work.

The most effective way to avoid arguments is to make sure you're on the same page as your spouse-to-be about your guest list. Politely question — don't attack — your spouse-to-be about someone on his or her list. Give him or her an opportunity to be heard, and you may realize it's not an issue after all. When the two of you are in agreement, dealing with Mom and Dad and their lists is much easier.

A similar approach can help you avoid (or minimize) your arguments with your parents. Start by giving your parents (and your in-laws) a chance to explain why they want to invite the guests you deem questionable — and don't forget to listen to what they say! Be respectful and kind with your words. If you need to excuse yourself from the discussion and let it rest for a few hours or more, don't hesitate to do so. Come back to it when everyone is calmer and has had time to think things over. Hopefully, then you can reach a compromise.

Being gracious to the people not invited

After you finalize your guest list but before you send invitations, make a phone call or a visit to anyone you think may have hurt feelings over not being invited.

Honesty is best. Of course, this conversation isn't an easy one to have with anyone, but it's better to address any hurt feelings than to not say anything at all. Be sincere and explain that your wedding is small and that if circumstances were different, you'd want them there. Hopefully, friends or co-workers will understand. If they're offended, however, it's probably best that you didn't invite them. Don't respond in defense — a simple sorry and hope you'll remain friends is all you need to say.

If you and your spouse-to-be find that you can't invite as many close friends as you would like because both of you have large families, consider hosting a BBQ or casual cocktail party when you return from your honeymoon. Include all the friends you couldn't invite to the actual wedding. Just be sure to mention that you don't want them to bring gifts.

Chapter 11

Carefully Composing Your Invitations and Announcements

*O*nce upon a time, engaged couples had two exciting choices for their invitations: black ink on ivory card stock or black ink on white card stock. Although these very similar options are still the traditional style for a formal wedding invitation today, couples planning a more contemporary or informal wedding have many more options available. As a result, the process of selecting your invitations can be as fun as any other part of planning your special day.

Whichever style of invitation you choose, you also need to know how to word your invitations; what to enclose (or not enclose) with the invitations; how to properly address the envelopes to avoid any misunderstandings about who's invited; how to handle unfortunate postponements or cancellations; and when to use wedding announcements. I explain everything you need to know about these topics in this chapter.

Etiquette dictates that guests over the age of 18 should receive their own invitations, so be sure to count them before placing your invitation order. You should also send invitations to the officiant and his or her significant other, and don't forget your attendants and your parents (yes, they get invitations, too). As a general rule, order about 20 percent more stationery (including enclosures and envelopes) than you think you'll need; you may decide to add to your guest list, or you may make mistakes in addressing envelopes.

Choosing a Proper Invitation Style

The invitation is typically the first hint to your guests about the style of your wedding (anything from black tie to informal; see Chapter 9), and you want it to have the best possible presentation so that everyone knows what to look forward to on your happy day. A stationery company or wedding planner can guide you toward your final selection according to your wedding's style, your budget, and your personalities, but the following sections cover some general guidelines to keep in mind.

Focusing on formal invitations

The most formal invitations for black tie weddings follow the time-honored techniques of engraving, which result in raised lettering that adds texture to the paper. Couples who choose the traditional, formal route use black or dark gray script on high-quality, medium to heavyweight paper. The paper color can be soft cream, ivory, or white. The paper is folded in half, like a card, with the invitation on the front; the inside is blank.

A slightly less formal invitation (but still appropriate for formal weddings) follows the same choices for ink, paper weight, and paper color, but it's printed on an unfolded, single-paneled card. Both of these black tie and formal invitation styles can be on plain (flat) or raised-paneled paper.

Embossing (also known as *dry embossing*) is a technique that makes a raised impression, without ink, into the paper — think monogrammed, expensive, and elegant. It's a lovely addition to the formal invitation and is most often used for a design motif, coat of arms, family crest, or return address.

Looking for less traditional

If your wedding style is semiformal, informal, or themed, you have quite an array of invitation choices. You can use your wedding colors or theme to make your invitations personal and individualized, even to the choice of font style. For these less traditional wedding styles, you can have your invitations printed (rather than engraved) on an unfolded, single-paneled medium to heavyweight card — any color is appropriate. You can also have them printed on designs or bordered paper, using colors that coordinate with the wedding. For an extra personal touch to a very informal wedding, you may even choose to handwrite your invitations (neatly, of course).

Even though having hot pink ink may seem like an exciting option to you, keep in mind that not every ink color is easy to read. And, typically, most ink colors other than black cost more, which is something to consider when you're on a budget.

Note: Even in today's stretched wedding traditions, sending invitations through online services (like e-mail) is frowned upon. Save online invitations for other events, such as parties, business or organizational meetings, and other less formal social events.

Wording Invitations Properly

When you're wording your wedding invitation, careful attention to detail is a must. Your invitation is a keepsake — not only for yourself, but also for your guests. You want to avoid the potential embarrassment of mailing 250 invitations that announce your parents as Mr. and Mrs. Sue Ellen Williams. People will notice errors, and you definitely don't want to spoil the overall appearance of your invitation. So make sure to proofread carefully!

In the following sections, I describe the spelling and abbreviation rules to adhere to, and I explain how to properly specify the wedding's hosts. I also provide pointers on special wording for special events (like military weddings), and I warn you about what you should *never* put on an invitation.

An invitation gives the specifics of who's getting married, who's hosting the nuptials, and where those nuptials will take place — that's it. The only acceptable addition is stating the dress code for the wedding; see Chapter 9 for details.

Spelling and abbreviation rules

As you're composing your invitations, keep in mind the following spelling and abbreviation rules for names, dates, times, and addresses.

Names

The rules for including names on an invitation are fairly simple and traditional. In terms of titles, spell out professional titles, such as Doctor and Reverend, and all military titles (General, Major, and so on). Acceptable abbreviations are the nonprofessional titles Mr., Mrs., and Ms.

In the event that the mother of the bride or groom is a doctor and the father isn't, traditionally, the woman doesn't use her title, and the invitation reads "Mr. and Mrs. Browning." However, in today's society, it's becoming more and more acceptable for the woman to use her title. Here's the proper wording — on two lines — with the word *and* to indicate that the two people are married:

> Doctor Marie Browning
> and Mr. David Browning

Don't include academic titles, such as PhD, on the invitation unless the person is a minister with a theological degree ("The Reverend Doctor Paul Stevens," for example). You don't usually use "The Honorable" when issuing an invitation to or for a judge; however, you may use Judge as his title. Using elected titles, such as Senator, Mayor, and Governor, are also acceptable.

Spell out the terms *junior* and *senior,* using lowercase, for a formal invitation (George Davis, senior). If you choose to abbreviate these terms because of space or for a less formal invitation, you should capitalize them (George Davis, Sr.).

Always use full names rather than nicknames (such as David rather than Dave). If you choose to include any middle names on the invitation, spell them out, too — no initials allowed. For example, don't list your father as "Mr. David P. Browning"; use "Mr. David Peter Browning" instead.

Dates, times, and addresses

For all types of invitations, from black tie to informal, spell out street names, such as Avenue, Boulevard, and Street, as well as state names. For black tie and formal weddings, spell out days of the week, dates, months, times, and smaller numbers in addresses (larger numbers call for numerals). Don't include the street address for hotels, churches, country clubs, or banquet halls. Use only the name of the venue and the state. Here are some examples for formal invitations:

> Saturday, the fifth of June, two thousand ten
>
> half after eight in the morning (add "in the morning" to avoid possible confusion)
>
> twelve o'clock in the afternoon (not "twelve o'clock at noon")
>
> eight o'clock (optional: "in the evening")
>
> one hundred eleven North Main Street

For invitations to semiformal and informal weddings, you can use numbers freely. However, still spell out days of the week, months, and street names. Here are some examples:

Saturday, June 5, 2010

8:30 a.m.

at noon

8 p.m.

111 North Main Street

American versus British spelling

You may have noticed some unusual spelling on wedding invitations you've received, and now you're confused: Is it honor or honour? Favor or favour? The best answer I can give you is that which spelling you use depends on your personal preference. The more traditional spelling is the British spelling with the *u* in both cases. Whichever spelling you choose, just make sure you're consistent throughout the invitation (honor/favor; honour/favour).

In a house of worship, such as a church or synagogue, you show reverence to God by using the word *honour,* as in "request the honour of your presence." At a location other than a house of worship, even if the ceremony is religious, you use the phrasing "request the pleasure of your company" instead. Both phrases are proper for formal invitations.

Specifying the hosts

The hosts finance your wedding, so, naturally, they get top billing on the invitation. The following examples illustrate different scenarios and the proper invitation wording for each situation.

Different cultures and religions have varying practices for how to word traditional wedding invitations. For example, in Hispanic cultures, it's common for both sets of parents to issue the invitations; the bride's parents are listed first. For Jewish weddings, the word *to* before the groom's name is changed to *and;* the groom's parents are also included under his name. Make sure you know any special protocol for your situation before ordering your invitations; it's always advisable to check with your officiant or a knowledgeable family member first.

The bride's parents as hosts

For a formal wedding when the bride's parents are hosting, use the format shown in Figure 11-1 for your invitations (with traditional wording and proper spellings).

> *Mr. and Mrs. Peter Sun*
> *request the honour of your presence*
> *at the marriage of their daughter*
> *Lily Yuh*
> *to*
> *Mr. Terry Allen Fischer*
> *Saturday, the eighteenth of September*
> *two thousand ten*
> *at five o'clock*
> *Fourth Presbyterian Church*
> *Chicago, Illinois*

Figure 11-1: An invitation with the bride's parents as hosts.

The groom's parents as hosts

When the groom's parents are hosting the wedding, use the format shown in Figure 11-2.

> *Mr. and Mrs. Edward Fischer*
> *request the honour of your presence*
> *at the marriage of*
> *Miss Lily Yuh Sun*
> *to their son*
> *Terry Allen Fischer*
> *Saturday, the eighteenth of September*
> *two thousand ten*
> *at five o'clock*
> *Fourth Presbyterian Church*
> *Chicago, Illinois*

Figure 11-2: An invitation with the groom's parents as hosts.

Both sets of parents as hosts

Today both the bride and groom's parents often share the financial responsibility of hosting the wedding, in which case you follow the format shown in Figure 11-3 for your invitations.

Mr. and Mrs. Peter Sun

and

Mr. and Mrs. Edward Fischer

request the honour of your presence

at the marriage of

Lily Yuh Sun

to

Terry Allen Fischer

Saturday, the eighteenth of September

two thousand ten

at five o'clock

Fourth Presbyterian Church

Chicago, Illinois

Figure 11-3: An invitation with both sets of parents as hosts.

If you have stepparents whom you don't want to feel left out or you don't want to include such a long list of parents, you can choose to use the following initial wording instead:

> Together with their parents
> Lily Yuh Sun
> and
> Terry Allen Fischer
> request the honour of your presence

A single or widowed parent as host

When a widow who hasn't remarried is hosting the wedding, her name appears by itself on the host's line (see Figure 11-4). A widow who has remarried uses Mrs. followed by her present husband's name. The same wording guidelines apply when a widower hosts.

Divorced parents who haven't remarried as hosts

When the bride's parents are divorced but not remarried, list the mother's name on the first line and the father's name on the third line. Separate the lines with the word *and* (see Figure 11-5).

Mrs. Peter Sun

requests the honour of your presence

at the marriage of her daughter

Lily Yuh

to

Mr. Terry Allen Fischer

Saturday, the eighteenth of September

two thousand ten

at five o'clock

Fourth Presbyterian Church

Chicago, Illinois

Figure 11-4: An invitation with a single or widowed parent as host.

Mrs. Elizabeth Sun

and

Mr. Peter Sun

request the honour of your presence

at the marriage of their daughter

Lily Yuh

to

Mr. Terry Allen Fischer

Saturday, the eighteenth of September

two thousand ten

at five o'clock

Fourth Presbyterian Church

Chicago, Illinois

Figure 11-5: An invitation with divorced parents as hosts.

Stepparents as hosts

When the bride's mother and stepfather are hosting the wedding, list both their names and then specify whose daughter the bride is (see Figure 11-6).

Mr. and Mrs. Robert Miller

request the honour of your presence

at the marriage of

Mrs. Miller's daughter

Lily Yuh Sun

to

Mr. Terry Allen Fischer

Saturday, the eighteenth of September

two thousand ten

at five o'clock

Fourth Presbyterian Church

Chicago, Illinois

Figure 11-6: An invitation including stepparents.

When the bride's father and stepmother are included on the invitation, the first part of the invitation may read as follows:

Mr. and Mrs. Robert Miller
and
Mr. and Mrs. Peter Sun
request the honour of your presence
at the marriage of their daughter
Lily Yuh Sun
to
Mr. Terry Allen Fischer

When the groom's parents are divorced and are being included on the invitation, use the preceding guidelines for appropriate wording.

Relatives other than parents as hosts

If family members other than parents or stepparents are hosting the wedding, follow the wording shown in Figure 11-7. Make sure to insert the correct relationship of the hosts to the bride or groom. For example, if the bride's aunt and uncle are hosting, use the phrase, "at the marriage of their niece Lily Yuh Sun."

Mr. and Mrs. Charles Edwards
request the honour of your presence
at the marriage of their granddaughter
Lily Yuh Sun

to

Mr. Terry Allen Fischer
Saturday, the eighteenth of September
two thousand ten
at five o'clock
Fourth Presbyterian Church
Chicago, Illinois

Figure 11-7: An invitation with relatives other than parents as hosts.

The bride and groom as hosts

When the bride and groom are hosting their own wedding, use the wording and format shown in Figure 11-8.

Special wording for special events

A few types of events require special wording on the invitation. The following sections cover military and commitment ceremonies (see Chapter 5 for more information on ceremony styles), as well as belated receptions.

Military ceremonies

Military wedding ceremonies are exciting events — all those uniforms walking around make the wedding even more memorable. You need to take extra care when wording your invitation, however, because protocol regarding rank determines how the names of the bride and groom should be listed on the invitations. (No matter what, make sure to spell out all ranks and branches of military, including the words *United States*.)

Miss Lily Yuh Sun
and
Mr. Terry Allen Fischer
request the honour of your presence
at their marriage
Saturday, the eighteenth of September
two thousand ten
at five o'clock
Fourth Presbyterian Church
Chicago, Illinois

Figure 11-8: An invitation with the bride and groom as hosts.

In the past, you didn't use a title lower than sergeant on wedding invitations, and you placed only the branch of military under the person's name. For example:

> Lily Yuh Sun
> United States Army

Today, however, a noncommissioned officer or enlisted man or woman of any branch may choose to use his or her title. For example, a corporal in the U.S. Army may write his name like:

> Terry Allen Fischer
> Corporal, United States Army

For an enlisted, noncommissioned officer or junior officer, place the title under the name with the branch of service following it. For example:

> Terry Allen Fischer
> First Lieutenant, United States Army

For ranks higher than lieutenant, place the title in front of the name, with the branch of service under the name. For example:

> Captain Terry Allen Fischer
> United States Army

With these guidelines in mind, use the appropriate wording specifying the wedding's hosts to complete the invitation (see the "Specifying the hosts" section). Figure 11-9 shows an invitation in which the bride and groom are in the military and the bride's parents are hosting the wedding.

Mr. and Mrs. Peter Sun

request the honour of your presence

at the marriage of their daughter

Lily Yuh

United States Army

to

Terry Allen Fischer

First Lieutenant, United States Army

Saturday, the eighteenth of September

two thousand ten

at five o'clock

Memorial Chapel

Fort Jackson, South Carolina

Figure 11-9: An invitation for a military ceremony.

Commitment ceremonies

A same-sex couple who wants to formally announce their union to family and friends may choose to have a commitment ceremony, usually followed by a reception. But how do you word an invitation to this event? Well, the wording isn't much different from the traditional wedding invitation. Follow the earlier rules for listing the host(s) and the names of the couple. Then just insert the type of ceremony the couple is having (commitment ceremony, for example). Figure 11-10 shows an invitation in which one set of parents is hosting a commitment ceremony. When two sets of parents are hosting the ceremony, use this initial wording instead:

Mr. and Mrs. Samuel Johnston
and
Mr. and Mrs. Robert Simmons
request the pleasure of your company

Mr. and Mrs. Samuel Johnston
request the pleasure of your company
at the Ceremony of Commitment
joining their daughter
Mary Beth Johnston
and
Laura Lynn Simmons
Saturday, the eighteenth of September
two thousand ten
at four o'clock in the afternoon
Marina Yacht Club
One Ocean View Boulevard
Fort Lauderdale, Florida

Figure 11-10: An invitation for a commitment ceremony.

You can substitute any meaningful name for your ceremony that you want to, including Commitment Ceremony, Civil Union Ceremony, and Celebration of Commitment.

Belated receptions

Sometimes having the reception immediately following the wedding simply isn't practical — especially if the wedding ceremony is in an exotic location (you lucky couple!) and only a few close friends and family are able to attend (lucky people!). In this instance, it's appropriate to host a belated reception after you return from your honeymoon trip for all your loved ones who had to stay home. When you're wording the invitation for a belated reception, you need to clearly indicate that the marriage has already taken place. You can do so by using the phrase "celebrating the marriage" (see Figure 11-11).

If your belated reception isn't formal, you can use your first name and your spouse's first name rather than the traditional "Mr. and Mrs." on the invitation.

> Mr. and Mrs. Peter Sun
> request the pleasure of your company
> at a reception
> celebrating the marriage of
> Mr. and Mrs. Terry Allen Fischer
> Saturday, the sixteenth of October
> two thousand ten
> at five o'clock
> Bay View Country Club
> 111 Marina Way
> Miami, Florida

Figure 11-11: An invitation for a belated reception.

Items you should never include on an invitation

Whatever you do, *don't* include information about where you're registered or a note that you want cash instead of gifts. Although you may think including this information in some way on the invitation is a good idea, doing so goes against all the rules of etiquette you're trying to follow by reading this book. If you'd like to suggest that your guests contribute to a particular charity instead of giving you gifts, include this info on your Web site, save-the-dates, or shower invitations.

Also never, ever, handwrite anything on the invitation, and never print "No children" on your invitation. Your guests should know whether their kids are invited by the way you address the invitation. (See the "Addressing Invitations Properly" section for details.)

Investigating Invitation Insertions

Whew! Congratulations are in order for perfectly wording your invitations. But you're not finished yet. You need to find out about everything else that has to go into the envelopes with your beautiful invitations — items such as the inner envelope, the reception and response cards, the response envelope, the map and directions, the hotel information, the pew cards (if you're using them), and that one intriguing item, tissue paper.

Registry cards, which disclose where you're registered, are never acceptable enclosures with your invitations. Including them is considered the same as asking for gifts, which is a major no-no — no matter what the stores tell you (for them, it's free advertising).

The inner envelope

The inner envelope doesn't have any glue, is slightly smaller than the outer envelope (which I discuss later in this chapter), and may or may not have a colored lining (which beautifully matches your wedding colors, of course). You don't write the mailing address on this envelope, so what do you do with it?

The inner envelope allows you to specify exactly whom you're inviting to your wedding. For example, although you address the outer mailing envelope to your friend, Miss Stacey Carmichael, you can indicate on the inner envelope that she can bring a guest of her choosing. In this case, on the inner envelope, you write "Miss Carmichael and guest" or, if you prefer, "Stacey and guest." Either option is appropriate for formal and informal weddings.

The inner envelope gives you a place to list the names of the children you're inviting; omit their names if you aren't inviting children to your wedding. (I explain how to address all invitations the right way in the "Addressing Invitations Properly" section later in this chapter.)

In all but formal and black tie weddings, budget-conscious couples may omit the inner envelope. If you choose to do so, you may include "and guest" on the outer envelope to show who's invited.

The reception card

A *reception card* is a formal invitation to your reception, and it's used when the reception venue is different from the ceremony's location or when there's a gap in time between the ceremony and reception. The reception card should be the same style and quality as your invitation, but it should be only half the size. Along with the reception's location, it should state whether you're planning a meal for your guests ("Luncheon reception," "Dinner reception," or "Cocktail reception"). If the reception immediately follows the ceremony, state so clearly; if the time of your reception is to be a few hours later than the ceremony, state that on the card, too. Figure 11-12 shows a sample reception card.

The inner envelope's pristine past

In the distant past, when people delivered invitations by various means other than the postal service, the outer envelope protected the inner envelope from wear, tear, weather, and dirt. Upon the invitation's arrival to its recipient's location, the butler removed the offensive outer envelope — revealing a pristine inner envelope — and presented the exquisite invitation (on a silver tray, of course) to his employer.

If your reception is at the same location as the ceremony, you don't need a separate reception card. Simply print the information on the invitation. You can write "Reception immediately following" or "Dinner and dancing immediately following."

If you're planning an intimate wedding to be followed by a larger reception, order a larger reception invitation, using the words "request the pleasure of your company at a wedding reception" (or "marriage reception"). Use a smaller card for the ceremony information and send it only to those folks invited to the ceremony.

> *Luncheon reception*
> *immediately following the ceremony*
> *The Atrium at Swan Lake*
> *4200 Lake Street*
> *Oakville, California*

Figure 11-12: An example of a reception card.

The response card

A *response card* is also known as a *reply card* or *RSVP*. It functions to alert you (and your caterer) to how many guests will be attending the reception and, in some cases, serves as a menu planner when guests are allowed to select their entrées. For any wedding reception that requires planning significant amounts of food, you need response cards. In addition to helping with food planning, the response card also helps you plan seating arrangements for your guests.

Response cards typically include the following (see Figure 11-13):

- ✔ A line preceded by an M gives guests a place to finish their titles and write all the names of the people invited who plan to attend (Mr. and Mrs. John Smith, Paul, Rebecca, and James, for example).

✔ Spaces before the words *accepts* and *regrets* or *will attend* and *will be unable to attend* give guests a place to check whether or not they're attending.

✔ A place to indicate food preferences gives guests an opportunity to choose an entrée if you're offering them a choice.

✔ An *on or before date* lets guests know when they need to return the response cards to the host; this date should be at least two weeks prior to the reception, or whenever your caterer needs a final count. Formal invitations spell out the date (such as "the first of June, two thousand ten"); less formal invitations can use numbers freely (such as "June 1, 2010").

The favor of a reply is requested
on or before the first of June, two thousand ten

M _____

_____ *accepts* _____ *regrets*
_____ *New York Strip Steak* _____ *Atlantic Wild Salmon*

Figure 11-13: An example of a response card.

When you begin receiving your response cards, make sure you keep track of them against your guest list so that you can see at a glance who's attending your reception and who isn't; doing so makes it easier for you to finalize your plans accordingly. After waiting a couple of days past the date you've set for the cards to be returned, contact the guests you haven't heard from. Not only do you need a final head count, but you also need to make sure their invitations didn't get lost in the mail.

Refer to Chapter 3 for information on using Web site RSVPs.

The response envelope

When you order your invitations, the response cards come with response envelopes for you to include with the invitations; use them. They help your guests return your response cards in a timely fashion. Neatly pre-address the envelope to the wedding host (no labels, please; and use the same format for these addresses that you use to address the outer invitation envelopes, which I explain in the "Addressing Invitations Properly" section later in this chapter). And don't neglect to put a first-class postage stamp on the envelope. Adding appropriate postage is not only a wedding courtesy, but it also helps your guests avoid having to locate a stamp, misplacing the response card, and never actually mailing the thing.

Omitting the stamps on the response envelope to cut costs may be tempting, but doing so is tacky and makes you look cheap — so don't do it.

The map and directions

After all your careful planning, you want to make sure people actually arrive on time to your event and are at the correct location. Unless you live in a small town and know for certain that everyone is familiar with the ceremony and reception sites, you need to include a map and written directions with your invitation. You need both because some people follow directions better with maps, while others follow directions better with words.

You can draw a map of your area by hand or print a copy off the Internet. Make sure the directions to the ceremony and reception are adequate for guests coming from different locations and that you include major highways, if necessary. Then have your printer print the map and directions on a smaller, heavier card than your invitation but in the same style so that all your insertions coordinate.

In addition to including directions from different locations to the ceremony site, include on the same map directions from the wedding site — point A — to the reception — point B — if the reception is at a different place. If doing so isn't possible, have printed maps and directions from the wedding site to the reception site ready for ushers to hand out after the ceremony.

Another option is to use an online service to create your maps. Several companies on the Internet provide specialized wedding maps to match your invitations. These maps can be as simple or as detailed as you want, from providing a basic map and directions to all your wedding events to giving your out-of-town guests a complete visitor's guide to your city. Type something like "wedding maps" into your favorite search engine to compare companies.

Hotel information for out-of-town guests

Thoughtful couples, such as you and your spouse-to-be, include hotel information with your invitations if some of your guests will require overnight accommodations. Don't worry; you don't actually have to pay for the rooms yourselves. What you do have to do is call around your area to find a selection of nice hotels of various price ranges at which you can reserve a block of rooms for your guests at a discount.

Ideally, you can include this information on your map/direction cards (see the preceding section). If you can't fit the hotel information with the map and directions, print another card (to match your invitations, of course) with the following information:

- ✓ Hotel names and locations
- ✓ Nightly rates
- ✓ The hotel reservation phone numbers
- ✓ Any information the guests need to have to reserve their rooms, such as "mention the Sun-Fischer wedding party" or any other reservation code the hotel may give you for your guests to use

If some guests need rental cars, the hotel information card is a good place for you to let them know what's available, or better yet, tell them where you've reserved a car in their name.

Pew cards

Typically used only in formal wedding ceremonies where many guests are expected, *pew cards,* which are also known as *within-the-ribbon cards,* are small, individually printed cards that you send along with the invitations to only those few special guests and family members for whom you've reserved special seating at the ceremony.

The guest is supposed to bring the card to the wedding ceremony, where he or she hands it to the usher. The usher then escorts the guest to the proper pew (or section, if you're not marrying in a church) that's reserved with a ribbon. The card may say, "Please present this card at Fourth Presbyterian Church on the eighteenth of September, two thousand ten." If you assign your guests a specific pew, you need to indicate that on the card; if you don't, simply write "within the ribbon," which means any seat in the reserved area (see Figure 11-14).

It's also appropriate to wait to send your pew cards until after you receive confirmation (via your response cards) that your special guests are coming to your ceremony. Doing so allows you to reserve an accurate number of pews.

Please present this card at Fourth Presbyterian Church
on the eighteenth of September, two thousand ten
John & Karen Colavitti
Bride's Section
Pew Number Four

Figure 11-14: An example of a pew card.

Tissue paper

No, including *tissue paper* doesn't mean you need to have plenty of tissues on hand for guests in case they shed happy tears at your beautiful wedding. The tissue paper I'm talking about here is the tiny piece of flimsy paper that flutters to the floor when you take the invitation out of the envelope.

Tissue paper (or *overlay,* as it's sometimes called) is available in several designs, but the most formal is sheer white. It's placed on top of the invitation itself. (See the next section for more on how to assemble your invitations.) You may omit the tissue paper to cut costs; however, its addition makes for a nice presentation.

Putting Everything Together in the Outer Envelope

Finally! You have your invitations and all the insertions that go with them in piles (seemingly endless piles, perhaps) on the table. But how in the world do you put all this stuff into the outer envelopes? Very carefully — and according to the proper assembly order, of course. Organization is key!

It's probably best to have only one or two helpers when you're assembling your invitations; too many people trying to keep all the insertion cards straight will only confuse you.

Before you start stuffing your envelopes, you need to properly fold your invitations (if they require folding) and stamp your response envelopes. Your response envelopes are usually preprinted, so you shouldn't have to address them by hand. After you finish those tasks, you're ready to start assembling. Follow these steps to do so:

1. **Lay out all your piles in the order you need to assemble your insertions and count each pile to make sure you have everything you need.**

   Find a work space where the dog or cat won't wander across them while you're working. I also recommend having no beverages or food in the area. Be sure to have your hands clean during the process to eliminate any smudges.

2. **Assemble one set of insertions in the following proper order (if you don't have every item shown, just skip it and continue to the next one):**

   - Invitation, face up

   - Tissue overlay on top of the invitation

   - Reception card, face up, on top of the tissue

   - Response card, face up in the fold of the response envelope flap, on top of the reception card

   - Map and directions card, face up, on top of the response card

   - Hotel information card, face up, on top of the map and directions card

   - Pew card, face up, on top of the hotel information card (included only in the invitations of the guests whom you want to have special seating)

3. **After you have one pile containing each element, hold the inner envelope with its back face up (the front faces the floor), and carefully slide your neatly stacked pile (which should be face up) into the envelope.**

   If you're using folded invitations, the fold should go into the envelope first. If you're using flat invitations, the left side of the invitation (as you read it) should go into the envelope first as you hold the envelope (back face up) in your left hand.

4. **Label each inner envelope with the names of the guests you're inviting — handwritten in black ink.**

   I explain how to address invitations properly in the next section.

5. **Have your guest list handy and check off your guests' names as you prepare their invitations so you can keep track of whose invitations you've completed, just in case you have a question later.**

6. **Repeat this process until you're done assembling all your invitations.**

After you've stuffed all your inner envelopes, you're ready to insert the stuffed inner envelopes into outer envelopes and address them. But don't just insert them any old way — you know etiquette calls for a proper way to slide the stuffed envelope into the next envelope. Hold the outer envelope with its front facing toward the floor, and slide the inner envelope into it with the guest's name face up and the top of the letters in the name toward the top of the outer envelope.

To keep your handwriting neat and to avoid frustration, you may want to address the outer envelope before you slide the (full) inner envelope into it.

Addressing Invitations Properly

After you stuff all your envelopes, you need to address them correctly. The following sections cover the most common scenarios you'll encounter when you address your outer and inner envelopes. But before you dive in, here are a few general guidelines for addressing invitations properly:

- Don't use the preprinted address labels you make on your computer. Wedding invitations are special pieces of correspondence that you should treat with special care, so you want your invitations to have a personal touch that only handwriting can convey. For very formal weddings, hiring a calligrapher to address your outer envelopes adds a nice, elegant touch. In fact, you can also have a calligrapher address the inner envelopes, if you choose. If you can't afford a calligrapher (and don't have neat handwriting yourself), ask a friend with lovely, legible handwriting to help. You can buy her lunch or give her a small gift as a thank-you.

- Handwrite the guest's home mailing address on the larger, outer envelope (with the glue for sealing it); write only the guests' individual names on the smaller envelope. Always use black ink.

- Follow the spelling and abbreviation rules used for the text of the invitation for the envelopes, as well. (I cover these rules in the "Spelling and abbreviation rules" section earlier in this chapter.) One minor note: The words junior and senior should appear only on the outer envelope, not the inner envelope. Also spell out names of states and the words *Rural Route* and *Post Office Box.*

- When you address the outer envelope with titles other than Mr., Mrs., Ms., and Miss, use full names. But for inner envelopes, use only the title and the last name.

- Include a return address (the last two lines only — no name) on the outer envelope's flap in case the invitation can't be delivered for some reason. This address is usually the host's unless you want the wedding presents to be sent directly to your address.

Although the guest's address should be handwritten, the return address is always preprinted on the envelope flap. No self-stick labels!

An entire family

For very formal invitations, when you're inviting an entire family, write only the parents' names on the outer envelope. For example:

Mr. and Mrs. Michael Edwards
200 Geneva Avenue
Chicago, Illinois 60164

Traditionally, you also have the option of writing "and Family" on the outer envelope, after the parents' names. However, some guests may think they can bring Grandma and Uncle along, too.

Whichever option you choose for the outer envelope, on the inner envelope, write everyone's individual names, using titles and last names only for the adults. Children's names go on the second line — from oldest to youngest. For example:

Mr. and Mrs. Edwards
Timothy and Tabitha

If you're planning an informal wedding, you may choose not to use the inner envelope, in which case you can use first names of close relatives or friends on the outer envelope. For example, you can write "Aunt Scarlett and Uncle Kevin."

If the children are younger than age 8, extremely formal invitations call for "Master Timothy and Miss Tabitha" on the inner envelope.

A married couple

When you're inviting a married couple with no kids, address the invitations like any other regular mailing, using Mr. and Mrs. followed by the husband's name. For instance:

Mr. and Mrs. Michael Edwards
200 Geneva Avenue
Chicago, Illinois 60164

On the inner envelope, write "Mr. and Mrs. Edwards." If you know them well, write only their first names ("Michael and Elizabeth").

A married couple using different last names

When you're inviting a married couple who don't use the same last name, write the woman's name first on the outer envelope. Use one line for the woman's name and one line for the man's name, and connect them with *and* to indicate the couple is married. For example:

> Mrs. Elizabeth Miller
> and Mr. Michael Edwards
> 200 Geneva Avenue
> Chicago, Illinois 60164

On the inner envelope, write "Mrs. Miller and Mr. Edwards" on one line if possible. If you know them well, you can write only their first names ("Elizabeth and Michael").

An unmarried couple

When you're inviting an unmarried couple, send them one invitation (usually to the person you know well). Write the names of the couple on two lines, but don't connect them with *and* (unless they live together). If you know both individuals equally well, list the woman's name first. If you know only one individual well, list that name first. For example, if you know Cathy well, and she and her boyfriend Stephen aren't living together, address their envelope in this way:

> Miss (or Ms.) Catherine Williams
> Mr. Stephen Brown
> 1124 East Fullerton Avenue
> Chicago, Illinois 60164

On the inner envelope, write "Miss (or Ms.) Williams; Mr. Brown" on two lines without the word *and* unless they're living together. If you know them well, regardless of whether they live together, use only their first names on one line ("Cathy and Stephen").

A same-sex couple

When you're inviting a same-sex couple, send one invitation, and write the names of the couple on two lines, with the name of the person you know well coming first. If you know both individuals equally well, write their names alphabetically by last name. Don't use *and* to connect the names unless they're legally married or have been together a long time.

> Mr. Walter Kramer
> Mr. Keith Rogers
> 1124 East Fullerton Avenue
> Chicago, Illinois 60164

On the inner envelope, write "Mr. Kramer; Mr. Rogers" (on two lines) or "Walter and Keith" on one line if you know them well.

A single guest

When you're inviting a single guest, write only the single guest's name on the outer envelope, followed by the mailing address. For example:

> Miss Stacey Carmichael
> 1124 East Fullerton Avenue
> Chicago, Illinois 60164

On the inner envelope, write "Miss (or Ms.) Carmichael and guest" or just "Stacey and guest" if you know her well. Of course, if you've decided that single guests can't bring dates, omit "and guest" entirely.

Indicating no children

When you want to indicate that you're not inviting children to your wedding, write the names of the adult(s) invited on the outer envelope, using the guidelines in the preceding sections. On the inner envelope, write only the names of the adult(s), such as "Mr. and Mrs. Edwards," and hope that the parents understand that kids aren't invited when they see that their children's names aren't written below theirs. Not writing the children's names on the inner envelope is the time-honored, subtle hint that only the parents are invited to the event.

Although it's perfectly acceptable to invite only the wedding attendant's children and immediate family members, if you extend the invitation to any other guests' children, you should invite everyone's children. Otherwise, someone's feelings will inevitably get hurt. Keep in mind that many of your guests who have children at home may be hiring babysitters at an additional cost so they can attend your wedding. If they arrive and see many other children at the reception, it may cause them frustration. (See Chapter 15 for details on how to deal with this and other tough reception-related situations.)

Knowing When to Mail Your Invitations

Mail your invitations six to eight weeks before the wedding day; doing so allows guests to set aside the date on their calendars and gives them ample time to plan their wardrobes and make travel plans for your big day. (If your wedding is scheduled on or close to a major holiday, such as Memorial Day, you may want to issue the invitations at least ten weeks prior to the actual date.) Also, be sure to mail them all at once. Doing so prevents possible hurt feelings that mailing invitations in batches may cause Aunt Edith if she doesn't get her invitation until several days (or weeks) after Aunt Martha receives hers.

Before you order your invitations, don't forget to calculate how long it'll take to address all the envelopes, especially if you have an unusually large guest list or are using a calligrapher. Ask your stationery provider how long it takes for the invitations to be proofed, printed, and shipped, and plan for additional time so you can hit the target of mailing finished invitations six to eight weeks before your wedding. Overestimating the time it takes to accomplish the whole invitation task is better than underestimating, which only adds to your stress.

Before you go out and buy a bunch of romantic heart stamps, take one completed invitation — you know, with all the inserts and both inner and outer envelopes — to the post office to be weighed. After you have the proper postage requirement, you can purchase your stamps accordingly.

Postponing or Canceling Your Wedding after Invitations Are Out

Wedding cancellations and postponements do happen, I'm sorry to say. Difficult times in life sometimes call for difficult decisions. What do you do at an unfortunate time like this, especially when the invitations have already gone out? Rest assured that you aren't obligated to tell everyone why you had to postpone or cancel the wedding. Simply word an announcement as follows, in the name of the wedding's hosts:

Mr. and Mrs. Peter Sun
regret to inform you that
the wedding of their daughter
Lily Yuh Sun
to
Mr. Terry Allen Fischer
on Saturday, the eighteenth of September
two thousand ten
has been postponed (canceled)

Be sure to send an announcement to everyone on your guest list.
If the wedding date is quickly approaching, you can make phone
calls to the guests to notify them. (See Chapter 2 for more information on gracefully canceling an engagement.)

Sending Wedding Announcements

Why send a wedding announcement instead of an invitation? The
two scenarios that call for wedding announcements are

- ✔ After an elopement (when you sneak away and secretly tie the
  knot to avoid all the hoopla)

- ✔ When you have family, friends, or acquaintances whom you're
  unable to invite to the wedding for any number of reasons (distance, budget constraints, limited number of guests, and so on)
  but you know they'd be interested in hearing that you got married

Traditionally, you send announcements either the day of the wedding or the day after, although it's considered appropriate to send
them anytime during the first year of marriage. Naturally, the
sooner you send them, the better. If possible, order them when
you order your invitations — they should be in a design similar to
that of your invitations. Don't send them to anyone who received
an invitation.

To save last-minute worries, have your announcements addressed
and ready to be mailed well before the day of your wedding. (But
don't mail them early!)

Either set of parents can announce the happy event, or you as the
bridal couple may announce your wedding. Follow a format similar
to the one you use for the invitation, with just a few changes: In an
announcement, you state only the person announcing the wedding,
the bride and groom's names, and where and when it took place.
You're not inviting people to anything. Figure 11-15 shows an
example of a properly worded wedding announcement.

> Mr. and Mrs. Peter Sun
> have the honour of announcing
> the marriage of their daughter
> Lily Yuh
> to
> Mr. Terry Allen Fischer
> Saturday, the eighteenth of September
> two thousand ten
> Fourth Presbyterian Church
> Chicago, Illinois

Figure 11-15: A sample wedding announcement.

Often, *at home* cards are included with the announcements. At home cards are smaller cards that give information, such as how the couple would like to be addressed (in other words, is the bride keeping her maiden name?), when the happy pair will return from the honeymoon, and the couple's address. Here's an example of an at home card:

> Mr. and Mrs. Terry Fischer
> will be at home (optional)
> after the fifteenth of October
> 1600 Geneva Avenue
> Chicago, Illinois 60164

Yes, you need two envelopes for the wedding announcements, too, and you should follow the same rules for addressing them that you do when you address the invitations. You can check out the rules earlier in this chapter.

Chapter 12

Registering for Gifts and Giving Your Own

In This Chapter
▶ Setting up a gift registry properly
▶ Knowing the etiquette of giving gifts to family and friends

*W*ho doesn't like presents? No one I know! When you get married, you receive — and give — a lot of them. In this chapter, I get you up to speed on the etiquette of gift registries and the protocol of selecting gifts for your family and friends before your wedding.

Behaving throughout the Gift Registry Process

A gift registry helps you and your spouse-to-be get started in your new home together, but it also helps the gift-givers by telling them what you want. Although many couples getting married today have already lived together for several years before tying the knot, a gift registry gives them a chance to create a wish list of items that complement what they already own. In the following sections, I explain various parts of the gift registry process.

Even if you aren't a shopper or aren't really interested in a gift registry, registering is still a good idea. Wedding guests expect to give gifts, and wouldn't you rather receive gifts you'll use rather than gifts that will just sit on your shelves?

Figuring out when to register

I recommend that you register soon after your engagement takes place — well before any shower invitations are mailed. However, if you're having a long engagement period before the actual wedding, wait until about three months before your shower invitations are sent.

 If you register too early, some of the items included on your list may not be available in the retail stores by the time guests go to make their purchases (which will likely frustrate them — and you definitely don't want unhappy gift-givers!). Check with specific stores for their recommended time frames for registering to help avoid any confusion.

Even if you're planning your wedding on a short schedule of only a few months, it's still appropriate for you to register. Just do so as soon as possible after your engagement to give guests plenty of time to shop.

Accommodating your guests with a range of stores and prices

The norm these days is to have a gift registry at two to three national chain stores. Doing so makes shopping easy for guests, no matter where they live, because they likely have at least one of these stores in their area. Even if they don't, they can always order gifts online.

 Some guests who live out of town or who can't make it to your wedding will want to send you wedding gifts by mail, so make sure you provide an address with each of your registries. You can use your own home address, your spouse-to-be's address, or one of your parents' addresses. Just make sure you use the same address for all your registries to make the process of keeping track of your gifts easier. (Check out the "Tracking gifts you receive before the big day and sending prompt thanks" section for more about this process.)

You aren't required to register for a plethora of items at every single store that has a wedding registry service. Although doing so may be convenient for your guests, managing so many registries would be overwhelming for you and your spouse-to-be. So choose stores that suit you as a couple, not just your guests.

 Need some ideas on where to register? For casual items, such as small kitchen gadgets, appliances, and bath accessories, register at places like Target or Wal-Mart. Well-known national stores, such as Macy's, Crate & Barrel, Bed Bath & Beyond, and Williams & Sonoma, carry fine dinnerware, as well as everyday dining pieces and much more. You may even choose to register at a one-of-a-kind shop in your hometown to support your community, but don't neglect to register at one national store (or more) for guests who live farther away.

It's always best to make an appointment with a registry consultant at each store you want to register at to find out about the specific registry process and to get helpful guidelines and tips. Always be patient with and kind to consultants because they're often being pulled in different directions by the many brides and grooms they're trying to help. After all, if you ever have a problem with your registry, you'll want a friendly consultant on your side!

Each of your registries should list items in different price ranges. Many of the national stores have lots of fun and useful, less expensive gadgets that make great gifts. Of course, it's okay to register for some pricier items, as well; often friends and family go together to purchase one larger, more expensive item, such as a new grill. Don't be concerned with having too many items on each list; your guests will appreciate having options to fit any budget.

Be considerate not to have only expensive items on your registry. Guests have varying budgets, and you should never assume they can splurge for wedding gifts.

In addition, if someone asks you directly what you want for a gift, answering truthfully and offering some suggestions is acceptable, but be mindful of the cost of the items you suggest. Although such a direct question may make you uncomfortable, try to answer gracefully, saying something like: "We appreciate your thoughtfulness about what to give us for a gift. Our gift registry includes many of our favorite choices, including a new toaster and can opener that will be great to have. Thanks so much for asking."

Avoid asking or registering for cash, honeymoon expenses, and so on because doing so may put off some of your guests. Some guests may want to select a personal gift they feel you may enjoy instead of using your registry, and if you request cash or honeymoon expenses, they may not feel free to do so.

Always be gracious and thankful of every gift you receive, no matter how much a guest has spent. I provide pointers on sending thank-you notes for gifts in Chapter 16.

Making selections together — and keeping the peace

Your gift registry should reflect your tastes and needs as a couple. Traditionally, couples register for china, crystal, dinnerware, utensils, glassware, and housewares, as well as bedding and bathroom items, but it's perfectly acceptable to register for more unconventional items, such as camping equipment, sporting gear, automotive equipment, or patio furniture. For example, my niece, Kelly, and her husband, Steve, who both love the outdoors, registered for and received a beautiful canoe as a wedding gift, and they were absolutely thrilled!

Search the stores' Web sites together for ideas for your registry before you go out to your local branch and start scanning items. Discuss your likes, dislikes, and must-haves with each other, and be kind and respectful each other as you uncover your different styles. Listen well, and have an open mind. Most importantly, be ready to compromise. For instance: If your heart's set on a particular china pattern, ask your spouse-to-be whether he likes it. If he's absolutely opposed because it reminds him of Grandma's dishes 30 years ago, be open to looking at another pattern — you have so many to choose from!

Even when your tastes are similar, your spouse-to-be may not be interested in shopping with you to establish a registry. As you may imagine, it's no fun dragging along someone who'll be bored; it can ruin the experience. So what should you do? Ask your mother, an aunt, a member of the bridal party, or a close friend who has been through the process of registering for a wedding to tag along instead. Even though Mom may not have registered before, she knows how to organize a kitchen and home. You can share the choices you made with your spouse-to-be by checking out the registry online later. If he or she truly doesn't like some of the things you've selected, you can delete them at any time.

Spreading the word about your registry appropriately

Getting the word out about your gift registries can be tricky, but don't worry! A few etiquette guidelines are in place to help you:

- First, it's *always* inappropriate to include any wording about your registry in your wedding invitation.

- Today it's acceptable to note where you're registered on a bridal shower invitation. Usually, where you're registered appears on an enclosure card with the shower invite or is noted at the bottom of the invitation in smaller type. Just remember to keep it discreet. (Flip to Chapter 13 for more on shower invitation protocol.)

- Listing stores where you're registered on your wedding Web sites is completely acceptable (see Chapter 3 for information on wedding Web sites).

 ✔ Telling guests where you're registered when they ask is fine.
 It's also appropriate to tell your close friends and family
 where you're registered so they can tell guests who ask them.

 ✔ Sending a mass e-mail announcing, "Shop now and avoid the
 rush at Macy's!" is definitely a no-no.

Monitoring your registry and knowing when to add items

It's a good idea to peek at your registry every so often to make
sure the correct items are listed and that there aren't any errors.
But if you want to be completely surprised when you open gifts at
showers and after the wedding, you can set up your registry and
then give the monitoring job to your mom, a family member, or a
close friend (asking politely, of course!). Your monitor can keep
you informed about any errors.

You (or your assigned monitor) should also check your registry
to make sure there are always plenty of affordable items left for
guests to purchase. If only expensive items are left on your registry
several months before your big day, you may hear about frustrated
guests — or worse, you may receive a third cutting board from a
little cooking shop in Wyoming where you didn't register.

Tracking gifts you receive before the big day and sending prompt thanks

Having a plan for how you're going to keep track of the gifts you
receive as they arrive is helpful. If thinking about this process is
overwhelming, ask your family or friends to help you keep track.
You can also find software that can make the job easier. If possible,
send your thank-you note the day the gift arrives. Doing so keeps
you from getting slammed with too many gifts (and thank-you
notes) at one time (until the wedding day, of course). See Chapter
16 for more information on how to organize this task.

Understanding when a gift registry may not be appropriate

For most weddings, a gift registry is always appropriate and even
expected. However, couples who are marrying for the second or
even third time may be very established in their homes and in
their finances. In this case, having a wedding registry may not be

appropriate. If you're in this situation, instead of creating a registry, you can choose a charity and give your guests the option to donate in your name by providing appropriate contact information. Simply spread the word about your favorite charity through family and friends.

Of course, some guests will still want to give traditional wedding gifts to couples who are marrying for the second or third time. So make sure you accept unexpected traditional gifts graciously, too.

What if it's the groom's second or third marriage but the bride's first? In this case, it's appropriate to have a wedding registry. Every first-time bride-to-be should have the experience of setting up a gift registry. But be sensitive to your spouse-to-be's feelings, discuss the issue, and compromise. If your spouse-to-be is a little uncomfortable with having another wedding registry, agree to have one, but keep it traditional and not so elaborate. Register only for items you need.

Picking Proper Gifts for Your Loved Ones before the Wedding

Giving gifts to your loved ones shows your appreciation and gratitude for everything they've done to help you and your spouse-to-be with your wedding. In the following sections, I provide some etiquette pointers on selecting appropriate gifts for your parents, your wedding party, your special helpers, and each other.

Your rehearsal dinner is the appropriate time to present gifts to your parents and wedding party members; see Chapter 13 for details. If your special helpers attend the rehearsal dinner, present their gifts to them at that time, too. If they won't be there, try to make arrangements to get together with them before the wedding.

Gifts to your parents

You wouldn't be getting ready to marry the love of your life without at least some help from your parents, so you and your spouse-to-be should try to find a special way to show them how much you appreciate them. Presenting your parents (and stepparents) with thank-you gifts is a nice gesture to thank them for all the help they've given you with your wedding.

Just make sure you don't show extreme preferences in either direction (toward one set of parents or stepparents) if you decide to give your parents their gifts during a group presentation at the rehearsal dinner. You can always choose to express your additional thanks after the wedding if doing so is more comfortable.

Sometimes the simplest gift is the best one. A pretty piece of jewelry for your mother to wear on your wedding day and a nice pair of cuff links for your father make for memorable gifts. If your budget allows, your gift can be more elaborate, like a weekend trip.

Whatever you decide to give your parents, be sure to express your sincere gratitude to all your parents. What does the trick? Give them a heartfelt thank-you card telling them that without their help and support, you wouldn't have reached this point in life.

Gifts to the wedding party

The bride should give a gift to her maid or matron of honor, to each bridesmaid, and to her flower girl. There are no rules about what the gifts should be, but you want to give them something thoughtful and meaningful, something that reflects your personality and that they can treasure forever. Jewelry the girls can wear on your wedding day or engraved picture frames make nice gifts, but so do framed poems about your friendships. Your gift can also be an item of your attendants' wedding attire or the salon services on the day of the wedding. A small, delicate necklace is perfect for your flower girl — she'll feel so special!

Whatever you decide, be sure to keep your gifts consistent for all your bridesmaids. If you want to, you can add a special touch to your maid or matron of honor's gift because she's closest to you. For instance, you can treat her to a special lunch and movie or visit to a hair and nail salon after the wedding.

One of the few jobs the groom has in all this gift giving is to purchase gifts for his groomsmen and ring bearer. Make sure you do this task at least one to two months before your wedding, especially if you're having the gifts engraved. The most popular groomsman gift is an engraved flask, but it's best not to give this gift full of alcohol. Include a light-hearted note with the gift asking your groomsmen to leave their flasks safely behind to enjoy after the reception is over. Pocket watches, cuff links, or any golf-related items can be engraved and make nice gifts, too. As with other gift buying and presenting, remember to keep the value of gifts the same. And for your ring bearer, a personalized tractor or train bank with a dollar bill inside is sure to be a winner!

If you and your spouse-to-be are working within a tight budget, you don't need to go overboard on gifts. A beautifully written card expressing your appreciation for their support is a very meaningful way to say thank you and makes for a nice touch when included with a small gift. Keep in mind that all gifts for your wedding party should be elegant and meaningful — the best time for joke gifts is at the bachelor or bachelorette parties.

Countless Web sites carry all sorts of traditional, unique, and memorable gifts for your wedding party. Just type *wedding gifts and accessories* into your browser, and you'll be sure to find the perfect gift in your price range in one of the results. Many shopping malls and jewelry stores also offer a wide variety of gift choices.

Gifts to special helpers

Special helpers deserve a thank-you, too! Your special helpers may do a reading during your ceremony, pass out programs before your wedding starts, seat guests, or attend to your guest book. Who your special helpers are and how old they are determine what types of gifts you should give them. Something thoughtful but not over the top says a heartfelt thank-you for their help.

Gifts that are appropriate include a pretty handkerchief for your aunt who does a reading, a unique silver key chain for your uncle who plays the role of greeter, and a pretty bracelet for your cousin who attends to your guest book. Remember that these gifts don't have to be expensive to be special and unique — a gracious note to say thank you goes a long way.

Recognizing your helpers' names in your program is a nice touch, too; see Chapter 6 for program pointers.

Gifts to each other

Is giving a gift to each other a must? Not at all. This is an optional tradition. Marrying each other is gift enough, right? If you and your spouse-to-be have decided to exchange gifts, you may opt for traditional items like jewelry, but most couples today are getting more creative. For example, you may decide to buy something together on your honeymoon, such as a private sunset cruise, a snorkeling trip, or maybe even matching outfits for the luau (okay, maybe not). Or you may decide to buy fun items that you'll definitely appreciate down the road, like a new rod for a husband's annual fishing trip or a day at the spa for a wife and her sister. The sky's the limit!

Chapter 13

Observing Etiquette Rules at Festivities before the Wedding

In This Chapter

▶ Surveying the protocol of bridal showers

▶ Delving in to rehearsal dinner etiquette

*P*lanning your wedding can get quite complicated and emotional, and your wedding day itself is a whirlwind, so you should try to make prewedding events, such as bridal showers and the rehearsal dinner, relaxing and fun! They provide a great opportunity for you to spend time with the people you care most about on a more intimate level than you'll be able to experience at the wedding itself. To make the most of these events, you need to know the rules of etiquette behind them, which I describe in this chapter.

Considering Bridal Shower Etiquette

The purpose of a bridal shower is to pamper the bride with a celebration of friendship and love. In this section, I discuss the basics of bridal shower etiquette.

Deciding when to hold a shower

Bridal showers may take place at any time during the engagement period, but they usually occur about two to three months before the ceremony (right about the time the wedding invitations are mailed; see Chapter 11 for more on invitations). Because the happy couple is busy with the details of wedding planning, scheduling a shower around this time, rather than at the last minute, is recommended.

If many shower invitees will have to travel a great distance for the ceremony (especially if you're having a destination wedding), having the shower a few days before the wedding is perfectly acceptable. Just be sure to notify guests well in advance so they can make the proper travel arrangements and make sure they arrive in time for the shower as well as the wedding itself.

Figuring out who hosts your shower

The maid or matron of honor and bridesmaids typically host the bridal shower, but it isn't uncommon for other friends to host it instead, especially when the maid or matron of honor doesn't live near the bride.

In most cases, it isn't appropriate for anyone in the bride's and groom's families to host a shower because it shouldn't look as if they're asking for gifts on the couple's behalf. However, this rule is much more relaxed today. For example, the bride's sister, if she's the maid of honor, may want to host a shower, or the groom's family, if they live far from the couple, may want to host a shower if the couple is visiting from out of town.

As a courtesy to the hostesses, make sure you provide assistance with setting a convenient date and theme and drawing up the guest list. Your only other shower responsibility is to tell the hostesses where you're registered for gifts so they can spread the word properly (see Chapter 12 for more on gift registering).

Understanding how formal a shower should be

The bridal shower's theme, location, and budget determine the shower's level of formality. Unless the shower is going to be a surprise, the hostess should discuss the details with the bride; if the shower is a surprise, the hostess needs to seek input from the bride's mother, sister, or other close family member.

Determining who's invited and whether you can have more than one shower

It's customary to invite the bride's and the groom's immediate female family members, including mothers, grandmothers, sisters, aunts, and cousins, to a bridal shower. The bridesmaids as well as any close female friends of the bride should also be invited. Having more than one shower is perfectly acceptable nowadays (particularly when family and friends live in several different faraway cities), but anyone who's invited to a shower also *must* be invited to the wedding — no exceptions!

If you or your spouse-to-be has a young daughter, it's completely up to you whether she's invited to the shower. You have to consider her age and where the shower is taking place. The shower is for and about you, so it's acceptable to want to enjoy it without having to cater to the needs and attention of a young child. On the other hand, in the case of a young stepdaughter-to-be, you may feel that it's important to share such an important event.

Of course, you hope that all members of a blended family can attend the shower and behave cordially. However, this cordiality simply isn't realistic in all families. If people who may have a conflict (for example, the groom's mother and the groom's stepmother) are invited to the same shower, be sure they both know the other person has been invited. One person may choose to graciously bow out or decide to host a shower of her own; don't discourage either of these offers. Or both people may choose to come to the same shower, but knowing who will be there ensures you won't have any tense surprises in the middle of the shower.

If you're having an additional shower, only the bridesmaids should be invited to both (they have to buy only one gift, though!).

Speaking of multiple showers: In addition to having a shower attended by family and friends, you may also have a shower thrown by your co-workers. In this case, you're not obligated or expected to invite people who come to the work shower to the wedding. Showers at work tend to be much more casual and shorter in length than traditional bridal showers. For example, I've seen work showers where few gifts are given and the focus is mostly on sharing good wishes and advice with the bride. Sometimes everyone goes together to give a group gift. If members of the bridal party don't work with you, they're not expected to attend your work shower.

What about the groom? Should he attend any of the bridal shower festivities? In a nutshell, the groom isn't expected to attend the bridal shower(s). He may make an appearance, particularly if he has family attending whom he hasn't seen in a long time, but this festivity really is for the bride and the women in her life.

Some people nowadays are opting for co-ed or couples showers, which are appropriate and becoming more popular; in such cases, the groom, of course, does attend. A co-ed shower may work best for you if this isn't your or your spouse-to-be's first wedding, you have children you want to include, a co-worker at either of your jobs is hosting it, or the shower is part of a destination wedding.

A shower for a same-sex couple may honor both members of the couple, or each person can have his or her own shower. If friends attend both showers, they aren't expected to bring gifts to both.

Sending invitations

The shower's hostess should mail (not e-mail) invitations at least four weeks before the event. If you have friends or relatives who'll be traveling far, let them know about the details even farther in advance — just don't forget to send them a formal printed invitation, too. (In the case of showers at work, e-mail invitations are acceptable, but written invitations are never inappropriate.)

The following basics should appear on a shower invitation (see Figure 13-1 for a sample):

- ✔ The bride's full name (and the groom's if it's a co-ed shower)
- ✔ The date
- ✔ The time
- ✔ The location
- ✔ The name(s) of the hostess(es)
- ✔ RSVP information (the name, contact information, and date to respond by)

It's also important to mention whether the shower is a surprise so guests will know to be there on time. If the location doesn't clearly determine the dress code, include a note on appropriate attire. Finally, you can list where the couple is registered.

If the shower has a theme (cooking, linens, or honeymoon, for example), the hostess clearly states it on the invitation. The guests don't have to buy a gift from that particular category, but most of them appreciate the guidance. For example, my niece and her fiancé planned a destination wedding in Costa Rica, so their friends hosted a couple's shower with a Costa Rican theme; gifts included everything from a beautiful tropical oil painting to a canoe!

> *Constance Natarelli and Maryanne Fleming*
> *cordially invite you to*
> *a bridal luncheon*
> *in honor of*
> *Michele Avecilla*
> *Sunday, May 23, 2010*
> *12 to 2 p.m.*
>
> *Smith's Restaurant*
> *123 Main Street*
> *Seattle, Washington*
>
> *RSVP by May 17: 555-978-1245 (Constance)*
>
> *Michele is registered at Target, Macy's, and*
> *Crate & Barrel.*

Figure 13-1: A bridal shower invitation.

Giving thanks after all your showers

At one time, sending thank-you notes wasn't considered necessary if you thanked someone in person. Today, however, because bridal showers are becoming larger and everyone has such busy schedules, writing a personal note is the only way to be certain that sincere appreciation is expressed, so you need to send a thank-you note for every gift you receive at your shower(s). Even if a person comes and gives you only a card, you still need to convey your appreciation for her effort and presence in a note. Your stationery and signature should reflect your maiden name, and the groom is expected to sign the note only if the shower was co-ed.

Be specific when writing a thank-you note for a shower gift (or for any gift.) Mention the item received, say something kind about it, and thank the giver for attending the shower. See Figure 13-2 for a sample thank-you note.

Dear Karen,

Thank you for attending my bridal shower and also
for the lovely serving dish! You're such a dear friend
and so thoughtful. Jim and I will think of you
whenever we set our dinner table!

See you at the wedding!

Love, Michele

Figure 13-2: A thank-you note for a shower gift.

Don't forget to send a thank-you note for a shower gift sent from
someone who couldn't attend the shower. You can say something
such as the following: "I missed seeing you at the shower, but your
well wishes were certainly felt. Thank you for thinking of us and for
the beautiful silver platter."

Don't use preprinted thank-you cards that allow you to fill in a
blank and sign your name!

Mail your thank-you notes as soon as possible after the shower.
Even if you don't get them out right away, definitely send the notes
before the wedding. I like to send notes immediately after receiving gifts because I find that the longer I wait, the less likely I am to
write a sincere note. Also, you'll be writing so many thank-yous
that the task will be much less daunting if you spread it out.

Making the Most of the Rehearsal Dinner

The wedding rehearsal and the dinner immediately following it are
opportunities for the happy couple, their immediate families, and
the bridal party to ensure that everyone is comfortable with the
final plans for the big day — and then to celebrate! In this section,
I describe the basic etiquette of the rehearsal itself as well as the
dinner immediately following.

The rehearsal dinner is the perfect time for the couple to
acknowledge their attendants and present them with their gifts.
Traditionally, you present gifts before dessert is served. If you
have gifts for your parents, give them out at this time, too. See
Chapter 12 for more about gifts for your wedding party and other
loved ones.

Easy rehearsal etiquette

You definitely need to rehearse your wedding ceremony so that you and everyone else involved can figure out the logistics before the actual event. The rehearsal is typically held the afternoon or night before the event, although some couples choose to have it two nights before if the venue is being used for another wedding when you'd normally hold your rehearsal. Keep it as close to the wedding as possible, so the details stay fresh in everyone's mind.

The following people are typically present at the rehearsal: the bride's parents, the groom's parents, all wedding attendants, including the maid or matron of honor, the best man, bridesmaids, groomsmen, flower girls, ring bearer, and ushers, your wedding planner (if you have one), your musician(s), and your officiant.

The officiant leads the rehearsal, guiding the wedding party through all the elements and protocol of the ceremony, including each person's role. Your venue's wedding coordinator (if your venue has one) can also offer direction on the following:

- ✔ The correct way for ushers to escort guests to their seats

- ✔ The appropriate time to turn back the veil if the bride wears one over her face

- ✔ The correct time for the maid or matron of honor to take the bridal bouquet from the bride and help with the bride's train

- ✔ The proper time for the best man and maid or matron of honor to give the rings to the bride and groom

- ✔ The correct order of the processional and recessional, as well as the proper pace to walk down the aisle

Being prompt to the rehearsal is the most important responsibility for all the attendees, including you and your spouse-to-be. But listening carefully to the person providing the ceremony instructions — typically the officiant or the wedding coordinator — is also critical. Questions are always encouraged, but try not to interrupt the speaker. You should have an opportunity at the end of the rehearsal to ask questions.

At the end of the rehearsal, remember to thank everyone who attended and took part.

Deciding who should host the dinner

Although the groom's parents traditionally host the rehearsal dinner, the expenses can be shared by both families if for some reason the groom's family isn't in a financial position to host the dinner. Another family member or the bride and groom can host the dinner and share the costs in certain circumstances, such as when the groom's parents are estranged or deceased. But it's never acceptable to expect a family member to pay for something that will create a financial hardship. (See Chapter 4 for more on the traditional division of expenses for all the parts of a wedding.)

When the rehearsal dinner is being held in honor of a same-sex couple, the couple needs to decide early on whose parents will be responsible for which events. If one person's family is paying for the bulk of the wedding expenses, the other person's family should host the rehearsal dinner.

Choosing the formality of the dinner

There are different schools of thought on how formal the rehearsal dinner should be; many people think it should mirror that of the wedding itself. Others don't think the rehearsal dinner should be more formal than the wedding. I happen to think the formality of the dinner is completely up to the couple and the host family. For instance, even if you're having a black-tie ceremony, you may want to enjoy a backyard barbecue after the rehearsal. On the flip side, if you're having a barefoot-on-the-beach wedding, you may want to serve a sit-down dinner for your wedding party.

If the rehearsal is taking place the afternoon or evening before the wedding, don't make too much work or fuss for the people hosting the event — they have enough to worry about with the wedding the next day. For instance, if you decide to have a casual backyard picnic or dinner at one of your parents' homes, consider hiring a caterer or bringing food from a take-out restaurant.

The most important things to consider when you're planning your rehearsal dinner are

- ✓ **Budget:** If your budget is tight, the rehearsal dinner can be as casual and informal as you want it to be. There's no need to break the bank.

- ✓ **Location:** Whether you choose to dine out or have the dinner in someone's home (both options are equally acceptable), make sure the location is close to the ceremony venue so the guests don't have to drive too far.

- ✓ **Time:** Be considerate of out-of-town guests who may have come a long distance. You don't want the dinner to run too late.

Knowing whom to invite and whether to send invitations

The bride needs to give the rehearsal dinner's hosts a list of names and addresses of the people to invite. You're expected to invite the following people to your rehearsal dinner: the bride's parents and grandparents, the groom's parents and grandparents, all siblings and their significant others, the wedding party (and their dates), all child attendants and their parents, any other wedding participants you have, the wedding planner (if you have one), and the officiant and his or her spouse. If you or your intended have children, they should also attend. Beyond that, the guest list truly depends on your budget, the location, and the type of event you envision.

If you can't include anyone outside of the expected list, you may want to either coordinate a separate dinner for your out-of-town guests or at least recommend some places where they can go for a nice meal. They'll appreciate your thoughtfulness.

As far as invitations go, if only the people participating in the rehearsal are invited to the dinner, you don't need to send formal invitations. A phone call with the details or an e-mail invitation is perfectly acceptable. If you plan to invite extended family and guests from out-of-town, however, the hosts should send some kind of written invitation — and they should do so anywhere from three to six weeks in advance so they can get a handle on the numbers and plan accordingly.

Your invitation should always match the formality of the event. If you go the backyard barbecue route, sending an e-mail invitation is fine, but keep in mind that not all guest have e-mail. If you're planning a more formal rehearsal dinner, you should send a separate printed invitation that specifies the formality of the dinner, along with other important details, such as time, location, and appropriate attire. Figure 13-3 has a sample rehearsal dinner invitation.

Making speeches and toasts

Anyone who wants to give a toast may do so throughout the dinner (not after), but because the dinner is typically hosted by the groom's parents, they're expected to give a speech and offer the first toast to the couple. The groom should follow, saying a few words of thanks to his parents and the bride's parents.

> The pleasure of your company
> is requested at the wedding rehearsal dinner for
> Michele Avecilla
> and
> James Edwin
>
> Friday, July 9, 2010
> 5:30 rehearsal
> St. George Church
> 456 Main Street
> Seattle, Washington
>
> 7 p.m. dinner
> Smith's Restaurant
> 123 Main Street
> Seattle, Washington
>
> Given by Christina and Jason Edwin
> RSVP by July 1: 555-978-9696

Figure 13-3: A sample rehearsal dinner invitation.

When someone offers a toast directly to the bride and groom, they do *not* participate in the toast. They may have glasses in their hands, but they don't raise their glasses, clink them with others' glasses, or sip their beverages. Instead, they bask in the glow of the tribute, smile, and thank the person toasting them.

In terms of toasts, the rehearsal dinner is absolutely one of those occasions where less is more; all you and your parents need to say is a brief thank-you and acknowledgement to the people who have helped the wedding come together: "We want to express our gratitude for all your support and everything you've done to help us get to our special day."

If you know there's a chance a guest may say something embarrassing or inappropriate, be prepared to have a family member or friend jump in or to find a humorous way to end the toast. This is no time to tell stories of your college shenanigans!

Part IV

Behaving on the Big Day and Beyond

The 5th Wave   By Rich Tennant

"Morris! You christen a ship, not a marriage!"

In this part...

Your time has arrived! In this part, I cover everything that actually occurs on your wedding day: from properly greeting and seating guests to correctly practicing the processional, recessional, and other ceremony rituals. I also lead you through the etiquette of receiving lines.

There's no question that the rules regarding wedding etiquette are ever changing, but one area that doesn't change is behaving appropriately at wedding receptions! Therefore, I include advice on giving a proper toast, cutting the cake, and being prepared for the unexpected, among other topics. Finally, I end with suggestions on celebrating after the celebration, including the etiquette involved in sending thank-you notes.

Chapter 14

Minding Your Manners at the Ceremony

In This Chapter

▶ Greeting and seating your guests

▶ Moving through the processional and the recessional gracefully

▶ Handling the receiving line with skill and ease

Whether you're having a small, informal wedding ceremony or a large production worthy of Hollywood awards, you need to follow a few time-honored customs as you plan this blessed occasion if you want to do it right. Having a dignified ceremony seems easy enough when you go to other people's weddings; but do you know who gets to sit in the aisle seats and who walks in first during the processional? No looking ahead for the answers!

Beginning with the arrival of the first guest and moving on from the processional to the recessional, this chapter gives you tips for gracefully handling etiquette related exclusively to your wedding ceremony. Here, you also find out everything you need to know about a receiving line: Why have one? Who's in it and where do they stand? What do you say to guests when they come through it?

Naturally, you practice all the etiquette in this chapter at the rehearsal. But informing the wedding party and family members ahead of time about what's expected of them at your ceremony will make your wedding day go much more smoothly. See Chapter 13 for more about the rehearsal and the dinner immediately following.

Greeting and Seating Appropriately

You want your guests to feel welcomed and appreciated for being a part of your big day, so making sure they're greeted warmly (but appropriately) when they arrive at your ceremony is very important. Then, of course, they have to be escorted to their seats. And like everything else having to do with weddings, there's a protocol for both of these customs. This section explains everything you need to know about appropriately greeting and seating your wedding guests.

Greeting guests the right way

Your guest book attendant is one of the first people your guests meet before they're taken to their seats, so make sure the guest book attendant is friendly and outgoing enough to get all the guests — including wedding attendants and parents — to sign this important keepsake. Advise the guest book attendant to greet people politely with "Good morning" or "Good afternoon" — this is no time for "Hey, what's happening?" If the guests aren't able to sign the book before the ceremony (because too many people show up at once, or because it's getting close to the ceremony time), your friendly attendant can happily gather missing signatures as guests leave the ceremony or at the reception. (Sometimes the guest book isn't taken to the ceremony site but is available for signing at the reception and has a designated attendant.)

After your guests sign the guest book (or perhaps before, if there's a long line), your ushers have the important responsibility of cordially greeting your guests and escorting them down the aisle to their seats. (So choose your ushers wisely! See Chapter 8 for details.) If you don't plan to have ushers, you can have the groomsmen seat the guests. Whoever does the ushering, make sure you advise them that the ceremony isn't the time for the "good ol' boy" slap-on-the-back type of greeting. "Good morning" and "Good afternoon" are suitable greetings; "Hey" and "What's up?" aren't.

Because the ushers are your welcoming committee, they need to be in place at least 45 to 60 minutes before the ceremony's start time. Tell them to arrive 15 minutes before the actual time you want them at their posts so they have enough time to pin on their boutonnieres and receive last-minute instructions before getting into position.

In some areas of the country, it's customary for the groom's parents to be the first to greet guests in front of the ceremony site, particularly if it's a small or informal wedding. At very informal occasions (usually not at a place of worship), the bride and groom may socialize with their guests before the ceremony — unless the bride doesn't want her groom to see her before the ceremony.

Make sure you tell all the people who are greeting and seating your guests to smile; after all, your wedding is a happy occasion. Your rehearsal is a great time to remind them to do so because they may be nervous and so focused on where to stand and what to do that they forget to smile.

Escorting guests to the correct seats

After your guests have been greeted and have signed the guest book, it's time to escort them down the aisle to their seats. This section explains the necessary protocol.

Knowing who sits where

If your wedding is large, you've probably designated certain guests to receive within-the-ribbon or pew cards (see Chapter 11 for more about these cards). These special guests present their coveted cards to the usher when they're ready to be seated; the ushers then lead them to their designated rows. (Immediate family members are usually seated about ten minutes before the ceremony.)

For guests who don't have pew cards (or for all your guests if you're not using pew cards), the usher may ask the guests the traditional question, "Bride or groom's side?" so that he knows on which side of the ceremony site to seat them. The bride's friends and family traditionally sit on her side of the ceremony site; the groom's friends and family sit on his side.

In a Christian wedding, the bride's side is on the left side of the aisle and the groom's side is on the right side of the aisle, facing forward toward the altar. A Jewish wedding is reversed. If you're conducting a wedding from other cultures or faiths, or a blended service, consult someone knowledgeable in the finer points of your desired ceremony — typically your officiant or wedding planner. Note that more and more couples today choose to mix their guests and eliminate the bride and groom's sides altogether, which is also an appropriate option.

What if your ceremony site has two main aisles? Seat the bride's friends and family on both sides of the left aisle, facing toward the front of the site, and seat the groom's friends and family on both sides of the right aisle (which makes the center section a mix of both groups of guests).

Seating the guests smoothly

After the usher has determined where the guest(s) wants to be seated, he proceeds as follows:

  ✔ When he's escorting a woman, he offers his inside arm to her. The inside arm is the arm on the side of the ceremony site that she requests. At a Christian wedding, for example, if she says bride's side, the usher offers her his left arm; if she says groom's side, he offers her his right arm. If the woman's husband or date accompanies her, he follows behind the usher and the woman.

When the woman and the usher arrive at their destination, they step aside to permit anyone accompanying her to enter the row first so that no other guests have to climb over her to get to their seats. Courtesy dictates that women get the aisle seats — they do offer the best views, after all. As the guests enter their row, the usher faces the back of the ceremony site. Then he walks back up the aisle to seat the next person in line.

If possible, the usher should try to seat families with small children and elderly guests on or near the aisles, too.

✔ When a man arrives alone, the usher directs him by saying something like, "This way, please," or, "Please follow me." The man either follows him down the aisle or walks with him side-by-side (the usher walks to the left of the guest), which appears less awkward than trailing behind the usher.

✔ When a group arrives together and wants to be seated together, the usher offers his arm to the oldest woman, and the rest of the guests follow them to their seats. If you have additional ushers, they can escort the other women in the group. As the guests enter the pew, the usher faces the back of the location.

Ushers should behave themselves with decorum and dignity; rushing down the aisle isn't allowed nor is horsing around with guests they know well. However, quiet small-talk during the trip down the aisle is permissible ("My, the church is beautiful." "The flowers are lovely." "Isn't it a perfect day for a wedding?"). To help keep all the ushers on task, the bride and groom may want to select a "head" usher to direct and give directions to the others.

When the ceremony site becomes full, the ushers can discreetly ask guests to move toward the center of the pews or seats so they can seat additional guests.

It's perfectly acceptable for guests to courteously seat themselves if your wedding is large and the number of guests waiting to be escorted down the aisle is multiplying like bunnies or if it's almost time for your ceremony to start. Simply ask your guest book attendant or another helper to let your guests know what to do.

Filling the seats in the right order

Ushers should fill seats or pews from the front to the back of the ceremony site, reserving the first few rows (within-the-ribbon rows) for close family members and special guests. If one side of the site fills up more than the other, ushers should seat new guests on the less filled side to make the rows look even — after politely asking guests if they mind, of course. The response cards your guests send back to you give you a clue about the possibility of having uneven sides ahead of time, and you should alert your ushers accordingly (see Chapter 11 for more on response cards).

Another alternative is to have the ushers seat everyone evenly from the front of the site to the back — disregarding the bride-or-groom preference. Well-mannered guests will comply with the bride's wishes; however, some clueless guest may insist on a seating preference. In a situation like this, the guest wins. (And the usher graciously accommodates the guest's preference.) Go ahead and designate your reserved rows with special ribbons or flowers, though, and remind your ushers that those rows are for honored guests and family members.

Guests who arrive after ushers have started to escort immediate family members to their seats (about ten minutes before the ceremony's start) may sit or stand in the back of the ceremony site (see the "Seating honored relatives" section for more info). If guests arrive after the processional has begun, they should seat themselves after the wedding party has made it to the front of the site and the bride has been presented to the groom. (And for heaven's sake, no tardy guests are allowed to parade down the white runner!) To eliminate needless interruptions, strategically station an usher or a trusted friend to intercept and advise late-arriving guests where to sit. Later guests may use the side aisles to slip quickly and quietly into seats without disturbing guests who are already seated.

Going down the Aisle: The Processional

The processional begins your journey to a new life. The bride, the groom, the wedding party, the officiant, and close relatives of the happy couple are all part of this breathtaking grand entrance. This section explains how it's done.

If your ceremony site has two main aisles, have the processional down the bride's side and the recessional (which I discuss in the later section "The Recessional and Other Postceremony Rituals") up the groom's side.

Seating honored relatives

About ten minutes before the wedding begins, the couple's immediate family members are escorted down the aisle to take their seats within the ribbon (the first four rows or so, which are specially reserved and adorned); five minutes before the ceremony, the mothers are seated in this area. I explain who goes where and how in the following sections.

Offering the *right* protection

Have you ever wondered how the groom and his family wound up sitting on the right side of a Christian ceremony site? Well, in medieval Christian weddings, the groom stood to the right of the altar to keep his right hand free to grab his sword in case he had to defend his bride. The tradition (without the sword, of course) continues to this day. En garde!

Understanding where family members sit

Rows reserved for family members have particular seating arrangements, according to each member's relationship to the couple. Create a seating plan for these front rows to avoid confusion when these special guests take their seats. The following seating protocol applies to both the bride's and the groom's sides:

- **First row:** Any unfortunate wedding party member who feels faint or ill or all the attendants during particularly long ceremonies sit here.

- **Second row:** Parents of the bride and groom are seated next to the aisle, and any siblings who aren't in the wedding are seated next to them.

- **Third row:** Grandparents of the bride and groom are seated next to the aisle, and any siblings who aren't in the wedding are seated next to them (if you want them to sit here instead of in the second row).

  Guests in the first three rows are seated in the ten minutes before the ceremony starts (any attendants who sit in the first row sit down after the processional, of course).

- **Fourth row:** Other honored guests, such as elderly relatives, aunts, uncles, cousins, godparents, a friend doing a special reading, or parents of children in the ceremony sit here.

Guests in this row are seated during the general ushering of wedding guests, not during the immediate family's seating just before the wedding.

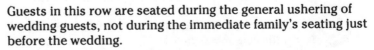

If your parents are divorced but haven't remarried, the seating is the same as noted in the previous list as long as both parents are on good terms. Divorced parents who have dates or who are remarried and remain friendly may also sit together in the second row. Otherwise, use the seating recommended in the following list (it applies to both the bride's and the groom's sides). Let your parents help you make this decision.

✔ **First row:** Again, any wedding party members who feel faint or ill or all the attendants during particularly long ceremonies sit here.

✔ **Second row:** The parent who raised you and his or her spouse or date (if there is one) are seated next to the aisle, along with any siblings who aren't in the wedding.

✔ **Third row:** Your other parent and his or her spouse or date (if there is one) are seated next to the aisle, along with any siblings who aren't in the wedding (if you want them to sit here instead of in the second row).

If divorced parents aren't on good terms and you think a squabble may break out between your parents, seat the parent who didn't raise you in the fourth row and move your grandparents forward to the third row.

✔ **Fourth row:** Your grandparents are seated next to the aisle, along with other relatives or honored guests (as noted in the previous list).

The grandparents are seated during the immediate family's seating right before the ceremony. Additional honored relatives and guests, however, are seated during the general seating of guests, not during the immediate family's seating.

In a formal Jewish ceremony, both the bride's mother and father accompany her down the aisle. The parents stand under the huppah with the bride and groom. Grandparents and siblings sit in the second row on each side of the aisle (the groom's side is the left when facing the front of the venue, and the bride's side is the right). Stepparents (if there are any) sit in the third and fourth rows unless they're close to the couple, in which case they may also stand under the huppah. Special guests sit behind the grandparents, siblings, and stepparents.

The most honored seats are next to the aisle, and they're reserved for grandparents and parents. Traditionally, stepparents aren't seated next to the aisle, although they may be escorted in during the family seating time and seated within the area of honor. The bride and groom can choose to elevate a stepparent to another seat if they wish to do so.

More reserved rows may be necessary for additional special friends or relatives, and you may want to include other steprelatives in the rows behind your immediate family. Make sure the ushers know which family members are stepfamily members and which family members are immediate family members so they know where to seat everyone; the rehearsal is the perfect time to draw up a plan.

Although everyone would like to believe differently, weddings are high-stress times for many families, and sometimes emotions and tempers flare. Use your best judgment (and caution) when seating estranged family members, taking care to try to avoid any possible situation that may put a damper on your special day.

If the ceremony site has two main aisles, parents and special family members and guests sit in the middle section, with the bride's family on the left and the groom's family on the right in a Christian ceremony (the reverse for a Jewish ceremony).

Bringing family members down the aisle

About ten minutes before the start of the ceremony, your closest relatives are escorted to their seats in the following order (beginning with the groom's family and alternating with the bride's; for same-sex ceremonies, it's up to the couple to decide whose family is seated first):

1. Ushers escort the groom's siblings who aren't in the wedding and then the bride's siblings to their seats. Ushers offer their arms to sisters, with brothers walking behind.

2. Ushers escort the groom's grandparents and then the bride's grandparents to their seats (the maternal grandparents are first). Ushers offer their arms to the grandmothers, with grandfathers walking behind.

3. An usher escorts the mother of the groom to her seat (the father walks behind, unless he's the best man, in which case he's with the groom before the ceremony starts).

4. An usher escorts the mother of the bride to her seat; she's the last person to be seated before the entrance of the wedding party, unless she's walking the bride down the aisle. (I discuss this important role in more detail in the "Deciding who walks the bride down the aisle" section.) If the father of the bride isn't walking the bride down the aisle, he either escorts the mother of the bride or walks just behind the usher escorting the mother.

If you want to, you can have your brothers and your spouse-to-be's brothers escort the grandparents and mothers to their seats instead of having the ushers do so. Either option is perfectly acceptable.

If you have steprelatives, ushers escort them to their seats in the following order (again alternating families with the groom's first): stepsiblings, siblings, stepgrandparents, grandparents, stepparent(s), groom's mother, bride's mother.

After the mother of the bride is seated, the ushers carefully unfurl the white runner (which is optional) down the aisle, and they no longer escort anyone down it. In fact, no one is escorted down the aisle after the family begins seating. (Any guest who arrives during this time should silently slide into a back row, as I explain in the earlier "Filling the seats in the right order" section.)

Knowing the right order of the bridal party

After the family members are all comfortably seated in their seats (and clutching hankies), it's time for your processional music to begin. Although you can choose from a couple of slight variations for how the wedding party makes its entrance (for example, informal, formal, Catholic, and Protestant), here's the basic, time-honored order of the bridal party's appearance, particularly in Christian ceremonies (see Figure 14-1):

1. **The officiant, groom, and best man take their places to the right of the altar when facing forward, usually entering the ceremony site through a side door near the altar; they face the guests.**

2. **Groomsmen can either take their places with the groom and best man (also through the side door) or escort the bridesmaids down the aisle (bridesmaid on the left facing the front, groomsman on the right). If the groomsmen escort the bridesmaids, they can either walk with them from the back of the ceremony site or start next to the groom and best man and meet the bridesmaids halfway down the aisle and escort them the rest of the way. When they arrive at the altar, they turn to face the guests.**

   Another option (for larger weddings) is to have the groomsmen precede the bridesmaids down the aisle in pairs. If your wedding party has an uneven number of men, one of them may lead the procession.

3. **Bridesmaids enter through the back of the ceremony site, either alone or with the groomsmen. For larger weddings, they may walk in pairs. After they arrive at the altar, they turn to face the guests.**

   Try to line up both groomsmen and bridesmaids by height — shortest to tallest. (The shortest walks in first.)

4. **The maid or matron of honor is the last of the bride's attendants to walk down the aisle. She either walks in alone or with the best man.**

5. The ring bearer walks in next before the flower girl.

6. The flower girl walks in just before the bride. It's common today to have two flower girls, in which case they walk in together.

   The flower girl and ring bearer may also walk together (the ring bearer is on the right when facing the front of the venue). It's also acceptable to have the maid or matron of honor walk behind this cute little couple. Depending on their ages, the flower girl and ring bearer may sit with their families instead of standing with the rest of the attendants.

7. Finally, it's the bride's turn to walk down the aisle. In a traditional Christian ceremony, the bride walks on her escort's left arm. Some couples choose to have the bride walk on her escort's right so that no one is between her and the groom when they arrive at the altar.

The basic Jewish processional is as follows (see Figure 14-2):

1. The cantor and rabbi take their places in the front of the ceremony site.

2. The bride's grandparents, followed by the groom's grandparents, may choose to take part in the processional instead of being seated beforehand; they lead everyone else down the aisle.

3. The ushers file down the aisle in pairs (according to height from shortest to tallest), followed by the best man and then the groom, who may or may not be escorted by both parents (either way is appropriate). His mother is on his right, and his father is on his left.

4. The bridesmaids may either walk individually or in pairs.

5. The maid or matron of honor comes after all the bridesmaids, followed by the ring bearer and then the flower girl, who comes in just before the bride.

6. The bride makes her entrance last. Her escort is on her right side. It's also appropriate to have both parents escort the bride down the aisle. In that case, the bride's mother is on her right, and the bride's father is on her left.

Make sure your attendants practice pacing themselves about four to six rows apart and walking serenely down the aisle at the rehearsal. Nervousness tends to make people rush down the aisle — which, as you can imagine, doesn't make for a very elegant entrance.

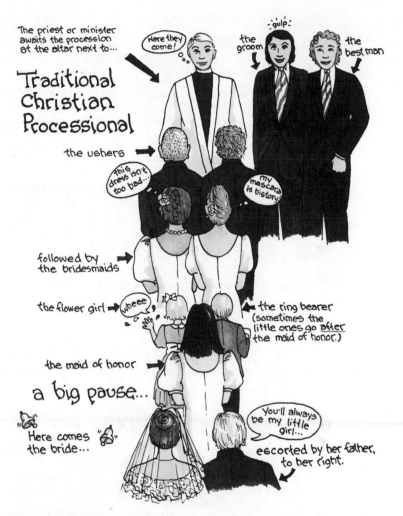

Figure 14-1: The basic order of a traditional Christian processional.

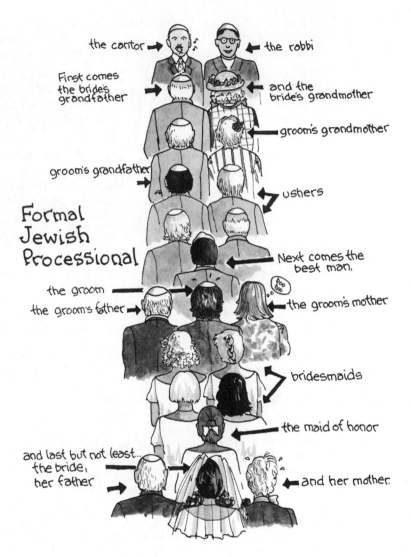

the cantor

the rabbi

First comes the bride's grandfather

and the bride's grandmother

groom's grandmother

groom's grandfather

ushers

Formal Jewish Processional

Next comes the best man,

the groom

the groom's father

the groom's mother

bridesmaids

the maid of honor

and last but not least... the bride, her father

and her mother.

Figure 14-2: A formal Jewish processional.

Deciding who walks the bride down the aisle

Traditionally, the father of the bride has the duty and honor of walking his daughter down the aisle; however, some situations call for different setups. It's the bride's job to decide who walks her down the aisle, and it's not always an easy choice. Here are some suggestions for different situations, all of which are appropriate:

- ✔ If your father is deceased, choose a close male relative, such as a grandfather, uncle, or brother. Or, you may select either your mother or your stepfather if your mother is remarried.

- ✔ If your parents are divorced and you remain close to your father, by all means, bestow this honor upon him. This option is appropriate even if your mother is remarried. You can give your stepfather a reading or allow him to make a toast at the reception so he doesn't feel left out.

- ✔ If your mother is remarried and you're close to both your father and your stepfather, you can have them share this privilege. For example, your stepfather may take you halfway down the aisle and then step aside to allow your birth father to walk you the rest of the way to your groom.

- ✔ If you're close to both your parents, you can have both your mother and your father escort you down the aisle.

- ✔ If the bride has children from a previous marriage, she may choose to have them walk her down the aisle.

- ✔ If you think choosing one person over another may hurt the other person's feelings, you may choose to walk alone.

In a same-sex ceremony, each partner can decide whether to walk down the aisle (with or without an escort) or enter with the officiant.

However you decide to process down the aisle, make sure you discuss your choice with all your parents and stepparents before the ceremony so that no one is unpleasantly surprised at the rehearsal. Be sensitive to everyone's feelings.

After the bride walks down the aisle, the officiant asks, "Who gives this woman in marriage?" or the more modern version, "Who presents this bride?" Your parents can step to your side, or your mother can be escorted to your side by the best man, to answer the traditional, "We/I do." Or, your parents may answer from their row. All options are acceptable and a matter of personal choice.

The Recessional and Other Postceremony Rituals

You've said your vows and shared your first kiss as a married couple; your picture-perfect, long-anticipated wedding ceremony is almost over — but not quite. Now it's time to walk back up the aisle during the recessional. To make your recessional just as memorable and lovely as your processional, keep in mind the etiquette guidelines I address in the following sections.

Stopping to greet your parents

The ritual of pausing during the recessional to greet your parents is guaranteed to cause guests to shed another tear or two. This greeting is an optional wedding element, of course, but taking a moment after you leave the front of the ceremony site to stop and hug each set of parents is a very thoughtful gesture of love and appreciation. You can also choose to offer a single rose or other keepsake flower to your mothers for an added touch. The etiquette patrol approves!

Some brides choose to present a flower out of their bouquet to their mother during the processional and another to their new mother-in-law during the recessional. Doing so is also appropriate, but the couple always greets the bride's family first. For same-sex ceremonies, it's up to the couple whose parents they greet first.

Following the couple up the aisle in the right order

While you're greeting your parents and the officiant is beaming benevolently, your attendants begin to pair up — bridesmaids with groomsmen — and they follow you up the aisle after you've finished greeting your parents. Here's the basic order of the recessional for most ceremonies, particularly Christian ones (see Figure 14-3):

1. Bride and Groom

2. Flower girl and ring bearer (if they remained at the altar)

3. Maid or matron of honor and best man

4. Remaining bridesmaids and groomsmen in the reverse order of how they walked in during the processional

5. Parents of the bride, followed by parents of the groom

6. Grandparents of the bride, followed by grandparents of the groom

As the bride, groom, and wedding party walk up the aisle toward the back of the ceremony site, guests should see all the women on the left and all the men on the right.

Jewish recessionals are similar; however, following the bride and groom are the bride's parents and then the groom's parents, followed by the bride's grandparents and the groom's grandparents. The rest of the bridal party processes in the same order as in the preceding list after the grandparents, with the cantor and rabbi at the end (see Figure 14-4). As the bride, groom, and bridal party walk up the aisle toward the back of the ceremony site, guests should see all the women on the right and all the men on the left.

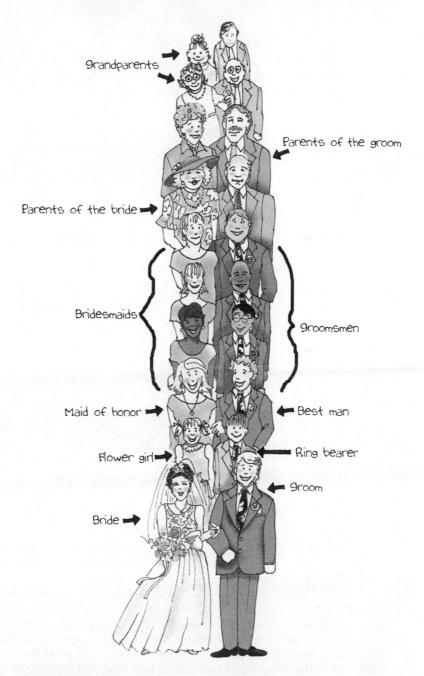

grandparents

Parents of the groom

Parents of the bride

Bridesmaids

Groomsmen

Maid of honor

Best man

Flower girl

Ring bearer

Groom

Bride

Figure 14-3: A basic Christian recessional.

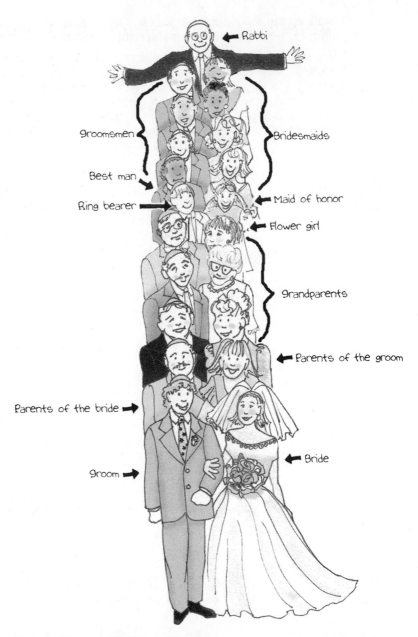

Figure 14-4: A basic Jewish recessional.

Yes, you're permitted to walk briskly back up the aisle — in sync with your joyous music. But please, no running! Tell your wedding party these instructions during your rehearsal, and make sure they're properly spaced as they walk back up the aisle — no crowding allowed!

Releasing guests from their seats

After the wedding party is out of the ceremony site, two ushers return to dismiss your guests, beginning from the front of the site with the family members seated within the ribbons. Ushers stand at the end of each row (facing the back of the site) and step forward to the next row when the row in front of it has emptied. Both sides of the aisle exit at the same time. Guests remain patiently seated until it's their turn to leave.

If you don't have a large number of guests (fewer than 150 or so), you may choose to release the guests yourselves. To do so, you simply return to the front of the church after the recessional and briefly greet your guests as they exit their rows; this ritual takes the place of the traditional receiving line that I describe in the "Walk the Line: Receiving Line Etiquette" section later in this chapter.

Signing the marriage license and paying the officiant

Your marriage license bureau can guide you appropriately on the issue of who needs to sign your license (the bride, the groom, and witnesses, for example) when you apply for or pick up your license. The clerk also can give you any necessary information on qualifying witnesses, if appropriate. Make sure you give your officiant your marriage license before the wedding; after the wedding, your officiant sends it to the appropriate government office for validating and filing.

Note: Don't forget to apply for a marriage license at your county's recorder office or marriage bureau at least one month before your wedding day; call ahead to find out how long a marriage license is valid and what forms of identification you need to obtain one.

You can pay the officiant either before or after the ceremony — either way, doing so is a duty for your best man. And because you're such a well-mannered and thoughtful couple, you enclose your cash or check in a nice thank-you card.

Walk the Line: Receiving Line Etiquette

So you don't plan to have a receiving line? I suggest you think again. How else will you be able to greet and personally thank all your guests who took time out of their busy schedules to come to your wedding? Don't think you'll be able to catch up with everyone at the reception — it's highly unlikely that you'll accomplish that mission unless you have fewer than 50 guests. Which would you rather do — spend the few brief hours at your reception inching along from table to table greeting chatty guests, or dancing, mingling, and having fun? That's what I thought.

Having a receiving line is the proper and gracious thing to do, particularly if you have more than 40 or 50 guests at the ceremony and you and your spouse don't release your guests from their rows after the ceremony (a ritual I mention in the "Releasing guests from their seats" section). In the following sections, I explain the etiquette you need to know to make the receiving line a breeze.

Picking the right time to line up

When do you line up to receive your guests? If you have a less formal wedding, immediately following the ceremony is just fine because it allows you to greet people as they come out of the site. Traditionally (and for formal weddings), however, you greet guests as they arrive at the reception, although doing so isn't always possible if the wedding party stops for photographs on the way.

Some reception venues discourage receiving lines, particularly if the reception is in the afternoon and they have to set up for another party after yours. (Lengthy receiving lines can eat up precious time.) Find out your reception site's preferences before you arrive on your wedding day. If your reception site frowns on receiving lines, have your line at your ceremony site, even if you're having a formal or semiformal wedding.

Knowing the correct order of the people in the line

Whom you include in your receiving line is up to you, but here's a clue: Keep it somewhat short. Doing so speeds things along, and, besides, no one wants to have to greet each and every attendant in your wedding party. Sad but true.

Here's the traditional receiving line order (see Figure 14-5):

1. The bride's mother heads the line as hostess. (You may choose to have the bride's father join next in line.)

2. The groom's mother stands next in line. (The groom's father stands next to her if the bride's father is in line.)

3. The bride and groom are last in line.

Figure 14-5: A traditional receiving line features the bride and groom with their mothers (including the fathers is optional).

Traditionally, fathers of the bride and groom, the best man, and the groomsmen don't join the receiving line; they socialize with the guests and introduce people to one another. The bride's father also directs guests to the hors d'oeuvres and beverages if the line is taking place at the reception site. However, the fathers may choose to cycle in and out of the line, taking their wives' places when they need a short respite.

Rules of etiquette have loosened over the years, and you're free to customize your own receiving line, within reason. For example, you can include grandparents (if they're able), you as a couple may stand alone to greet your guests if you're hosting your own wedding, or you can include your maid of honor and best man, too. The bridesmaids may choose to stand after the bride and groom, as well. And if you have your heart set on a receiving line with your entire bridal party, alternate bridesmaids with groomsmen (ladies first). Only the cutest members of your wedding party (the children) are let off the hook, unless they're the children of you or your spouse and wish to participate. If someone other than your parents or your spouse's parents are hosting the wedding (like an aunt and uncle), they stand at the head of the line.

If your parents are divorced, a little careful planning is in order. The simplest way to handle this situation is to have only the mothers of the bride and groom (and the bride and groom) in the receiving line. If you want to include the fathers in the line, place the bride's parents on either side of the bride with their spouses (if they have them), and place the groom's parents on either side of the groom with their spouses (if they have them) so guests aren't confused about who goes with whom. (If any parent brings a date who isn't a spouse, the date doesn't stand in line.) The mother of the bride is always first.

The receiving line is another time when you need to be sensitive about divorced parents' situations — especially if they're not on friendly terms. You definitely have to think this ritual out ahead of time; discussing it with your parents may be necessary.

Greeting guests in line politely

The receiving line isn't the place for extended conversations; short comments suffice because you want to keep the line moving. Most of the time, your guests speak to you first, commenting about the ceremony, how great you look, or what a wonderful couple you make; they likely offer congratulations, too. Make sure you thank them. Your job as a couple is to introduce your parents to guests they may not know and to tell all your guests how pleased you are that they came to your wedding. (You can say thanks in a number of ways: "So glad you could come," "Thanks for coming," "So happy you're here," just to name a few.)

If you encounter an extra-chatty guest, you can use physical communication signals as well as verbal ones to end the conversation. The ideal thing to do is to smile, shake hands, thank the person for coming to the wedding, gently nudge him or her through the line, and close by saying, "It's so nice to see you. I look forward to catching up with you soon."

That's it! You made it through your ceremony and the dreaded receiving line. Congratulations and best wishes; you may now celebrate at your reception! (Check out Chapter 15 for how to celebrate with class at the reception — and still have fun!)

Chapter 15

Celebrating with Class at the Reception

. . . .

In This Chapter

▶ Making introductions and toasts

▶ Cutting your cake carefully

▶ Knowing the etiquette of dancing and tossing the bouquet and garter

▶ Mingling with and accepting gifts from your guests

▶ Preparing yourself for glitches

▶ Leaving your reception gracefully

. . . .

*A*fter you say your "I do's," exchange the official kiss, and take your formal photographs, it's time to start the party. Everyone gets to relax and celebrate the marriage with a few time-honored traditions. In this chapter, I describe what you need to know to have a well-mannered and fun reception.

Announcing the Parents, the Wedding Party, and the Happy Couple

First things first: You need to decide whether you want the DJ or band leader to announce you and your new spouse at your reception or you want a friend or family member to act as MC (Master/ Mistress of Ceremonies); either choice is appropriate and accept-able. Having someone other than the DJ act as MC may work out well if you have a person whom you want to be a part of your wedding day but can't quite figure out where he or she fits.

Of course, you need to make sure the family member or friend you choose is someone who'll be able to maintain composure throughout the announcements; an extremely nervous (or intoxicated) announcer will embarrass everyone involved.

Whomever you choose to make the introductions, be sure that he or she knows the proper titles and name pronunciations of the people being introduced and has a written list with the correct order. Here's the order in which important folks are typically announced:

1. Traditionally, the parents of the bride are announced first, followed by the parents of the groom. If any parents are divorced, make sure you decide ahead of time whether they're going to be announced together, separately, or with their current spouses.

2. After the parents are introduced, the wedding party comes next. The DJ or band leader announces the bridesmaids along with their groomsmen escorts in the order they walked during the ceremony. Usually, the introduction includes the person's name and connection to the bride or groom. The DJ or band leader may say, for example, "Bridesmaid Shelly Lewis, sister of the bride, escorted by groomsman John Dean, brother of the groom." Including the attendant's connection to you adds a nice touch, especially because many of your guests may not know how the people in the wedding party are significant in your life. However you decide to introduce your party, keep it brief and simple. Your guests (and you) will be ready to move on to the meal and dancing.

3. The big moment — when you and your new spouse are introduced — follows the bridal party introductions. How you're introduced at the reception is how people will expect to refer to you in the future, so put some thought into this decision. Consider whether you want to be introduced as "Mr. and Mrs. Frederick Smith," "Mr. Frederick Smith and Mrs. Samantha Jones-Smith," or some other variation (see Chapter 16 for more about name options). If you or your spouse-to-be has a title (Dr., Rev., and so on) you should be introduced as "Dr. Frederick Smith and Mrs. Samantha Smith" or "Mr. Frederick Smith and Dr. Samantha Jones-Smith."

In the case of same-sex weddings, most couples choose to be announced as "the brides Kate Jones and Stephanie Smith" or "the grooms Kevin Jones and David Smith." If one partner is legally taking the other's name, they can be announced as "Misters Kevin and David Smith." If the couple chooses to have both spouses hyphenate and join their names, they can be introduced as "Misters Kevin and David Jones-Smith."

If you and/or your spouse has a child or children you'd like to include in the introductions, introducing them after the bridal party seems to work best so that you and your new spouse can have your moment together at the end. If the child is very young, you may want to have them introduced with their grandparents instead. Of course, if it's important to you to have your son(s) or daughter(s) presented with you and your spouse, go for it. This area of etiquette is changing all the time, and there aren't really any fixed rules — just guidelines based on practicality.

Some couples choose to be introduced during a specific song and then go straight into their first dance. I recommend against this practice; it's most appropriate to hold off on dancing until after dinner is served. After you're introduced, you should go to the bridal table.

Don't Burn the Toast!

After the introductions, the beginning of the reception is marked with the traditional toasting and is usually signaled by the pouring of champagne or cider by the servers. If bottles of bubbly beverages are already on the tables, the MC should announce that it's time to fill the flutes. Otherwise, guests may toast with whatever they're drinking at the time. Then it's show time!

The best man always proposes the first toast, followed immediately by the maid or matron of honor. Each of them should start by standing and tapping a glass to get everyone's attention. Five minutes or less is the perfect length of time for each toast. (There's nothing wrong with working out a cue with the DJ, the wedding planner, or a guest to let each toaster know when he or she has hit a certain time limit.) Each toast should end with a raising of glasses, cheers, clinking of glasses all around, and a kiss by the bride and groom. All the guests and bridal party members should rise to toast to the bride and groom, who remain seated. The bride and groom do *not* drink a toast to themselves.

The worst best man's toast I ever heard ended with the best man sobbing into his champagne, talking about how much he loved the bride and alluding to an affair he had with her while the groom (the best man's brother) was out of town. You *don't* want something like this to happen at your wedding. Even if this story isn't one the best man can truthfully tell during your reception, you want to make sure he and everyone else who's toasting are suited to the task of giving a speech. Make sure they write down at least an outline and are clear on what you expect them to say (or not say, as the case may be). It's fine for each person to refer to notes while speaking.

Appropriate toast topics include a description about how you and your spouse met or when the two of you realized you were in love. It's also appropriate for each speaker to give a word of advice or share a poem or quote. Unsavory anecdotes are strictly off limits.

In general, all toasts except the best man's are optional. Most of the time, however, the maid or matron of honor also offers a toast. And letting a few other people make toasts isn't unheard of. So, in terms of etiquette, who else can make a toast at your reception? The most common speakers are the following:

- **Father of the bride:** A wedding reception never quite seems complete until the father of the bride makes a toast. Although it's perfectly acceptable for him not to speak, there's something really lovely in hearing the father of the bride address the guests and his daughter's new spouse. I've heard some speeches as simple as this: "Thank you for sharing this day with us; I could not be happier for my daughter." Typically, the mother of the bride doesn't speak, but if she requests to do so, she does so after the father's toast.

- **Groom's parents:** The groom's parents usually don't make a toast at the reception because they traditionally speak at the rehearsal dinner. Of course, they may speak if they want to and if it's okay with the bride and groom. If they choose to toast, they do so right after the father of the bride.

- **You and your spouse:** You and/or your spouse may want to make a toast of your own, especially if you're hosting your own wedding. Doing so adds a wonderful touch. Traditionally, as part of this toast, the groom thanks the bride's parents for their love and support. Even if you're not hosting your reception, giving your own toast can be a great opportunity to thank the people who contributed so much to your wedding and, of course, to thank your guests who came to celebrate with you.

It's perfectly fine — and a very good idea — to give the MC a specific list of people who are going to give toasts, along with strict instructions that last-minute additions won't be made by anyone other than you or your spouse. Laying the ground rules ahead of time and making a game plan will help you feel confident that only happy stories and good wishes will be expressed during the toasts.

If you're concerned about a relative or friend who has a history of making scenes or inappropriate comments at gatherings, feel free to seat the person far away from the head table and post a friend or family member at his table with instructions not to let him take the floor. You may even let word get around that time will be limited at the reception so only a few people will be able to speak. You also should let your MC, wedding planner, and a close friend know about this person so they can be prepared to stop any inappropriate behavior as soon as — or perhaps even before — it starts.

Cutting Your Cake without Messing Up Your Manners

Cutting the wedding cake is a time-honored tradition that few people choose to leave out of their reception. It isn't necessary (or expected) for you to provide any other dessert than cake, but it's perfectly acceptable to serve other treats, especially if you and your spouse have certain favorites.

The couple usually cuts the wedding cake right after the meal, although some reception venues encourage the bride and groom to cut their cake just after the introductions. In most cases, doing so allows the wait staff sufficient time to have the cake slices ready to serve to the guests right after the meal.

Traditionally, the bride cuts the first two slices of cake with a decorated cake knife. The groom places his hand over the bride's hand during the cutting. He then feeds the first bite to his bride, and she, in turn, feeds him a small bite. Today many brides and grooms even choose to feed each other at the same time.

Some people think it's funny to smash cake all over their new spouse's face, but doing so not only looks silly and immature— it also ruins the bride's make-up and can damage her dress. It's best to use utensils and respectfully feed each other small bites of cake.

If you choose to have a cake with different flavored layers and you know a guest has an allergy to a specific layer, make sure the servers are aware of this allergy so they can deliver an appropriate piece of cake to your guest.

Depending on your reception venue, the servers may slice the cake and then serve a piece to each guest at his or her table, or the servers may just place the slices on the cake table and invite guests to select their own pieces.

The dish on having a groom's cake

The groom's cake began as a heavy fruit cake that would be cut at the wedding and sent home with the guests in cake boxes or bags. Legend had it that if each unmarried female guest slipped a piece of the cake under her pillow on the night of the wedding, she might have dreams of the man she would someday marry.

In today's wedding world, the groom's cake can be a separate small cake cut at the rehearsal dinner or reception. Guests can choose to enjoy it instead of the wedding cake. You can decorate the groom's cake anyway you want; for example, you can relate it to sports, college logos, or the place where the groom met the bride.

Some brides choose to have cupcakes arranged in the shape of a wedding cake instead of the traditional confection. This arrangement is a lovely (and often less expensive) alternative to a regular wedding cake. You may either have a top layer made for your cutting or simply feed each other bites of a specially decorated cupcake; either practice is acceptable. You can have the cupcakes served, or you can let guests come up and choose their own. Again, either practice is appropriate.

May I Have This Dance?

Some couples may choose not to have music or dancing at their reception, which is acceptable, but most couples uphold the tradition of having a first dance. Your first dance as a married couple is such a sweet moment and traditionally occurs after dessert. The MC announces you, at which point you make your way to the center of the dance floor. A slow dance is most appropriate, but you may choose another traditional style, like a ballroom dance.

Make sure the DJ or band has the correct version of your song. At one wedding I attended, a traditional version of Elvis Presley's "Can't Help Falling in Love" was supposed to play during the bride and groom's first dance, but, instead, the DJ put on a modern, techno version. The pictures of the bride and groom's reactions may have been priceless, but shock and disappointment are not expressions you want to see in your wedding pictures.

Many couples find it fun to take dance lessons in preparation for their first dance or choreograph a number together; if doing something like that interests you at all, go for it! However, there's no need to feel pressure to put on a show if doing so doesn't fit your personalities.

After the bride dances with the groom, her father should come and join her on the dance floor for the father-daughter dance. Either the bride or her father may choose the song. If the bride has a stepfather with whom she'd also like to dance, he may either cut in or share the next dance with her. Whatever the bride decides to do, she should arrange everything ahead of time to avoid any misunderstandings or hurt feelings during the reception. If some-one other than the bride's father (or stepfather) walked her down the aisle, she may choose to share this dance with that person, although it's also fine to leave this dance out.

After the bride dances with her father, the groom shares a dance with his mother. The groom or his mother can pick the song — it's up to the groom what he wants to do. Again, the groom can choose to dance with his stepmother, too, if he wants to. After the mother-son dance, the bride may want to have a song during which she dances with the groom's father and the groom dances with the bride's mother; this dance is completely optional, though. After all the traditional dances have taken place, the floor is opened up for everyone to dance (the MC should make an announcement).

If you or your spouse wants to include your child (or children) in any of the dances, go for it! It's a lovely gesture. You may even want to have the kid(s) pick the song. This dance should happen after you've danced with your spouse and each of you has danced with your parents. This dance may also be a nice time to have the MC announce you as "The Jones-Smith" family (or however you'd like to be addressed in the future).

When the reception is in honor of a same-sex couple, the couple still has their first dance together, but after that, it's up to the couple how to include their parents and in which order. If this situ-ation applies to you, make sure everyone is aware of the lineup and the cues they should look for ahead of time.

Tossing the Bouquet and the Garter

The bouquet and garter tosses usually take place later in the eve-ning, after people have been dancing awhile. The MC makes an announcement and gathers all the young, single women for the bou-quet toss. The bride may want to have a second bouquet made (one made of silk flowers is fine) so she can preserve the one she used in the ceremony. The bride turns her back toward the women and tosses the bouquet high over her head for one of them to catch.

The single men then come forward for the garter toss. The groom starts by removing a garter from the bride's leg. He then turns his back to the crowd and throws the garter over his shoulder. Superstition states that whoever catches the garter will be the next man to get married.

Please display restraint during the garter removal, and keep in mind that most of your guests aren't interested in watching an amateur version of a burlesque show — save that for your honeymoon.

It's perfectly acceptable if the bride and groom want to skip the bouquet and garter tosses altogether, or at least keep one and eliminate the other. Many couples don't like these traditions and choose to use fun alternatives. For example, it's becoming popular to give the garter and bouquet to the longest married couple present instead of throwing them out into the crowd. You can, of course, choose to practice both traditions — there's nothing wrong with honoring a well-established marriage as well as passing the torch of your commitment onto another set of people. Remember to order enough bouquets and garters to cover whatever choice you make.

The Importance of Mingling

Your guests come to your wedding to help you and your spouse celebrate your marriage, right? Many of them spend a lot of money on clothes, gifts, and travel simply because you're important to them, and they want to share the day with you. The least you can do is spend a second or two of face-to-face time with these guests.

One of the easiest ways to make sure you get a chance to see everyone (outside of the receiving line, which I discuss in Chapter 14) is to eat first, while the guests are being served, and then walk around to the tables while the guests are eating. This way, your guests are seated and you can make a sort of game plan for getting around the room, which helps save time and ensures you don't miss anyone. You and your spouse should do your best to visit all your guests together. It's also a good idea to keep conversations short and move on gracefully when people are eating. After a brief exchange, you can exit with a simple "I'll let you get back to your meal."

You *must* plan to mingle throughout the reception. Yes, there's much to be accomplished in a short time frame, but this gesture is an important part of wedding protocol, no matter what style of wedding you have. Your attention will make guests feel special, and taking a couple of moments for all your guests gives them an opportunity to congratulate you. Plus, the two of you get to show off your beautiful attire and rings, which is just plain fun! After you've mingled with everyone, it's time for dancing and celebrating.

Accepting Gifts Directly from Guests at Your Reception

Many guests bring gifts to the reception (although it's not the preferred way to give gifts; better etiquette is to send gifts directly to either the bride's home or the address where she registered to have her gifts sent). So you need to have a table set up to accommodate packages, as well as a basket or box to hold cards.

Usually the best man and maid or matron of honor are responsible for transferring the gifts from the wedding site to the hotel or home, wherever the bride and groom want them to go. But you may assign another family member or close friend to this job. It's a good idea to make sure someone checks the ceremony site for stray gifts just in case someone brings a gift or card there and accidentally leaves it in a pew or on a chair (or in the bathroom, vestibule, or any number of places). At the reception site, be sure to ask the banquet event manager to place the gift table or card box in a secure location, away from all public doorways or entrances.

Some guests may hand you gifts directly even though doing so is inconvenient for you — and inconsiderate on their part! If you run into this kind of situation, here are a few guidelines to follow:

- ✔ If a guest directly hands you a card or gift at the reception, say thank you and then make sure your maid or matron of honor or best man puts it with the other gifts right away.

- ✔ If a guest hands you a gift because she forgot to attach a card and she wants to make sure you know the gift is from her, write her name on the outside of the wrapping or stick a note on it to make sure you send a thank-you note to the proper person (see Chapter 16 for details on thank-you notes).

- ✔ If a guest hands you a gift and wants you to open it in her presence, gently decline and explain that you don't want to lose the gift and that you'll make sure it's put with the others right away. Explain that you want to give the gift opening your full attention later.

  If the guest is insistent, open the gift and say thank you. Remember, though, that you still need to send that guest a thank-you note, and don't forget to make sure the gift is transferred with the others.

Being Prepared for the Unexpected

The reality of weddings is that anything and everything can go wrong — I don't say this to scare you. I say it to help you understand the reality of the situation. Take a minute to think about what you'll do if the flowers don't show up, Aunt Sally makes a scene (again), or there's a recall on chicken and your dinner menu is ruined. These things can happen. Hopefully, they won't, but, if they do, you have to stay calm, keep your manners intact, and focus as much as possible on your spouse and all the things that are going right at your wedding.

 You need to designate someone who's prepared and capable of taking care of any disasters that may take place; this person can be a wedding planner or a family member or close friend who isn't in the wedding party. Your go-to person should know the agenda for the day, as well as who's expected to be where and when (you should give this person a copy of the day's itinerary and a list of important contact numbers before the big day). Your go-to person may also have to act as a go-between for you and your vendors. Most importantly, though, this person should be levelheaded and able to remind you that flowers are nice but not necessary, someone is keeping a close eye on Aunt Sally, and the caterer is rearranging the appetizers, salad, and side dishes to make a filling and wonderful meal from which the chicken will scarcely be missed.

In the following sections, I describe how to avoid some major potential problems (if possible) and give you pointers on how to handle problems with grace if they do occur.

 You may never forget the things that go wrong at your wedding, but your guests will hardly notice, especially if you hold yourself together. You want them to remember a gorgeous, happily married, and well-mannered couple — not a bride who threw a crying fit over some missing chicken. Do your best to maintain a sense of humor. At the end of the day, all that matters is that you married the love of your life. Any bumps along the way will only be cause for laughter down the road, so try not to let them get the best of you.

Avoiding wardrobe malfunctions

You never know when someone may lose a button or when intricate detailing may start to come off a dress. And it's easy to snag or rip the fabric of the bride's dress when the maid or matron of honor is putting up the dress's bustle or taking off the train. To prevent these possible wardrobe malfunctions from ruining your day, make sure you have the following items *on hand* (not in the trunk of someone's car or back at the hotel) throughout your wedding day just in case you or your attendants need them:

- A small sewing kit that includes buttons, scissors, and thread
- Extra bobby pins
- Double-sided tape (for fixing hems)
- Safety pins
- A small marker (to fill in any shoe scuffs)
- A stain-remover pen
- Static remover

Usually, when you have everything you need to fix a malfunction, you don't end up needing it. It's when you leave the tools behind that disaster is sure to strike.

Recovering from an embarrassing moment

Cringe-worthy moments happen to everybody . . . you just hope they don't occur while a hundred or so of your family members and closest friends are watching you. If you or your spouse happens to slip up (or just plain slip) during your wedding day, or a glitch in the planning occurs, the best thing to do is ignore the incident and move on. However, if you happen to commit a major faux pas, such as calling a guest by the wrong name, apologize immediately, mention how overwhelmed you are, and move on. Your (gracious) guests will follow your lead. After all, people are very understanding of what's expected of you on your wedding day. Note that the apologies and corrections to these situations depend on the situation at hand; use your best judgment for each incident.

For most people, the easiest way to ensure they don't embarrass themselves is to keep the alcohol intake to a minimum. Doing so may be difficult at your reception because so many people want to toast with you. Just remember to eat and alternate every glass of champagne with a glass of sparkling water or cider (put it in a champagne glass and no one will know the difference). The bartender, a server, or the maid or matron of honor should help make sure you always have an alternate beverage nearby.

Handling issues with your vendors

Communication between you and your vendors is very important. Make sure you discuss the necessary details with each of your vendors (and have a signed agreement with each of them) before the big day — doing so helps eliminate uncomfortable situations during the reception. Meet with each vendor approximately three weeks before your wedding day to make sure you're on the same page.

If a problem arises with a specific vendor during the reception, let your wedding planner or go-to person handle it for you. After all, the last thing you want to be doing at your reception is running around trying to fix problems. (See Chapter 17 for more information on getting along with vendors.)

Asking a guest to leave

You know your friends and relatives. As you read this section, you're probably already making a mental note of one or two people who may behave improperly at your wedding.

If you have a guest who has an issue with alcohol, you may want to identify him or her to the bartender. Wedding bartenders have seen it all and can water down their drinks or discreetly limit a particular guest's consumption. If you have a guest or two in mind who simply like to cause a scene, have a relative keep an eye on them or distract them when they appear to be getting wound up. Helping your guests stay in line isn't something you should have to worry about on your wedding day, so don't think twice about delegating the task.

If all else fails and a guest continues to be a nuisance, you and your spouse may have to have the guest removed from the reception. If you don't have formal security at your wedding or a wedding planner, designate a couple of the groomsmen, or a senior family member, to act as unofficial "bouncers."

If someone does have to be asked to leave, be as discreet as possible; you don't want to draw attention to the situation or embarrass the individual.

It's a good idea to have phone numbers for taxi companies or shuttle services to make sure the guests being removed can get home safely.

Dealing with uninvited guests

Few actions are ruder than going to a wedding as an uninvited guest. Doing so goes against all the rules of etiquette. But sometimes people surprise you and show up uninvited.

If any uninvited guests show up at your wedding, you have a few options for how to handle the situation, including the following:

✔ You may choose to let your planner or caterer accommodate them in a way that's convenient — but the planner and/or caterer shouldn't be expected to extend themselves in any way.

✔ You may choose to ignore the uninvited guests completely or have a designated family member confront them, saying something like: "Oh, we weren't expecting to see you here. How did you know where the reception was being held?"

They may be embarrassed enough by that time to leave in a timely matter. If the guests are so clueless they choose to stay, just try to ignore them and go about your day.

✔ You may choose to have the uninvited guests escorted from the reception if they start to cause any kind of problems (see the preceding section for guidelines).

If an uninvited guest brings you a gift, you may simply want to return it to the giver — no further correspondence is necessary. If you decide to keep or exchange the gift, however, you need to send a thank-you note.

You may be able to avoid the arrival of uninvited guests by putting someone in charge of checking a guest list before guests enter the venue. You can also require guests to present their invitations before they can enter the reception (just make sure you make this requirement abundantly clear on the invitation so your guests don't leave their invitations behind). These methods are the best way to keep someone in particular out of your wedding (an ex or an estranged parent, for example).

Deciding what to do about uninvited kids

What should you do when invited guests bring their uninvited children? You have to make a choice — you can let them stay or make them go. If you made it clear on your invitations that your reception is a formal or adult-only affair and some guests still bring their children, they're either completely clueless or they were in a situation in which they had to make the choice between coming to your wedding with their children or skipping the celebration altogether. If you choose to let them stay, be gracious and don't belabor the fact that they ignored your wishes; more than likely they know they did so and were in a tough spot. Have your planner, maid of honor, or go-to person speak with the wait staff immediately and explain the situation to make accommodations for the guests.

If you decide to ask them to leave, ask your go-to person or wedding planner to do so discreetly and early on. Your messenger can explain that the venue simply isn't set up for or doesn't allow children. Make sure your messenger extends an apology for not making that clear enough in the invitation (even if you spelled it out in bold, red ink).

If you know some of your guests have young ones to consider but you don't want the tykes at the wedding, you may want to pass on information for local babysitters well in advance of the wedding, particularly if your guests are traveling from far away. Or, if you can afford the sitter yourself, you can make arrangements to have a babysitter on call and nearby. Just make sure the sitter you hire is licensed or comes with some type of credentials. If your reception is in a hotel, have an extra room reserved for the kids and babysitter.

Departing the Reception Properly

Some couples stay until the last dance is played and enjoy the time celebrating with family and friends; others want a dramatic getaway scene. How you choose to depart your reception is completely up to you — both options are perfectly acceptable.

If you decide to go for the getaway scene, ask your MC to make an announcement so that all your guests can gather to see you off. You won't have time to individually say goodbye to everyone, so waving as you go past is all you need to do. If your guests are able to stay after you and your spouse depart, the MC should make it clear that the celebration will continue (though after you're gone, most guests will likely follow).

After you've waved goodbye to everyone, your best man or go-to person needs to make sure your getaway vehicle is waiting for your escape. If you didn't include an end time on your invitations, it's perfectly acceptable to have the DJ or band let your guests know when they have to leave. A great way to do so is to have the DJ announce the last song of the evening before he plays it.

Make sure you assign someone the job of being the last one to leave. This person needs to make sure any leftovers are taken care of, centerpieces are collected, and abandoned coats, shoes, and purses are gathered. Don't assume the items left behind will be able to be picked up the next day.

Chapter 16

Acting Properly after the Wedding

· ·

In This Chapter

▶ Sending mannered thank-you notes and following other gift protocol

▶ Handling a name change (or lack thereof) with grace

· ·

So the cake's been eaten, the dances danced, the pictures taken, and you and your beloved are officially married! Sounds like it's time to sit back and relax, right? Wrong. Now that the main event is over, you have a few more tasks to see to, including properly thanking your guests and officially changing your name. I explain what you need to know in this chapter.

Wrapping Up the Gift Process

After you return from your honeymoon, you don't have any more calls to make to vendors or last-minute details to deal with, so you may be asking yourself, "What on earth do I do now?" And you may be feeling a bit blue because all your hard work and planning (as well as one of the biggest days of your life) are over. But now's not the time to be sad! You need to focus on all the wedding gifts you and your new spouse received and start writing the very important thank-you notes.

Keeping track of gifts

When you first register for wedding gifts (see Chapter 12 for an introduction to the process), you have to choose an address where guests can send gifts. It may be your own home address or your parents' address. Wherever guests send your gifts, someone (typically the bride, her parents, or a family member) writes down who sends each gift and what each gift is as soon as it arrives. If the couple already live together and have gifts mailed to their home, they should handle this gift-tracking process themselves. Also, whoever keeps track of the gifts needs to keep the enclosure cards and gift receipts with the corresponding gifts.

Keep this list handy and be organized about keeping track of your gifts. When it's time to write thank-you notes after the wedding, you need to refer to this list again and again, and you'll be very thankful you have it. (I discuss these thank-you notes in more detail in the "Sending the all-important thank-you notes" section in this chapter.)

If you receive a fair number of gifts before your wedding, sending immediate thanks is entirely appropriate and will make the thank-you process after your wedding a lot more manageable. Flip to Chapter 12 for more about tracking gifts and giving thanks before your wedding.

Some gifts may arrive without enclosure cards. No need to worry! The packaging slip, which accompanies each gift, should list a return name and address of the store from which the gift was sent. If you can't identify the gift-giver, simply call the store and ask for your registry consultant. He or she should be able to tell you who sent it. But don't think you can get out of writing a thank-you note just because the enclosure card wasn't there! Be sure to make the extra effort to find out who sent every gift that doesn't have an enclosure card and provide proper thanks. No excuses, no exceptions!

Exchanging gifts

It's perfectly okay to exchange gifts that you absolutely know you won't use. If you've received duplicate gifts, for instance, exchange them for something you registered for but didn't receive. Or, if you've changed your mind about a few things since you first registered and have decided you no longer need the matching serving platters, simply return your gifts to the right retail store, which will refund you either cash or store credit, depending on its return policies. You may have some feelings of guilt for exchanging gifts, but most gift-givers want the newly married couple to make use of their gifts, even if it means exchanging them for something more useful and favorable.

Of course, you don't want to publicize that you're exchanging someone's gift because doing so may hurt that person's feelings. At the same time, however, don't lie about exchanging a gift, either. So when Aunt Dorothy comes over for dinner and asks you if you've used the electric cheese grater, just be honest. Be sensitive and show a lot of appreciation for her generosity in giving a gift no matter how small or large, and express to Aunt Dorothy that you exchanged her gift for a beautiful salad bowl, which you're using to serve her salad at dinner. (Of course, even when you exchange gifts, you still need to send proper thank-you notes, which I explain in the next section.) If Aunt Dorothy is very close to you, consider keeping the gift rather than hurting her feelings. You may not need that cheese grater at the moment, but in a few years, you may wish you had it!

You don't have to keep a gift that's completely unwanted or not to your particular décor. If you choose to exchange or return it, however, remember that your thank-you should be for the gift you received, not the one you exchanged it for.

If you receive a damaged gift that has been insured, let the gift-giver know so he or she can collect on the insurance and send you another gift. If you received the damaged gift from a department store, return it to the store for a replacement. In this case, you don't need to mention the damage to the gift-giver.

Before you make a mad dash for the mall, make sure you understand each store's exchange and return policies. Your registry consultant should've provided you with this information when you first registered. Some stores require that you return or exchange all gifts within a certain period of time after your wedding.

In addition to having different return and exchange policies, some stores also give you an additional discount for purchasing items left on your registry, a practice known as "buying out your wedding registry." Stores usually have time limits for these kinds of discounts, so be sure to check with the store to find out the details. Before you go to buy out your registry, print an updated version of your registry from each store. That way you can see what you received and what you still need to complete your registry.

Sending the all-important thank-you notes

If you remember only one thing from this chapter, remember this: Sending thank-you notes for wedding gifts is *absolutely necessary*. And, contrary to what many people think, both the bride *and* the groom should be involved in writing them. No matter how small or large a gift is, and whether you keep it or exchange it for something else, you must send a thank-you note to the person who gave it to you. No exceptions! Even when you see a family member or friend soon after receiving his or her gift and you offer a verbal thank-you, etiquette still requires you to follow up with a written thank-you note. Some of your guests will probably tell you not to worry about sending them thank-you notes, but you still need to send short, written notes — your guests definitely won't mind receiving them! I explain the etiquette you need to know when you're writing thank-you notes in the following sections.

Allow me to be honest — most couples dread writing thank-you notes. For some newly married couples, the whole task can be downright intimidating. They think their notes have to be perfect with just the right wording, which isn't necessarily the case. Remember that an imperfect note that comes with heartfelt sentiment is better than a perfect note that was never written.

The importance of a handwritten note on stationery

When you're ready to write your thank-you notes, remember that sending handwritten thank-you notes is the best way to show your personal appreciation.

Never, never, never send a preprinted thank-you note; doing so is impersonal and lazy and sends the message that the gift you received didn't mean much to you. And, for the same reasons, never ever send an e-mail to say thank you for a wedding gift.

Before you can start writing your thank-you notes, you have to pick out some nice stationery. Of course, you don't want to send someone a thank-you note on a piece of loose scrap paper that you tore from your old college notebook. Not only does doing so send the message that you don't care about the recipient, but it's also just plain tacky. You should select your thank-you cards with the same care you did for all your other wedding stationery. You may even want to order thank-you cards when you order your wedding invitations so they match the rest of your wedding stationery.

If you received monogrammed stationery as a wedding gift or a shower gift, step one of the thank-you task is done! This stationery is perfect for writing thank-you notes. If you didn't receive any nice stationery as a gift and you need to purchase some, you can go to a variety of stores to do so; card and gift shops and even large retail stores like Target and Wal-Mart carry very nice thank-you cards in bulk and at a reasonable cost.

In any case, your stationery should reflect your personality as a couple and can be creative or formal. For instance, some couples use a picture from their wedding or honeymoon as a postcard, which they use to write their thank-you notes. If your wedding was more formal, sending a monogrammed thank-you card is appropriate.

Sending thank-you notes to all the right people

Thank-you notes go a long way to show your guests that you appreciate them and their efforts to choose gifts specifically with you and your spouse in mind. Also, they provide true confirmation to your guests that you received their gifts. Each note doesn't have to fill the entire card; it just needs to be sincere and meaningful to the recipient.

You must send a thank-you note for each gift you receive, even if a person gives you more than one gift. For example, if Aunt Susan gives you a bridal shower gift and two weeks later sends a wedding gift, recognize each gift with a separate thank-you note. (Chapter 13 has tips on writing notes for bridal shower gifts.) However, when someone gives you two or three items as part of one gift, you just have to write one thank-you note to that person.

Sending thank-you notes to all the people who went out of their ways to make your wedding day a success is a lovely gesture and will surely be appreciated and remembered. These people can include vendors, officiants, planners, and so on.

Saying thanks the right way

In your note, make reference to the specific gift that person gave you and describe how you plan to use it (see Figure 16-1 for an example). And don't forget to sign both your names. If the gift is monetary, it's best to say "thank you for your generous gift" rather than "thank you for the 50 bucks." If you have a specific item you plan to purchase with a particular monetary gift, let the giver know about it. You can also thank your guests for the time they took to share in your special day, as well as for their gifts.

Dear Aunt Jean and Uncle Ned,

Thank you so much for the four place settings of our formal china. We look forward to welcoming you into our new home and serving you a meal on those beautiful dishes as soon as we are settled. We really appreciate your thoughtfulness.

Love,

Amy and Richard

Figure 16-1: A sample thank-you note for a wedding gift.

Your thank-you card for a gift you exchanged should *not* indicate its return. Simply thank the giver for what he or she gave you.

For group gifts, you need to send a thank-you to each person who contributed to the gift. If you don't, some of the group probably won't ever see the thank-you. Simply use the same format you use when sending individual notes.

Sending thank-you notes as soon as possible

Send thank-you cards as gifts arrive or as quickly as possible after returning from your honeymoon. Specifically, you need to send your notes within two weeks after returning and absolutely no later than three months from receiving the gift. The sooner, the better!

What's in a Name Change?

For some brides, changing their last names is a given. But for other brides, deciding whether they want to change their names may be one of the most difficult decisions they've been faced with so far. I provide etiquette pointers on issues related to name changes in the following sections.

Keeping a few considerations in mind before you make a choice

It's tradition for a bride to take her new husband's last name. You may have no problem with this custom, but if you have any hesitations in changing your last name, discuss this issue with your spouse-to-be, preferably soon after becoming engaged. By doing so, you can discuss the issue and mutually agree on a decision before you begin planning your wedding. The name-change issue can be a sensitive subject, so it's important to make your choice understood, especially when you aren't taking your future husband's name.

The bride may not want to change her name for any number of reasons. For example, if the bride is an attorney and has been in practice for some time, or if she owns her own business, and clients and potential clients recognize her maiden name as the name of her practice or business, she may want to keep her maiden name professionally with the option of changing her name legally. She may also choose to hyphenate or otherwise combine her maiden and married names. Either option is perfectly acceptable; after all, there's no law stating that a bride must take her husband's last name.

If the bride decides to change her name, she has a few options to work with. She doesn't have to completely lose her maiden name. For example, Shirley Marie Reed is marrying Scott Johnson. Shirley can change her name to

- ✔ Shirley Marie Johnson (switching her last name for her husband's; traditionally the most common option)

- ✔ Shirley Marie Reed-Johnson (hyphenating her maiden and married names)

- ✔ Shirley Reed Johnson (using her maiden name as her new middle name)

In the same way, same-sex couples may choose to keep their own names or make changes or hyphenations as they wish.

You have several options for notifying others of your name change. For instance, you can add a note to your thank-you notes, indicate your new name on your return address labels, or include a note in your local newspaper wedding announcement.

After you change your name, some people may occasionally call you by the wrong last name. The proper way to handle these situations is to nicely tell them you were recently married and have changed your name — and of course tell them your new name.

 Changing or keeping your name is a personal choice. Be confident about your decision, and people should respect it. But be prepared for varying opinions and always be kind but firm with your response. After all, it's your name! If someone makes a rude comment to you about your choice for a new name, let the person know it was a personal and mutual decision between you and your spouse and that you're both happy about your choice.

Making the switch official

If you decide to change your name, remember to do the following before you're married:

- ✔ Notify your work of your new name so someone can begin to process new business cards and change your e-mail address. It's a good idea to write in your e-mail signature "Shirley (Reed) Johnson" for a few months after your name change to help clients recognize that it's still the same Shirley.

- ✔ Let your close family members and bridal party know that you'll be changing your name in case anyone checks with them about a monogrammed gift.

✔ Make all your honeymoon reservations, especially airline tickets, in your maiden name because your passport and license will still have your maiden name on them.

After you're married, you need to obtain an official copy of your marriage license to change your name on your social security card and your driver's license. As with all legal matters, rules differ by locale, so it's important to check with your local or state government to make sure you take all the necessary steps.

After you've received your new social security card and driver's license, you need to change your name with credit card companies, banks and financial institutions, insurance companies, utility companies, creditors, and any other organizations that have record of your maiden name. Be sure to keep your marriage license handy because you'll have to provide it when you make these changes.

Figuring out how to address your new in-laws

Continue to call your in-laws exactly what you've been calling them throughout you and your spouse's relationship. When, and if, they want to be called by their first names or by "Mom" and "Dad," they'll let you know. After the marriage, if they haven't mentioned the subject, it's appropriate for you to ask them what they want you to call them.

Part V
The Part of Tens

The 5th Wave   By Rich Tennant

"After all that planning and preparation, it seems inappropriate
to have a sign that says 'JUST' married."

In this part...

If you're looking for fast and furious etiquette tips, this part is for you! Here I cover tried and true ways to get along with your wedding planner (if you have one) and vendors. I also offer advice on how to courteously and amicably fire someone — if (Heaven forbid!) all else fails. If your upcoming nuptials are the second time around for you, check out this part for appropriate etiquette guidelines for a second (or third) marriage.

Chapter 17

Ten Tips for Working with Your Vendors and Wedding Planner

Knowing how to gracefully work with all the people you've hired to help plan and take part in your wedding should ease a lot of your anxiety. Heed the advice in this chapter, and you'll be on your way to the wedding you've always dreamed of.

Set Priorities

You can't get what you want from others if you don't know what's most important to you for your wedding. Have a brainstorming session during which you write out every fantasy you have for your wedding. Find the common theme in all your imagined scenarios and write it down to make sure you and your team of vendors and planners carry out what's most important to you. Physically keeping a list of must-haves can help you and your vendors keep the main goals in mind throughout the planning process.

Be Honest

Be honest with vendors about your priorities and about your budget from the get-go. If you let your vendors know upfront what your budget and expectations are for the day, they can tell you whether or not they can work within your guidelines.

If you consider some things to be non-negotiable for your wedding (a certain song being played, a particular color being used, and so on), you *have* to speak up right away — politely, of course. Say something like: "Mary (your planner), I really value your suggestions on the ceremony entrance song, but it's never been one of my favorites. John (your spouse-to-be) and I discussed this a few days ago, and we'd prefer to have 'Canon in D' played at that time."

Be Flexible

The flip side of being honest with your vendors is that you have to be prepared for them to be honest with you. For example, do you have your heart set on a life-sized ice sculpture of you and your beloved? Well, after your vendor looks at your budget and other important factors, he or she may try to explain to you that you can't afford a life-sized sculpture but that you can have either a miniature one or your silhouettes sliced out of a watermelon. Embrace the creativity and experience your vendors bring to the table.

Get Everything in Writing

Having a written contract is the most important thing you can do to ensure a successful relationship with your vendors and/or wedding planner. If something goes awry, a signed contract can help you smooth out snags with tact. Keep the following guidelines in mind when you're working with a vendor to get a written contract:

- ✔ **Explain what services you expect of your vendors in their contracts.** Some planners only organize weddings. If you want them to work on the day of your event, say so in your contract.

- ✔ **Make sure all your needs are addressed in your vendor contracts *before* you sign them.** Make sure you read and receive copies of all contracts; you're the one paying the bill. Study the contracts carefully and negotiate for inclusions or deletions of items to meet all your concerns before signing them.

  Also, make sure your contract with your wedding planner *doesn't* include a clause that forbids vendors from working directly with you. Eliminating this clause is essential in case you wind up needing to fire your planner.

- ✔ **Put contingency plans in your contract so that you know who will pick up the slack if your vendor suddenly can't fulfill his or her part of the agreement.** For example, if your bakery goes out of business the week before your wedding, you don't want to have to find someone at the last minute to make your wedding cake.

✔ **Include a clause about what will happen if the wedding gets canceled or postponed.** As much as you don't want to think about this situation, having a set plan in place is a good idea for everyone involved.

Remember the Golden Rule

When people are planning their weddings, they say and do things that even they'd consider appalling in most situations. Your vendors and wedding planner are people, too, so treat them the way you want to be treated in return. Call them when you say you will, pay them when deposits are due, and let them know immediately (and politely) if something isn't happening the way you anticipated.

Hope for the Best

As you plan your wedding, imagine everything going right on the big day. By envisioning these beautiful parts of the day, you'll appreciate what an important part your vendors play in the planning process. Hoping for the best helps you treat your vendors with courtesy and respect, which helps them make all your hopes a reality.

Prepare for the Worst

Preparing for the worst means you can go through the day feeling confident that if something unexpected does arise, it won't ruin the whole event. For the most part, you'll prepare for the worst when you make your original agreements with your vendors, but you can also make a few plans yourself. For example, you can have the numbers for taxi services on hand in case the limos don't show up. Also, if you have a wedding planner, he or she should be ready to fix any problem that may occur.

Have a Sense of Humor

Trust me, you and your spouse-to-be will laugh about almost every mistake, omission, and blunder after the fact. You may as well get a head start and laugh off the little inconveniences that arise while you plan your wedding. Laughing off the little things will help you maintain a better relationship with your vendors, too, because it shows that you trust them to make the right decisions at crunch time.

Plan for Payments

Don't ruin a great working relationship with a vendor by mishandling the payment process. Your contracts need to spell out exactly when you need to pay your vendors and how you need to do so (by check, cash, credit card, and so on). If any of your vendors expect to be paid at the event, make sure you label the payment and select a responsible person to handle it. You also need to get a receipt or some other written acknowledgement from your vendors proving that they received your final payments.

When All Else Fails: Gracefully Firing Your Vendors or Planner

If you've tried to follow all the other tips in this chapter but you still can't work productively with a vendor or wedding planner, you may have to fire him or her. In this situation, keep the whole process simple and professional. Instead of screaming, focus on moving forward and, possibly, finding a new vendor.

The best way to fire a vendor is to document your reasons, write a simple letter, and firmly state your desire to end your working relationship. You may forfeit any deposit (or other) payments made, but if you're entitled to any money back, clearly state how much you expect and when and how the vendor should deliver it.

You may also need to cite your contract regarding repayment. If you decide to refuse to make a final payment based on something that happens at the wedding or reception, make sure someone gets documentation (pictures of the ruined cake or a recording of the caterer's inappropriate behavior, for example) because withholding payment after services are rendered is much harder to do when you have a contract. Just because things aren't *exactly* the way you wanted them isn't justification for getting out of a contract.

If you need to fire your wedding planner, tread lightly. This person may have close relationships with some of your other vendors and you may have to be prepared to replace them, as well. As hard as it may be, don't get emotional and clearly state why working together is no longer an option. Say something like: "Because we don't seem to be on the same path for developing a successful wedding day, I think the best way to proceed is to cancel our agreement."

Chapter 18

Nearly Ten Guidelines for Getting Married the Second Time Around

In This Chapter

▶ Having the wedding you want with realistic expectations in mind
▶ Understanding etiquette for attire, invitations, and more
▶ Showing respect for all previous marriages

So you've found new love — congratulations and best wishes to you! In this chapter, I provide a few guidelines for celebrating marriages the second time around.

Realize You May Meet Some Resistance

Some people out there don't believe second (or other higher order) marriages warrant an actual wedding. That's fine. Those people don't have to participate in your special day. When you get married, you should be surrounded by people who love and support you and your intended. Make it clear to your loved ones that their blessings and presence really mean a lot to you, but don't press the issue if someone still chooses not to participate in your wedding. (Chapter 2 has guidelines for dealing with folks who object to your marriage.)

The last thing you want to do is cause an even greater rift between you and an already-unsupportive individual. And you don't want to have someone at your wedding who really doesn't want to be there.

If the person who objects to your wedding is one of your parents or, worse, one of your children, moving on may be really difficult. If the children involved are adults, take the time to hear and address their concerns; then make it clear that you're still going forward with your wedding. If your children (and/or those of your future spouse) are young and will be living with you after you're married, you may need to get some outside help from someone like a family counselor to prepare for becoming a blended family. Even if all the kids are fine with the idea of the marriage, they still may not want to attend the actual wedding; in this case, you may just have to let it go, no matter how sad and difficult doing so may be.

Don't Be Shy about Having the Wedding You Want

You may not want to have a big, splashy wedding the second time around . . . and that's okay. On the other hand, you may want to have a fancy, formal event, and that's okay, too. Don't feel like you have to play things down or keep it casual just because you've been married before. You can have the wedding you want the second, third, even fourth time around. Just make sure you let your future spouse know what's important to you and why.

If you haven't been married before but your spouse-to-be has, don't feel like you have to give up all your big-wedding dreams just because he or she has done it all before. This wedding has nothing to do with the past — it's all about the future.

Have Realistic Expectations

If your parents forked out $40,000 for your first wedding, don't expect their contribution this time around to be nearly as generous. In fact, you shouldn't ask them to finance your second wedding at all, but you're free to accept their help if they offer it. The older you are and the more independent you are of your parents, the more you should expect to shoulder the costs of your second marriage.

Also, if you invite people who attended your first wedding to your second wedding, know that their gifts may not be as lavish this time around. Some people may decide to give just a card or some other small gift because your house is probably well furnished already.

Consider Your Ceremony Carefully

If you're having a religious ceremony for a second marriage, consult the officiant to make sure you fulfill any special requirements.

(See Chapter 6 for tips on how to work well with an officiant.) Even if you decide not to have a large bridal party your second time around, you can still include family members or special friends who may have been in your previous wedding. If it's the second time around for the groom, but the bride hasn't been married before, go ahead and enjoy all the bells and whistles of a huge wedding (if that's what you want). Just make sure you plan them tastefully.

Whether you, your spouse-to-be, or both of you have children from a previous marriage, you need to consider whether the children will play a special role on the wedding day. Do you want to make them part of the ceremony? Speak to the children to see how they feel about being in the wedding, and most importantly, talk to your officiant, as well, to get his or her ideas on how you can thoughtfully include them, keeping their ages in mind.

Select Appropriate Attire

In terms of attire, etiquette doesn't distinguish much of a difference between a second wedding and a first wedding. The most important guideline to remember about selecting a second wedding dress is to make it match the formality of both your wedding ceremony and your reception (as I explain in Chapter 9). This guideline goes for the groom's style and the entire wedding party, as well.

If you're the bride and this is your second wedding, you can still wear a white dress and a veil; just remember to select a veil that blends well with the gown and the ceremony style you choose.

Extend the Invitation Yourselves

If the bride and/or groom have been married before, no matter how old they are, they usually extend the invitation to their wedding ceremony themselves, either in the wording of their printed invitation or with a personal note. (Check out Chapter 11 for how to word your invitations.)

Know Whether to Invite the Ex

Inviting the exes can present an uncomfortable situation for family members, especially when you or your spouse-to-be have children from a previous marriage. It's important for the second wedding to demonstrate that you're starting a new family, and the presence of an ex-spouse can certainly confuse the overall picture.

Even if you're on good terms with your ex, you don't want your guests to be uncomfortable; therefore, it's best not to invite the exes. This same rule applies to ex-in-laws and relatives; however, all situations are different, so you need to carefully consider whether to invite any and all exes before you send your invitations.

Decide Whether to Ask for Gifts

Most people who are remarrying are more established than first-timers in terms of kitchen appliances, bed clothes, and the like. So if you and your spouse-to-be have everything you need for your new home, either you can choose to register at a hobby-related store specializing in something like outdoor gear, or you can choose not to request any gifts. However, if you decide not to request gifts, never state "No gifts, please" on your invitation — doing so is completely against etiquette rules. Simply spread the information by word of mouth that you don't need anything. Keep in mind that some guests will choose to give gifts even if you don't need anything.

If this marriage is the first for one of you, however, or if you'd appreciate some help starting your new life together, gifts are always appropriate, and you can register using the tips in Chapter 12.

Be Respectful of Your First Marriage

Although your second wedding is a new beginning for you and your spouse-to-be and all your guests are thrilled that you've found love again, you don't need to bash your former spouse or make fun of him or her in any way.

If you share children with your former spouse, you need to work especially hard not to say anything negative about that person. Your former spouse may be an obnoxious human being who treated you very badly, but you need to work out those issues in therapy, not at the altar. Your children are a part of your past with your ex, so make sure you don't do or say anything that may upset them. If your children are at the wedding, word your vows carefully to focus on the future you have in front of you instead of belittling your past.

Index

BUSINESS, CAREERS & PERSONAL FINANCE

Accounting For Dummies, 4th Edition*
978-0-470-24600-9

Bookkeeping Workbook For Dummies†
978-0-470-16983-4

Commodities For Dummies
978-0-470-04928-0

Doing Business in China For Dummies
978-0-470-04929-7

E-Mail Marketing For Dummies
978-0-470-19087-6

Job Interviews For Dummies, 3rd Edition*†
978-0-470-17748-8

Personal Finance Workbook For Dummies*†
978-0-470-09933-9

Real Estate License Exams For Dummies
978-0-7645-7623-2

Six Sigma For Dummies
978-0-7645-6798-8

Small Business Kit For Dummies, 2nd Edition*†
978-0-7645-5984-6

Telephone Sales For Dummies
978-0-470-16836-3

BUSINESS PRODUCTIVITY & MICROSOFT OFFICE

Access 2007 For Dummies
978-0-470-03649-5

Excel 2007 For Dummies
978-0-470-03737-9

Office 2007 For Dummies
978-0-470-00923-9

Outlook 2007 For Dummies
978-0-470-03830-7

PowerPoint 2007 For Dummies
978-0-470-04059-1

Project 2007 For Dummies
978-0-470-03651-8

QuickBooks 2008 For Dummies
978-0-470-18470-7

Quicken 2008 For Dummies
978-0-470-17473-9

Salesforce.com For Dummies, 2nd Edition
978-0-470-04893-1

Word 2007 For Dummies
978-0-470-03658-7

EDUCATION, HISTORY, REFERENCE & TEST PREPARATION

African American History For Dummies
978-0-7645-5469-8

Algebra For Dummies
978-0-7645-5325-7

Algebra Workbook For Dummies
978-0-7645-8467-1

Art History For Dummies
978-0-470-09910-0

ASVAB For Dummies, 2nd Edition
978-0-470-10671-6

British Military History For Dummies
978-0-470-03213-8

Calculus For Dummies
978-0-7645-2498-1

Canadian History For Dummies, 2nd Edition
978-0-470-83656-9

Geometry Workbook For Dummies
978-0-471-79940-5

The SAT I For Dummies, 6th Edition
978-0-7645-7193-0

Series 7 Exam For Dummies
978-0-470-09932-2

World History For Dummies
978-0-7645-5242-7

FOOD, HOME, GARDEN, HOBBIES & HOME

Bridge For Dummies, 2nd Edition
978-0-471-92426-5

Coin Collecting For Dummies, 2nd Edition
978-0-470-22275-1

Cooking Basics For Dummies, 3rd Edition
978-0-7645-7206-7

Drawing For Dummies
978-0-7645-5476-6

Etiquette For Dummies, 2nd Edition
978-0-470-10672-3

Gardening Basics For Dummies*†
978-0-470-03749-2

Knitting Patterns For Dummies
978-0-470-04556-5

Living Gluten-Free For Dummies†
978-0-471-77383-2

Painting Do-It-Yourself For Dummies
978-0-470-17533-0

HEALTH, SELF HELP, PARENTING & PETS

Anger Management For Dummies
978-0-470-03715-7

Anxiety & Depression Workbook For Dummies
978-0-7645-9793-0

Dieting For Dummies, 2nd Edition
978-0-7645-4149-0

Dog Training For Dummies, 2nd Edition
978-0-7645-8418-3

Horseback Riding For Dummies
978-0-470-09719-9

Infertility For Dummies†
978-0-470-11518-3

Meditation For Dummies with CD-ROM, 2nd Edition
978-0-471-77774-8

Post-Traumatic Stress Disorder For Dummies
978-0-470-04922-8

Puppies For Dummies, 2nd Edition
978-0-470-03717-1

Thyroid For Dummies, 2nd Edition†
978-0-471-78755-6

Type 1 Diabetes For Dummies*†
978-0-470-17811-9

* Separate Canadian edition also available
† Separate U.K. edition also available

Available wherever books are sold. For more information or to order direct: U.S. customers visit www.dummies.com or call 1-877-762-2974.
U.K. customers visit www.wileyeurope.com or call (0) 1243 843291. Canadian customers visit www.wiley.ca or call 1-800-567-4797.

WILEY

INTERNET & DIGITAL MEDIA

AdWords For Dummies
978-0-470-15252-2

Blogging For Dummies, 2nd Edition
978-0-470-23017-6

Digital Photography All-in-One Desk Reference For Dummies, 3rd Edition
978-0-470-03743-0

Digital Photography For Dummies, 5th Edition
978-0-7645-9802-9

Digital SLR Cameras & Photography For Dummies, 2nd Edition
978-0-470-14927-0

eBay Business All-in-One Desk Reference For Dummies
978-0-7645-8438-1

eBay For Dummies, 5th Edition*
978-0-470-04529-9

eBay Listings That Sell For Dummies
978-0-471-78912-3

Facebook For Dummies
978-0-470-26273-3

The Internet For Dummies, 11th Edition
978-0-470-12174-0

Investing Online For Dummies, 5th Edition
978-0-7645-8456-5

iPod & iTunes For Dummies, 5th Edition
978-0-470-17474-6

MySpace For Dummies
978-0-470-09529-4

Podcasting For Dummies
978-0-471-74898-4

Search Engine Optimization For Dummies, 2nd Edition
978-0-471-97998-2

Second Life For Dummies
978-0-470-18025-9

Starting an eBay Business For Dummies, 3rd Edition†
978-0-470-14924-9

GRAPHICS, DESIGN & WEB DEVELOPMENT

Adobe Creative Suite 3 Design Premium All-in-One Desk Reference For Dummies
978-0-470-11724-8

Adobe Web Suite CS3 All-in-One Desk Reference For Dummies
978-0-470-12099-6

AutoCAD 2008 For Dummies
978-0-470-11650-0

Building a Web Site For Dummies, 3rd Edition
978-0-470-14928-7

Creating Web Pages All-in-One Desk Reference For Dummies, 3rd Edition
978-0-470-09629-1

Creating Web Pages For Dummies, 8th Edition
978-0-470-08030-6

Dreamweaver CS3 For Dummies
978-0-470-11490-2

Flash CS3 For Dummies
978-0-470-12100-9

Google SketchUp For Dummies
978-0-470-13744-4

InDesign CS3 For Dummies
978-0-470-11865-8

Photoshop CS3 All-in-One Desk Reference For Dummies
978-0-470-11195-6

Photoshop CS3 For Dummies
978-0-470-11193-2

Photoshop Elements 5 For Dummies
978-0-470-09810-3

SolidWorks For Dummies
978-0-7645-9555-4

Visio 2007 For Dummies
978-0-470-08983-5

Web Design For Dummies, 2nd Edition
978-0-471-78117-2

Web Sites Do-It-Yourself For Dummies
978-0-470-16903-2

Web Stores Do-It-Yourself For Dummies
978-0-470-17443-2

LANGUAGES, RELIGION & SPIRITUALITY

Arabic For Dummies
978-0-471-77270-5

Chinese For Dummies, Audio Set
978-0-470-12766-7

French For Dummies
978-0-7645-5193-2

German For Dummies
978-0-7645-5195-6

Hebrew For Dummies
978-0-7645-5489-6

Ingles Para Dummies
978-0-7645-5427-8

Italian For Dummies, Audio Set
978-0-470-09586-7

Italian Verbs For Dummies
978-0-471-77389-4

Japanese For Dummies
978-0-7645-5429-2

Latin For Dummies
978-0-7645-5431-5

Portuguese For Dummies
978-0-471-78738-9

Russian For Dummies
978-0-471-78001-4

Spanish Phrases For Dummies
978-0-7645-7204-3

Spanish For Dummies
978-0-7645-5194-9

Spanish For Dummies, Audio Set
978-0-470-09585-0

The Bible For Dummies
978-0-7645-5296-0

Catholicism For Dummies
978-0-7645-5391-2

The Historical Jesus For Dummies
978-0-470-16785-4

Islam For Dummies
978-0-7645-5503-9

Spirituality For Dummies, 2nd Edition
978-0-470-19142-2

NETWORKING AND PROGRAMMING

ASP.NET 3.5 For Dummies
978-0-470-19592-5

C# 2008 For Dummies
978-0-470-19109-5

Hacking For Dummies, 2nd Edition
978-0-470-05235-8

Home Networking For Dummies, 4th Edition
978-0-470-11806-1

Java For Dummies, 4th Edition
978-0-470-08716-9

Microsoft® SQL Server™ 2008 All-in-One Desk Reference For Dummies
978-0-470-17954-3

Networking All-in-One Desk Reference For Dummies, 2nd Edition
978-0-7645-9939-2

Networking For Dummies, 8th Edition
978-0-470-05620-2

SharePoint 2007 For Dummies
978-0-470-09941-4

Wireless Home Networking For Dummies, 2nd Edition
978-0-471-74940-0